BEYOND WINNING

Beyond
Winning

Memoir of a Women's Soccer Coach

S. S. Hanna

University Press of Colorado

© 1996 by the University Press of Colorado

Published by the University Press of Colorado
P. O. Box 849
Niwot, Colorado 80544
Tel. (303) 530-5337

The University Press of Colorado is a cooperative publishing enterprise supported, in part, by Adams State College, Colorado State University, Fort Lewis College, Mesa State College, Metropolitan State College of Denver, University of Colorado, University of Northern Colorado, University of Southern Colorado, and Western State College of Colorado.

Library of Congress Cataloging-in-Publication Data

Hanna, S. S., 1943–
    Beyond winning : memoir of a women's soccer coach / S.S. Hanna.
        p.   cm.
    ISBN 0-87081-398-6 (cloth : perm. paper)
    1. Hanna, S. S., 1943– . 2. Soccer coaches—United States—
Biography. 3. College teachers—United States—Biography.
4. Soccer for women—United States. I. Title.
    GV942.7.H33A3 1996
    796.334'092—dc20
    [B]   96-25316
                                                                        CIP

Excerpt from "The Waste Land" in *Collected Poems 1909–1962* by T. S. Eliot, copyright © 1936 by Harcourt Brace & Company, copyright © 1964, 1963 by T. S. Eliot, reprinted by permission of the publisher.

Excerpt from "Howl" in *Collected Poems 1947–1980* by Allen Ginsberg, copyright © 1984 by Allen Ginsberg, reprinted by permission of HarperCollins, New York.

This book was set in Galliard and Tiepolo.

The paper used in this publication meets the minimum requirements of the American National Standard for Information Sciences—Permanence of Paper for Printed Library Materials. ANSI Z39.48–1948
∞

10 9 8 7 6 5 4 3 2 1

This Book Is for Rita

A strong and tender woman,
an athlete, a sailing dove.

There will always be
a soft spot in our hearts
for Kansas, beautiful Kansas,
land of your birth,
where the fence posts
are made of stone
and the land has muscle-tone.

Stop and feel
the sway of a Kansas wheat
field before harvest,
stop and listen
to the sounds of yeast at work

As we prepare and break
bread in The Old Homeplace.

Contents

Prologue

Words from Saul Bellow and Angi Moyer

Years ago, I wrote a seriocomic book manuscript that desperately needed a foreword by a famous writer. So I sent it to my favorite novelist, Saul Bellow, who was at the University of Chicago. In the cover letter, I noted all the other works of this sort that he probably received, and I apologized for even asking him to consider writing a foreword to the manuscript.

"Far from thinking your letter of 8th March 'forward', as you seemed to fear," Bellow began a letter to me dated 15th May and sent from Jerusalem, "I decided to take your typescript with me to Scotland in the hope of finding time to read it between meetings, lectures and seminars. In the event the Scottish Art's Council programme left me no time at all so the manuscript followed me to Jerusalem."

Bellow went on to say kind things about the book manuscript but declined to write a foreword to it. He concluded his letter with these words: "Though the Nobel Prize for Literature was an honour that I sincerely appreciated, the lecturing and travelling that it involved were infinitely more disruptive to my writing routine than I had expected. I feel now that I must be ruthless about getting on with my next book and hope you will understand."

I understood all right. And though disappointed with Bellow's response, I was also delighted by it. For how many other writers could claim that a book manuscript of theirs traveled with a Nobel laureate, going from Chicago to Scotland to Jerusalem, tucked away between the laureate's socks and underwear?

This incident came to mind when I started to write the prologue to this book on coaching women's soccer. I wondered: Should I ask a famous person—an athlete, a coach, a reporter, a novelist, a poet—to write a foreword to the book? After some thought, I decided to dismiss all prospective candidates and write my own prologue, spiking it with the wisdom of our star player.

Ideally, a toupee is more than a lid for those who part their hair in a circle. Likewise, college sports is more than a show for those who play on national television. To be sure, television dominates the lives of a tiny minority of colleges, especially those with big-time sports programs. But the vast majority of the United States' collegiate athletes and coaches participate in small-college sports programs. Such programs are seldom explored on national television or even in books.

Beyond Winning is a slice of life from small-college sports. No two sports programs are identical, but many share similar tensions, rewards, challenges, setbacks, triumphs, and aspirations. By profiling the life of a program in women's soccer, this book reveals and reflects the ways of many other small-college sports programs throughout the United States.

About ten years ago, I established and coached the women's soccer team at Geneva College, a small liberal arts school in western Pennsylvania. I kept a detailed diary and took extensive notes on our program. This book reworks that material into a narrative that reproduces conversations, sketches characters, sets scenes, and pursues issues. A person doesn't have to know a thing about soccer to connect with the book's central concerns.

Specifically, the narrative interprets the soccer season, graphs its suspenseful moments, integrates academics with athletics, footnotes the struggles around gender equity, traces the penetration of coaching into family life, assesses the wisdom of men coaching women in college sports, argues for some bold and innovative reforms regarding participation in varsity sports, and grapples with the fun of coaching a small-college sports program that's liberated from the "win-at-all-costs" mentality that tyrannizes big-time college sports.

That fun factor was highlighted one summer afternoon by Angi Moyer, a player who had come up to my English department office to return several books she had borrowed. At one point in our conversation, Angi, referring to the players on the team, said, "To us, you were a heck of a lot more than a coach: you were part van driver, part trainer, part manager, part teacher, part cone carrier, part entertainer, part reporter, part water bucket monitor. Oh, you had such a mixture of identities that people in the dog-breeding business would call you a mutt."

"Thanks a lot," I said, and looked out the window of that clapboard Victorian house that we call Fern Cliffe Hall. "Here I thought I was at a small liberal arts college basking in that noble tradition of the scholar-coach, but you're making me into a mutt."

"No, no," Angi said with a smile, "a scholar-mutt."

"Yeah, that."

"Seriously, Coach," Angi continued, "if you'd ask me to sum up our season, I'd do it by twisting an old expression."

"An old expression?" I asked.

"Yep."

"Which one?"

"The one dealing with a crock," she said.

"A crock?"

"You got it, Coach: a crock." Angi looked around the L-shaped, book-lined office, stared at a picture of James Joyce that along with those of other modern writers decorated a wall, then said slowly and distinctly, "Our season, if you stop and think about it, was a crock of—"

"Oh, please, Angi, please don't say it."

"But it's not what you're thinking, Coach."

I looked at her, dressed in jeans patched with the antiwar symbol of the late sixties, the era of her birth, and said, "OK, go ahead. Complete the expression."

"Our season," she said, "was a crock of wit."

"It was, wasn't it?" I smiled and glanced at the caterpillar below the nose of John Steinbeck. He surely could have grown a better-looking mustache than that, I thought, made eye contact with Angi, and said, "Sure, we had problems, but we had lots of fun, too, didn't we?"

"We did, and you better capture that fun—or at least a bit of it—in this thing that you're going to write," she said as she drifted toward the door. Before leaving, she added, "All sorts of people write about those big and nasty programs; few bother with programs like ours that tend to be humble but extraordinary." She waved and said, "I'll write from Europe. Bye."

Two days later Angi joined Amy, another player, and flew to Europe for the summer. They went not to play soccer but to tour the continent: packs on their backs, boots on their feet, hitchhiking on their minds.

As they began their tour, I began to write this book about our women's soccer program. I wrote from the point of view of the coach, for that's the one I knew best. Most sports memoirs appeal to either men or women. Given its content, this one might appeal to both genders inside and outside of sports, inside and outside of higher education. It might even appeal to those interested in a prose style flavored by a dash of irony and self-deprecating humor.

To write a nonfiction account from the point of view of the coach, one must first become a coach. Coaching jobs at the college level, as a rule, are difficult to find. Rejection letters, as a related rule, seldom lead to a job. *Seldom* is a key word here, for such letters enlivened my search for a coaching position.

This book opens with the story of that search.

Part I

Baseball and Soccer

1

The Search for the Job and the Players

On a rainy western Pennsylvania afternoon in late May 1986, I sat in one of those wooden Siamese benches (the kind where opposing buttocks share a backboard), sipped brown water—the restaurant called it coffee—tapped my fingers on a Styrofoam cup, and reflected on how rejection letters had led to a head coaching job in women's soccer at the college level.

Coaching soccer had never interested me, even though I had played the sport at the club level. While growing up in Milwaukee in the fifties, I had loved baseball, played it in high school, and coached it in the organized playground leagues of the city. In college, I earned a varsity letter in football as the team's kicking specialist, kicking field goals and extra points in a manner that *The Milwaukee Journal* once described as "not soccer style, not straight ahead style, but unorthodox, like a kid taking a swipe at a tin can."

In graduate school, I lost interest in athletics and immersed myself in studying for a Ph.D. in literature. The job market for Ph.D.'s in the early seventies was horrible. Like many other scholars, I found myself drifting from one non-tenure-track teaching position to another, searching for a salary, an identity, and a sense of purpose. I began my teaching career at a liberal arts college in Oklahoma; there, I taught English and founded the Kickapoo Spur Press, publisher of a "Little" magazine that my students and I established and edited. ("Little" is the name given to literary magazines with small circulation.) Following my sojourn in Oklahoma, I accepted a postdoctoral summer fellowship from the National Endowment for the Humanities to do research and writing in Amherst, Massachusetts. After that, I clinched a job at Sterling College, a small school on the prairies of central Kansas where I had agreed not only to teach English but also to serve as an assistant football coach for the Warriors of Sterling College. Besides teaching and coaching, I helped my students establish and edit *The Great Plains Review*, another "Little" magazine. During my fourth year at Sterling, a financial crisis hit the college, and sensing that the administration saw me not as a sacred cow but as potential hamburger, I journeyed to another small liberal arts college, in Virginia, and in due time moved north to Beaver Falls, Pennsylvania, home of the Golden Tornadoes of Geneva College.

Tension governed my first year at Geneva. I expected to be cut from the staff, a casualty of declining enrollment, but I wasn't. Instead, the president cut himself. Following his resignation, an interim president came, and he kept me on for another year; then a third president came, and he granted me tenure. During the summer of my second year at Geneva, I wrote a book manuscript profiling my life as a gypsy scholar, teaching English, coaching football, and working at the writer's craft. No publisher seemed to be interested in my seventy-thousand-word manuscript that dealt with the life of a clearly obscure college professor. So I abridged the text and added three chapters on all the problems and ironies that I had experienced in trying to publish the unabridged version. The new chapters tried to universalize the frolics and frustrations that most writers, professors, and artists experience in marketing their work. Two publishers expressed interest in the revised version, and I decided to go with Iowa State University Press, which planned to publish it under the title *The Gypsy Scholar: A Writer's Comic Search for a Publisher.*

Ambitious professors and writers often get rejected while pursuing academic appointments, publishing commitments, and prestigious fellowships. Unambitious ones do not. The publishers' responses to the manuscript of my life as an intellectual migrant worker elevated me to the realm of the ambitious professor and writer. The ambitious refuse to be cowed by past rejections or the prospect of more rejections on future projects. This realization, coupled with the enthusiasm of the folks at Iowa State University Press, led me to search for another undertaking in which I could gather more experiences and write them up into a nonfiction book aimed at a general audience rather than a narrow scholarly one. Accordingly, I turned to the idea of coaching not football (as I had done in Kansas, and happily so) and not soccer (for I knew little about *coaching* that sport) but baseball, the sport that I had played and coached in Milwaukee, the sport that I had come to enjoy while watching the Milwaukee Braves rise to the status of world champions—a team that featured Hank Aaron, Eddie Mathews, Warren Spahn, Del Crandal, Lew Burdette, Joe Adcock, Billy Bruton, Wes Covington, and other stars of years past. To us kids who grew up in Milwaukee in the fifties, the Braves were our "boys of summer."

I knew that finding a head coaching job in college-level baseball would be difficult enough, but finding one where I could teach English part-time and coach baseball full-time would be even more difficult—not as difficult perhaps as locating the mother of the Unknown Soldier, but close to it. Still, I tried hard. I ruled out the universities with major sports programs and the colleges that wished they had such programs. I telephoned a friend who was a head baseball coach at a small liberal arts college in Tennessee and asked him about publications that listed baseball coaching vacancies for small colleges. He was unaware of any. My friend believed that most baseball jobs, like cheap apartments in the student ghettos of university towns, seldom get advertised: they get passed on to friends or friends of friends. "Your best bet," he told me, "is to write the academic deans or vice presidents of small colleges and let them know of your intentions. If I were you, I wouldn't fool with the athletic directors; go right to the top, to the deans or presidents, if need be."

That certainly was sound advice. Because my potential appointment to the faculty of a small college would have to be in both the baseball and English programs, such a position would have to be initiated and coordinated by the chief academic officer at the college. I prepared a one-page curriculum vitae that listed my academic and athletic experience and my publications. After reproducing two hundred copies of the vita, I drafted a one-page cover letter in which I proposed the idea of my being hired as a head baseball coach and an English teacher-writer who would write a nonfiction book on the baseball program under my leadership. I further noted: "Though books on baseball sell vigorously, books on small college baseball are rare as albino cockroaches. The proposed idea would bring national attention to your college, not via an article in a magazine or a story on the wire services or even a chapter in a book, but via an *entire* book devoted to your college and especially its baseball program." I concluded by writing: "Now remember, if your college has been championing a losing tradition, so much the better. Indeed, I promise to do all I can to preserve that tradition which, parenthetically, might inject the book with its essential charm."

Before printing the letter, I turned to the *Higher Education Directory* (which lists the names and addresses of the main administrators of accredited institutions), isolated the names of the chief academic officers or presidents of two hundred small colleges throughout the country, and typed those names and addresses on envelopes. That done, I printed out a personal form letter for each administrator.

In time, I ended up using all two hundred vitas, spending fifty dollars in postage, and laughing at some curious and amusing responses to my cover letter, quirky cover letter, as it might have appeared to some administrators.

"Today I received a crazy letter from an administrator at a small college in West Virginia," I told my wife during lunch at Pizza Joe. "He doesn't want to hire me to coach baseball but wants to trade me his book on baseball cards, of all topics, for *The Gypsy Scholar* whenever it comes out. This is the kind of person who'd buy my baseball book—or maybe he'd want to trade for it—if I ever write it."

"Before you write it, you've got to get the job," she said.

"That I do, I do," I said, and bit into a slice of pizza.

The 200 baseball-English query letters harvested 160 rejection letters (actually, they were no-vacancy-type letters, a mild form of rejection). I kept the most promising ones and filed them for future contact. Two such letters had come from presidents of Phi Beta Kappa colleges in Wisconsin and Indiana. The Wisconsin president wrote:

Dear Professor Hanna:

I am sorry to be so late in responding to your letter, but I have circulated it among colleagues in various departments before responding and—the wheels of the gods grinding slow in this case—am only now in a position to write. It is fair to say that we are intrigued by your interesting offer, though I must also tell you that for reasons of staffing within athletics and the English Department, it appears that we will not be in a position to respond affirmatively to your inquiry. I trust that some institution will find itself in a position to do so and wish you all the best in your endeavors.

Best wishes for the new year—at Geneva or wherever you may be.

Sincerely,
[signature]
President

And the Indiana college president, to whom I had failed to forward a curriculum vitae, wrote this response:

Dear Dr. Hanna:

Yours is an extremely interesting proposition, and I have had some conversations about it on campus. Briefly, we have vacancies neither in the Athletic Department nor the English Department, and that is the effective barrier to proceeding directly with the intriguing experiment which you propose.

I would like to put your letter in my active file of faculty prospects, and it just might be that at a later date we could pursue something like this. I would appreciate it if you would send me a copy of your conventional style vita.

Yours sincerely,
[signature]
President

For the most part, the colleges with Phi Beta Kappa chapters were more encouraging and receptive than the colleges struggling to maintain their regional accreditation. Still, not a single response led to a head coaching job in baseball, but the letters did lead to a head coaching job in soccer. If a friend ever asked me how to get a head coaching job in soccer, I would reply, "That's easy: write two hundred letters—the quirkier the better—searching for a job to teach English and coach *baseball.* If your results turn out to be like mine, you'll get a soccer job."

At Geneva, the vice president for development is also in charge of athletics. He and I would frequently meet and exchange small talk in the college's mailroom. He would be there waiting for checks from donors to a fund-raising project, and I would be there waiting for checks from editors; more often than not, I would instead receive manuscripts—my manuscripts, many of which went out and came back with disturbing faithfulness. When the avalanche of baseball-English rejection letters began to pour in, the vice president took note of my negative prosperity. I explained to him my odd proposal, and he kept that explanation in mind.

Sometime in early May, when most of Geneva's students were preparing to take their final examinations and go home for the summer, the vice president called and asked, "Are you still looking for that coaching job?"

"Sure am," I said.

"We now have one in—"

"Baseball?"

"No, no, Joe isn't leaving as far as I know," the vice president said, referring to the head baseball coach.

"What sport?"

"Soccer—but not men's," he quickly added.

"Good."

He hesitated. "We're planning to start a women's soccer team and compete at the varsity level come September. What do you think? Are you up to it?"

"Well, you know, I played and coached football in college. I also played soccer, but I know little about *coaching* soccer, but I'll learn. Let me think about it, talk to my wife and kids about it, and I'll get back to you in a week's time," I said.

"And, by the way," the vice president said before ending the conversation, "you'll get a little extra pay for coaching."

A week or so afterward, I called the vice president and accepted the job. A few days later, I received the following letter in my campus mailbox:

Dear Dr. Hanna:

This will confirm your appointment as head coach of our new women's soccer program. I am excited about this program and for your enthusiasm as well. You will be compensated with $800 at the end of your season. It is hoped that this is satisfactory with you.

In this position you will report to Miss Kim Gall, who is responsible for women's athletics. A schedule has been prepared by her. An important aspect of this program is its student recruitment value. Please contact the director of admissions and arrange for a set of procedures to help you in this regard.

Best wishes and we're not expecting an undefeated season *this year*.

Sincerely,
Charles N. O'Data
Vice President for Development

I took the letter home and shared its contents with my wife and four children, ages five to nine. To really impress the children, I converted the pay for coaching soccer to Italian liras and quoted that amount. "What do you think?" I asked my family as we neared the end of our dinner.

"Sounds like lots of money," nine-year-old Rita said.

"Yeah," Sam said.

"After taxes," my wife observed, "you'll end up with peanuts."

"You'll get peanuts, Daddy?" five-year-old Paul asked quizzically.

"No, honey," I said, "that's an expression that means the pay isn't very good."

"But you made it sound so good," Rita said.

"Well," I said to my wife, "I could write a letter expressing some reservations about the pay, or I could decline the job now that I know the pay." After a slight pause, I asked my family: "Should I decline the job? Should I tell the vice president that I don't want to coach?"

"No, no!" the kids shouted. "Go for it, Dad!"

My wife added, "Let's face it: you're not teaching at a small college like this one for the money. Besides, you're going to coach partly to get a topic to write about, right?"

"That's right," I replied as the empty dishes were being passed to me. (It was my turn to wash them that evening.)

"I know this is *not* a baseball job," she said, "but that could be a blessing in disguise. I can think of many books on baseball from *The Boys of Summer* on down, but I can't name one title on women's soccer. And starting a new program and all might be fun and adventuresome. And you won't have the pressure to win—not that first season anyway."

"Fun and adventuresome": those words reverberated in my mind as I gathered the dishes and silverware and began to wash away. All sorts of questions competed for my attention. What could I do to make Geneva's soccer program an enjoyable experience for the players, for my family, and for myself? How could I make the program different from other athletic programs that I had participated in? How many players would try out for the team? What would they be like? Would I relate to them? Would they enjoy a program coached not by a physical education instructor but by a creative writing professor?

To make a program fun, I thought, a coach must have creative control. I felt fortunate in being the head coach of the program. At Sterling College, I had served as an assistant football coach and thus carried out the philosophy and wishes of the head coach, whose personality and outlook defined the tone of the program. At Geneva, I expected to unfurl my own vision for the soccer program, to experiment, innovate, take risks. Being the only coach, I expected to take full responsibility for the program's quirks and failures.

I thought Geneva's players would enjoy the program if they all participated in every contest, contributing to the losses and the wins, seeing their skills develop. As a coach, I expected to integrate all the healthy players in all the contests regardless of their physical talents. Moreover, I expected to integrate them meaningfully and not simply shove them in for a token appearance that parents or fans might miss if they happened to sneak a look into their popcorn bags to see what unpopped kernels remained at the bottom.

As I continued to soap and scrub and rinse those dishes, I continued to think about coaching soccer. The team's schedule flashed into my mind. I remembered that we had several road trips, two of which were at nationally known schools: Oberlin College and Slippery Rock University, known for different reasons, I presumed. I thought it might be fun—and refreshing—if I did more than simply drive the players to the site of a game, coach them during the contest, and drive them back. I thought it might be fun to do some research on the away schools and to share that research with the team members before embarking on the road trips. Such an approach might enhance the players' educational experience, leading them to learn more than soccer skills.

Many coaches of big-time sports programs often treat their athletes merely as people with physical skills, but I wanted to treat Geneva's women soccer players as complex human beings: sensitive, thoughtful, curious, emotional, beset by fears, fraught with hopes, eager to learn. Many coaches also tend to be lemon-sucking, rules-conscious disciplinarians, and even though their players spend a lot of time with them on the field and in the locker room, the coaches still end up projecting a one-dimensional appearance to their teams. In trying to make Geneva's soccer program fun, I thought it might be wise to be loose and flexible in my leadership style. I wanted to avoid the tyranny of rigid rules; I wanted to laugh with the players, to invite them to laugh with me and even at me, to help them connect with the wit and irony of numerous situations that we were likely to encounter during the season.

Many athletic programs I had known featured a motivational slogan that was used throughout the season. At Sterling College our football slogan (selected by the head coach) proclaimed: "101% EFFORT." As coaches, we demanded 101 percent effort from the players at all times, and we alerted them to that demand by plastering the slogan all over the locker room, by using it in our speeches, and by referring to it when we evaluated their performances. On occasion, when a receiver in practice would drop a pass that had hit his hands or punched the numbers on his jersey, our free-spirited quarterback would seek me out and mutter, "Coach, that was a 101 percent *drop.*"

As I neared the end of the dish washing, I found myself mentally flipping through a lot of slogans, searching for one that might be appropriate for our soccer program. In the end, I decided that rather than having a slogan for the season, it might be fun to devise a slogan or a theme for a given week of practice leading up to a game—or for select games.

The words of a small-college football coach from Arizona navigated my mind. "My wife becomes a widow with the kids during football season," the coach once told me. I vowed to avoid that trap. Indeed, I thought it would be fun to involve my wife and children as much as possible in my coaching activities. My wife, a registered nurse, could help with injuries, with taping of ankles, and similar concerns, especially on game day. The children could occasionally come to practice and the home games. They could help with ball retrieval, supply the players with drinks, position the cones on the field, tease and be teased by the players. The athletes I had known at Sterling tended to be excellent role models for children; they were disciplined, determined, hardworking, organized, goal-oriented, uneasy with failure. I expected Geneva's players to fit into a similar mold, thus being a positive influence on our kids. I even thought it might be enjoyable for the team if I occasionally brought along one of the children on a road trip. Coaching, I suspected, could well be a fun family affair.

After washing the dishes, I headed to the word processor and wrote a quick "Afterword" to *The Gypsy Scholar.* In the cover letter I asked the editors at Iowa State University Press to note on the book's dust jacket that I coached women's soccer as well as college football. That elusive baseball job would have made me not a gypsy coach—coaches are gypsies almost by definition— but a utility coach, akin to a utility infielder in baseball. But the baseball job would have to wait for another day.

"What fun," my wife said at a family dinner in mid-August, when the responsibilities of coaching and traveling and losing began to settle into our thoughts. "You're going to be the mid- wife of the women's soccer program."

"What does that mean?" little Sam asked.

"Let your dad explain" was her reply.

In late August, I started to think seriously about my new re- sponsibilities as the first soccer coach for the women's varsity program at Geneva College. Student recruitment, as the vice president for development had written in the appointment letter, was a crucial factor that led Geneva to start the program. In a highly competitive market for students, the college hoped to at- tract more students and to keep them for all four years. One of the best ways to do that, the obvious reasoning went, was to in- volve the new recruits in meaningful activities. Certainly the col- lege did not expect the women's soccer program to be a money- maker, but to be that "meaningful activity" with which some students could create a dimension of their Geneva identity.

Like most small liberal arts colleges, Geneva is a two-sport school: football and basketball. Most of its major organizations and activities—such as band, homecoming, cheerleading, post- season tournaments—center on these two sports. Soccer and baseball for men, volleyball and softball for women, track and tennis for both—all draw miserable fan support. And lack of winning is not the reason. Indeed, even though the baseball and soccer teams win often and there is no admission charged to these games, the fans stay away. Keeping this in mind, I set a goal for our women's soccer team: to resist playing winning soccer—a practical, realistic, honest, predictable, and conve- nient goal—and to play, instead, interesting soccer, the kind that might attract fan support. As fate would have it, our circumstances, our players, our schedule, our fans, and my coaching quirks conspired to make that an attainable goal.

That first year, I ruled out attempting to recruit high school seniors with soccer experience simply because my appointment had come so late in the academic year, and most students, soccer players or otherwise, had made commitments to other colleges. So I resolved to recruit players, with or without soccer experience, from the Geneva student body. Accordingly, I went to the bookstore, bought some markers and poster paper, and asked my daughter, Rita, to help me make the posters.

"Should I use my artistic flair, Dad?" she asked when we sat down to make the posters.

"Sure," I said, "but do it my way."

"Boy, you sound like a coach already," she said as we began to work, sketching the following data on the posters:

Geneva is starting a varsity
program in WOMEN'S SOCCER.

All those interested
in joining the team,
please contact Coach Hanna
in the English Department.

No experience necessary.
Beginners will be welcomed.
All positions are open.

First meeting: Registration Day
at THREE sharp at the English
desk in the field house.

First Practice: August 26.
First Game: September 7.

I planned to place the posters in the female dorms and houses on campus and throughout the field house, where students would register for the fall semester. I also planned to display them in the lobby of the dining room and in heavily traveled rooms and hallways in the student center. Finally, I planned to list the new soccer program in the campus bulletin, which contained all sorts of announcements, activities, last-minute instructions to students, special academic and social alerts, and the like.

One evening in late August, Rita and I placed the posters in the appointed locations. That evening at dinner, Rita asked, "Daddy, I wonder how many will show up for the team after reading our posters?"

"Yes, *Coach* Hanna, what're you expecting?" my wife asked.

"Oh, I'm sure some will," I said, "and after our first meeting, word of mouth will get others. I'm not worried in the least."

"We'll see," my wife said.

"We'll *all* see," Rita added, speaking for herself and the three boys whose attention was focused on their food.

"One thing I've got to do pretty soon is take care of those three things that begin with the first letter of Sam's name, the three—"

"Dad, don't say that—we're eating now," Sal interrupted, jerking his words with uncharacteristic anger.

"No, no, honey, by that I mean the shirts, shorts, and shoes."

"Oh," he said with a sigh.

"I've got to order these or ask the women's athletic director to order them."

"Order them yourself," Rita said, "but make sure Mom picks the colors and the designs."

"Don't you need to see first how many players come out and their sizes and all?" my wife asked.

"You're right; I should've thought of that," I said, passing a plate of food to Rita for seconds.

"But how should you know, Dad?" Rita asked. "It's only your first year at this head coaching business."

"And I hope it's going to be a fun year," I said.

"We're all hoping for that," Sal said.

"That we are," his mother agreed. "And if coaching women's soccer in Pennsylvania is anything like coaching men's football in Kansas, then we're in for a lot more than fun. A lot more."

Nine women showed up for that first meeting held at the periphery of the English registration desk at the field house. I gave the students index cards and told them, "Please write your name, height, weight, age, year in school, home state, major, soccer experience, and position that you wish to play." When they returned the cards, I immediately flipped through them and said, "We've got four and a half people with experience and four and a half with no experience whatsoever."

"How in the world did you come up with that, Coach?" Angi, a junior writing major, asked. Most of the players smiled, which indicated to me that Angi might have stumbled on what had puzzled them, too.

"That's easy," I said. "One player didn't write 'yes' or 'no' for 'Experience'; she wrote 'more or less.'"

"Got you, Coach," Angi said, winking.

I called out the names of the nine players, fumbled the pronunciation of a couple, then asked if they had any nicknames that they would like me to use. "Most of you are from Pennsylvania or neighboring states," I said, "but we've got one player here from as far away as Texas. And that's Amanda Widener, and according to her card, she'd like to be called Amy. Where's Amy?"

"Right here, Coach," Amy said, waving her arm as if she were signaling for a fair catch in football.

"You've had experience, it says here, Amy. " I looked at her five-foot, ten-inch frame: broad-shouldered, strong, self-confident. She listed her class status as sophomore, her weight at 172 pounds, and her age as twenty-one, making her the oldest player on the team. Her friendly smile invited me to ask, "What kind of experience did you have?"

"What do you mean by that, Coach?"

"Did you play on a club team or in high school or at another college?" I asked.

"I'm transferring from a college in Texas; they didn't have women's soccer down there. My experience came from playing with a *men*'s team in Texas, Coach." That remark must have intimidated the beginners; it made me realize that Amy—thanks to her commanding physique and experience—might be a team leader. That, of course, remained to be seen.

"What position did you play then?" I asked.

"Goalie and fullback," she said.

"I notice," I said to the group as a whole, "some of you didn't indicate what positions you wish to play."

"That's right," one of the beginners said. "I didn't do it, Coach Hanna, because I don't even know the names of the positions, but I'm willing to learn."

"I'm curious," I said to the beginner, "have you had any athletic experience in high school?"

"Yes. I ran track."

"Splendid," I said. "We'll be doing a lot of running in soccer. Your track experience should serve you well."

"I know the positions, Coach," Lori Toth, another beginner, said, "but I thought I'd play where I'm needed."

"That's fine." I looked at Lori and glanced at the index card she had just completed. She listed her height as five feet, six inches and her weight as 170 pounds; she was an eighteen-year-old freshman from Pittsburgh majoring in elementary education. In my mind, I assigned Lori to a fullback spot or maybe even goalie, the two positions Amy had played.

I stroked my cheek and then said to the assembled athletes, "Let me see if I understand you correctly: what you're telling me is that we've got two levels of beginners." I smiled and added, "We've got beginners, and we've got be-gin-ners."

"Or, to put it differently," Angi said, "we've got people who *think* they know that they don't know how to play soccer, and we've got others who *know* they know that they don't know how to play soccer."

Most of the players smiled as I began to explain the program to them, the reasons that the college had started it, how I came to be the coach, the schedule of the home and away games, and other relevant data. Then I leveled with them: "We don't even have enough people here to field a team. We need to get more players, many more if possible." I challenged them to recruit at least two players each and to bring them to our next meeting, to be held the following day at four in my office or, if enough people showed up, in the classroom below my office. I concluded the meeting by asking for a volunteer to accompany me to the bookstore to get more poster paper and markers in order to make still more signs on the program.

On the way to the bookstore, Lori, the volunteer, told me, "Dr. Hanna, I'm sure we'll have a lot more people there tomorrow. This just hit everybody so suddenly, and most kids today are worried about getting their classes and all."

Her innocent remark made me aware of a serious error that I had already made as coach, an error of omission. I realized that the minute that I had accepted the coaching appointment in late May, I should have written a letter to all the college's female students and described the new program in detail; I should have mailed the letter to their home addresses and invited those students interested in playing soccer to reply; and I should have followed up their responses with conditioning drills for the summer months.

"Not doing all that stuff," I told my wife one evening after the kids had gone to sleep and she was reading one of her medical journals and I was watching one of those animal programs on PBS television, "was a major mistake. I wish I had thought of sending them a letter in May or June."

"Thought of it is *not* enough," she said.

"That's right," I said. "I wish I had *done* it."

"If that's going to be your only mistake all season," she said, "then you're in better shape than I thought."

"Well, no, that won't be the only one, I suspect, but it's a major one."

"Sure is," she said.

"Don't agree so quickly."

"You mean you don't want a 'yes' person around?"

"Yes."

"The mistake—major, minor, or otherwise—is made and you don't need to cry over spilt milk."

"But this is more like a slit tit, with milk and blood everywhere. It's that major," I said.

"You spent most of your summer remodeling *When She—*"

"You mean to say 'revising'?"

"If I'd wanted to say 'revising,' I would've said that."

"I suppose they're one and the same, as in that Third World film whose subtitles translate 'a woman's period' as 'her dot of mathematics.'" She smiled at my reference to this peculiarity (concocted, no doubt, by a censor-conscious translator) that I had previously shared with her.

"Seriously," she said, referring to my comic novel, "you spent most of your summer on *When She Went Men-Bashing*, and what you ended up doing is bashing yourself in a manner of speaking. Touchingly ironic, isn't it?"

She returned to her reading and I continued to watch the animals on television. Writing a first novel, I thought, is no problem, just as buying a lottery ticket is no problem, but getting that novel professionally published is, just as winning the lottery is. "As you predict," I said, interrupting her reading once again, "that probably won't be my only mistake."

"So far," she said, "your score is no runs, no hits, one error."

"Oh, the metaphors of baseball! How wonderfully they speak to our follies and irrelevance," I said, and headed to the refrigerator for that late evening snack I had been trying to resist. Snack in hand, I returned to the animal program and told my wife, "There they go again; they're mating, which goes to prove that there's some kind of wisdom in the opening lines of *The Gypsy Scholar*: 'All college professors would love to publish as often as animals mate on the nature programs of PBS television.'"

The next day, thanks to word of mouth, posters, active recruiting, schedule clarification, or whatever, seventeen women stood inside and outside my office. All seemed eager to play soccer. Two out of the eight new players had had serious club experience. This fact at once pleased me and made me nervous. I was pleased that their experience would help us become a good team, but it would also lead them to compare my coaching with that of their previous, no doubt much better, coaches.

In the classroom below my office, I introduced myself to all the players and assured them that I could play soccer, I could dribble and pass, shoot and head the soccer ball, and I knew all the fundamentals of the game, but I had not coached it. I mentioned that in college I had earned a varsity letter in football and I did it "not by eating steroids and playing the line, but by being the team's delicate five-nine, 145-pound little kicker of field goals and extra points. But," I added, "I coached football for the Warriors of Sterling College in Kansas, so coaching as such is not new to me, but soccer coaching is. All this by way of saying that this program is a learning experience for all of us. We're all going to develop our physical and social skills; I hope we're in this program to have fun, to get to know each other individually and as a team, and who cares whether we win or lose. I, for one, do *not* care. To be sure, if victories come our way, we'll take them, but we won't lust after them. I can assure you," I told the players before we turned our attention to more mundane matters, "you'll hear no 'Win one for the Gipper' speeches from me. Not this afternoon, at any rate."

That afternoon in late August, the players completed all sorts of forms. The first one listed their sizes for shoes, shirts, and shorts; the instant those forms were completed, I asked a player to run them down to the director of women's athletics so that she might order the stuff at once. Then the players completed the "Geneva Athletes Information" sheet requesting data on their background, experience, majors, hometown newspapers, high school coaches, and the like; they also completed forms for physical examinations, insurance, and grade eligibility review. After I examined the players' class schedules, we agreed to practice daily from three-thirty to five-thirty. Because I had no assistant, no manager, and no secretary, and because I expected little attention from a trainer (Geneva's only trainer was too busy with the large and demanding football team and other fall sports), I told the players that I expected to serve them in these roles and

I would appreciate their assistance whenever possible. I also told them that my wife—a registered nurse—had agreed to help out in such areas as taping ankles and tending to injuries during home games and that my kids had offered to help with water, ice, ball retrieval, equipment gathering, and so forth.

"Questions?" I asked. "Are there any questions before we break up this meeting?"

"Yeah," one player said. "What about locker rooms, Coach?"

"There's none available to us at this time, as far as I can tell. Women's volleyball and, soon, basketball, and of course physical education classes use what's available," I said.

"But what're we expected to do now?" she asked.

"Come to the field dressed for practice." I took a deep breath and added, "I know all this is inconvenient, but we're a brand-new varsity sport, and I'm an English teacher, not a physical education instructor, and even though the women's athletic director invited me to the weekly coaches' meetings, where I could air our problems and aspirations, I won't be going. No time. So, what I'm saying is this: for this season, let's make do as best we can and let's try to stay out of people's hair much as they have no trouble staying out of mine." All the players smiled as they glanced at my bald head. "It might be rough for now, but we'll manage. In the near future, I'm sure we'll get locker rooms, scholarships, more coaches, a manager. We'll get all that the men's team has, and we'll get it either because the college administrators—an all-male crew—believe in our program or because they fear what might result if they fail to obey the dictates of Title IX; that's the law that prohibits schools that receive federal funds from discriminating against students on the basis of gender. Having said all this, I'd like to make one crucial notation: Geneva's history in dealing with women's sports is an exceedingly positive one, and whatever problems or inconveniences we're likely to encounter this year will be due to the fact that we're a new program that gestated for three months instead of nine."

"Are you saying that we're just a fetus, Coach?" Angi said.

I smiled. "You said that."

"So for now, for this season," a player asked, "we're to dress in the dorm?"

"Right," I said.

"Or any other place you wish," another player added.

"And showers?" someone asked.

"Oh, yes, take those in the dorms, too," I said.

"Of course, we can go to the dining room without showering and take them afterward," a player said.

"That's right, Coach," another player added. "We can't take a shower and eat when practice ends at five-thirty, and we've got to walk up and down these hills."

Following much discussion on the issues of showering and dining and the urgency of both—and in that order—I agreed to end practice at five. "Okay," I said, "we'll quit at five, daily. How's that?"

"Wonderful," one player said.

"Just wonderful," another added.

"That's what I like about you, Coach," Angi said. "You set these stern requirements and you stick by them."

Several players laughed; others hesitated and gave Angi an uneasy look; all applauded the new practice schedule.

"Okay," I said, "a couple of things before we break up." I looked at the players, most of whom seemed eager to leave the meeting. "For the next few days, until the shoes come in, you've got to come to practice with tennis shoes or sneakers, or if you have your own soccer shoes, use them, please. Another thing: if you need to tape your ankles for whatever reason, go down to the field house as early as possible before practice; the trainer and taping people are always busy with football players this time of the year. Third: I'll need a couple of players to come down to the field house before every practice and help me carry water, balls, cones, first-aid kit, and the like to the lower field, the field below where the football team practices, the field all the way down by the gas station at the bottom of the hill. I don't know what condition it's in. It looks bad, but that's going to be our lot; there's no other place to practice."

"Will we play our varsity games there?" Angi asked.

"No, no," I said. "Our home games will be at the Thirty-third Street field, where the men practice and play their games." I smiled and added, "Frankly, I don't like the men's field at all; it's a combination baseball field/soccer field; the baseball infield cuts through the soccer field, so when it rains, the infield gets muddy, and when it's sunny, it's dusty. It's what you might call a 'Have-you-stopped-beating-your-husband?'-type field."

"A what?" Amy asked.

"Say that again, Coach," Angi said. "I bet these women like the sound of that beating your husband bit, but they're too shy to admit it at this stage of the season."

"You'll get used to Angi as the season unfolds," I told the team, then added, "One final thing—and this might seem silly, but it's important: I don't want you anywhere near the weight lifting room. I don't care what your high school coaches might have said; all I know is that I don't want you to mess up your muscles lifting weights, bulking up to gain strength or whatever. I envision our team relying not so much on strength and power but on passing and finesse. Passing is as crucial to soccer as water is to fish. And passing requires grace and beauty and flexibility and timing and intuition and trust: feminine traits possessed by few football jocks, save the gifted quarterbacks, the Joe Montanas of this world, and the elusive and leaping wide receivers, the Jerry Rices, who exhibit those traits and exhibit them in abundance." I looked around the room, noticed the puzzled looks on the players' faces, and continued: "I know that this anti–weight lifting advice sounds strange coming from a coach, but I remember when I coached football in Kansas, so many of our players lifted weights so much that they walked around campus with their arms and elbows in triangular patterns, commanding all onlookers to yield. They lumbered around the prairies and their arms moved slow and smooth as robots. Instead of looking like normal human beings with natural elongated and attractive muscles, they looked like they had tumors sprouting everywhere. I'd love for you to earn nicknames like 'Hotshot' or 'Magic Foot,' but my advice is calculated to help you avoid the nickname that's often earned—and richly deserved, I might add—by the pumping iron boys: 'Tumorsville.'"

"Coach," a player said, "you just ruined my first date with a football player." Then she quickly added, "Come to think of it, I didn't want to go out with that guy, anyway."

"Tumorsville," I heard a player mumble.

"Let me see if I understand you correctly, Coach," Angi said, using an expression that I had often used in class discussions or in casual conversations to set up what I thought was going to be a witty remark. "What you're saying is that body-building classes is a misnomer; what they should be called is 'body-tumoring' classes. Is that correct?"

"Correct," I said, chuckling. "I certainly don't want our goalie to earn the nickname 'the Sterling Sieve,' not unless all our fans have a good sense of irony." With that comment, the meeting ended at about five, just in time for dinner at Alex's, the Geneva dining quarters, located in Alexander Hall.

Lori Toth, the player from Pittsburgh who had accompanied me to the bookstore and volunteered to make several recruiting signs, lingered in the room and began to talk to me: "You know, Dr. Hanna, you've got a lot of students here who've never played soccer before and who aren't really jock types. I'm one of them, and you put a lot of us at ease in this meeting, and I think your style of coaching is going to please a lot of us, making us very happy to be part of the team."

"I'm curious," I told Lori. "If you've never played soccer before, why would you come out now? Soccer, you know, is a grueling, physically demanding sport."

"Oh, yes, I know," she said. "I've always wanted to play organized sports at the varsity level, but frankly, I wasn't good enough to make our high school basketball team. We had no soccer team in high school, but when I saw your signs and read, 'Beginners will be welcomed,' and '*No* experience necessary,' and the 'no' was underlined, I said to myself: This program is for me. I want to play organized, competitive sports, but to do so, I've got to make the team first."

"Did you run track or play on any organized sport in high school?" I asked, looking at Lori's dark hair, packed in a tight bun and anchored to the back of her head. Her round face, free of makeup, was handsome and suggested a winsome personality.

"No, Coach," Lori said. "Our high school didn't have a track team for women. If they did, I probably would've gone out for it."

"But they had a track team for men, didn't they?" I asked.

"They did."

"Did many women go out for the men's team?"

"None that I know," she said. "And even if they had, they would've probably been cut anyway, no matter how good they were."

"That's not only sad," I said, "but it's illegal. Title IX forbids schools that receive federal funds from discriminating on the basis of gender."

"But many men—especially coaches—still have problems with women competing on their teams or against them, for that matter. To be honest, Coach," Lori said, "I wouldn't want to compete against men. I want to compete against other women."

"So, the ideal thing," I reasoned, "would've been to start a track team for women. Is that what you're suggesting?"

"Sure is."

"I agree," I said. Then I asked, "You're a freshman, Lori?"

"Yes, though I prefer being labeled a 'first-year student' instead of a 'freshman' or a 'freshperson,'" she said, smiling.

"Do you have plans to go out for any other sport besides soccer during your college career?" I asked.

"No way," she said, "and I say that for two reasons: time and talent. I won't have enough time to devote to another sport after soccer, and I surely don't have the talent to go out for basketball or volleyball here at Geneva."

"What about softball?"

"I don't care for it," she quickly responded, "and there're no intramural squads in volleyball or basketball for women here, so soccer sounded like an ideal sport to learn, especially for someone like me. You see, I want to be an elementary education teacher and a little knowledge of soccer would certainly help me relate to the kids in recess when they play kick ball. Of course, if I know soccer, I'll teach them soccer."

"Well, I'm really glad you came out for the team, and the way I hope to run the team is the way sports should be run, in my opinion, at a small liberal arts college. Oh, it might be fun to win and all, but that's not going to be our focus; our focus will be to enjoy the sport, the activity, to involve *all* the players—regardless of their physical abilities—in the practices and the games, and to nurture our physical fitness while building camaraderie and lasting friendships."

"That's what I mean, Coach, when I say that your style put a lot of us beginners at ease. We're hoping to have an enjoyable season," she said. Lori started to head toward the door but suddenly paused and said, "Coach, do you mind if I ask you what might appear to be a personal question but really isn't?"

"Well, that depends on the question, but go ahead, ask."

"Please don't feel offended by this," Lori said with a tremble in her voice, "but I'm just wondering: Did the college search for a woman to coach this program?"

"I suspect they did, but I really don't know for sure," I said. "I do know that Geneva loves to have women coaching women at the college level. We have a woman in charge of women's athletics, and we have a woman coaching basketball and a woman coaching volleyball and a woman coaching softball and a woman coaching track, but they probably couldn't find a woman to coach soccer, especially in light of the low pay for the job. Eight hundred dollars for a three-month-plus season wouldn't attract many coaches; after taxes, the pay comes out to less than fifty dollars a week."

"I can't imagine they'd offer that to the coach of the men's program," Lori said.

"Neither can I." After a pause, I added, "The fury from disobeying the dictates of Title IX hasn't kicked in yet in the women's movement nationally, but when it does, look out! There'll be all sorts of legal battles. Geneva at least is starting a women's soccer program in the late eighties. That's a step in the right direction, I'd say."

"I agree," Lori said. "Are you going to be the permanent coach for the program?"

"That I don't know," I said. "From what I understand, if I hadn't accepted the job in May, they were going to wait another full year before starting the varsity team. So I must have been their last choice or, as my wife believes, their *only* choice."

"A lot of us are glad you took the job, Coach, because we want to learn to play, and the sooner we learn, the better," Lori said.

"Yeah, learning a sport can be a lot of fun," I said, "and women's sports in general are a great deal of fun. I love to watch our women play."

"Do you get to see them often?"

"Sure do. I go to most of the basketball games and to some volleyball and softball games."

"Do they win a lot?" she asked.

"Not really, but watching how well they play together and how nicely they develop during the season is satisfying in itself. Oh, don't get me wrong: they get their share of wins, but they don't threaten to be district champs year after year. You see, in a small college like ours, when you get to know the students as individuals, it's satisfying to see them play and grow."

"And I bet," Lori said, "a lot of the players like to see their teachers in the stands."

"You're right," I said. "And because they do, I commit myself to going, and I do it in a strange way: I begin my English classes with a little chitchat with the athletes in a given class; I ask them about their game schedule for the week, and I promise them that I'll attend their games. Promising them in front of the class reminds the other students of the games and forces me to keep my word, and I keep it—cheerfully. I take all four of my kids—"

"How old are they?" Lori asked.

"Five to nine," I said. "Rita's the eldest. They love the games and they often bring their friends along. And at the end of a game, the players usually mingle with the fans, and they visit with their friends and parents and teachers and little kids. That's what makes small-college sports so special."

"Sounds like fun," Lori said.

"It really is," I agreed. "It's a lot of fun for our family, and it's a joy for the athletes. I strongly believe that our athletes need the support not only of their parents and friends but of their professors as well. And, by the way, I'm not the only professor who shows up at the women's games; several others do also, and they come with their kids or their grandkids. There'll be a number of professors and administrators at our soccer games: just wait and see."

Lori started to head toward the door. I gathered the clipboard and forms that the players had just completed. "See you tomorrow at practice, Coach," she said.

"Will do," I said as we parted ways.

On the way to my office, I thought about how glad I was that Lori and other beginners had the courage to come out for the team. Sure, I'd love to have a team of experienced players, players who'd been playing soccer since childhood, but those players were hard to come by. Women's sports, even in the late eighties, desperately needed an infusion of funds to develop them. Funds have a way of creating interest in a sport among coaches who know that they'll be adequately compensated for their labors and among players who know that they'll get competent coaching as well as uniforms, equipment, fields, buses for travel, food for away games, medical attention during games, coverage in the local newspaper, and so forth.

Developing women's sports in colleges and high schools and even in grade schools is still a major problem, and it's the kind of problem that could be solved by throwing money at it. There are still far too many high schools fielding soccer teams for men but not for women. Women are now permitted to play on the men's teams, but in reality, most of them see little or no action in the men's varsity games. Indeed, most women would love to have "a league of their own" at the high school and college levels. If the men's teams receive funds for scholarships, for coaches' salaries, for facilities, for trainers, and for other concerns, the women's teams should also. In fact, women should get *more* money for their sports in order to balance out the incredibly huge sums that the men receive for football.

In the office that afternoon, I leaned back in my Victorian armchair and glanced at two pictures on a shelf: one of Rita, the other of her softball team. Both pictures rested near the books of my favorite poet, T. S. Eliot. The team picture showed a dozen or so girls, ages nine, ten, or eleven, decked out in their red spikes and green and white uniforms emblazoned with "IZZO MONO-GRAM SERVICE," the team's sponsor. I noted the smiles and freckles and braces and wistful looks on the faces of those girls, who were kneeling or standing in front of their dugout at their home field on College Hill. Rita's picture, placed in the corner of the team picture, showed her soft smile, a bat on her left shoul-der, her ponytail dangling out of her one-size-fits-all ball cap.

As I looked at these pictures, I told myself that these girls and thousands like them have every right to expect that the oppor-tunities available to boys their age will also be made available to them—opportunities to develop their athletic talents and to qualify them for college scholarships in sports. I recalled the team's games, and I remembered how the parents would often talk about the emerging equity in sports.

In the mid-eighties, all of us saw what one father called "an honorable eagerness for equity" developing in sports at the youth level, but we wondered if that same spirit was also present at the college level, where a young person's athletic abilities could save the parents huge sums of money. One parent who identified herself as a "conservative Christian" once told us how uneasy she felt about "some of the goals of the women's move-ment," but then she quickly added, "I strongly—yes, strongly—support all that the movement does in behalf of equity in sports. If this makes me a 'Christian equity feminist,' if such a label ex-ists, then that's what I am."

My eyes wandered to the picture of the Sterling College football team I had helped coach, and I thought how unlikely it would be for a woman to coach a college football team; the players expect men to coach them. Likewise, Lori had every right to expect a woman to coach the women's soccer team. Indeed, a female coach could join others in the women's movement and make a strong case for women's sports, but a male coach in the women's movement might be perceived by some as an oxymoron of sorts.

I also thought how I'd love to be perceived not as an intruder in the women's movement but as a coach who cherishes equity, one who'd argue in behalf of Title IX from the equity perspectives shared by parents of daughters who play sports, by coaches of women's programs, and by sensitive and ethically minded citizens who had no vested interest, save a sense of fairness and an awareness of all the benefits that competitive sports could bring to girls and women in such areas as exercise, teamwork, discipline, leadership, enjoyment, friendship, and responsibility.

That afternoon, I also wrote a detailed entry in the "Soccer Season Diary," which I would keep throughout the season in the hope of later writing about Geneva's first year in women's soccer. The entry on that first classroom meeting stated in part:

Met with seventeen players today. What a nice surprise from yesterday's nine. All seem to be enthusiastic about the soccer program. They filled out all sorts of forms among them. . . .

Also, shared with the players my happy-go-lucky, have-fun, and enjoy-the-sport philosophy of coaching. They seemed pleased with that. One player stayed for a few moments after the meeting and told me how that philosophy put many of the players at ease. She disturbed me slightly when she *implied* that she would prefer a woman as a coach for the program. Her ambivalence perplexed me. I suspect other players share her ambivalence.

They loved it when I took stabs at football players. I got a big laugh when I told the story of the college class that had so many football players in it and an anti-football French language professor. The prof. prefaced his remarks before returning the students' first test by saying, "Half the members of this class are stupid. These tests show that." An angry football player sitting in the rear objected by shouting, "Hey, you can't say that. You're insulting us. You've got to take that back." And sure enough, the prof. did by saying, "Okay, I take that back. Half the members of this class are *not* stupid." To which the objecting football player replied, "That's better. Much better."

During the meeting, I stressed to the players the importance of academics, the urgency to do well in their studies; I reminded them that "at little Geneva College, you're student-athletes and not resident-athletes as the case seems to be at many large universities." I mentioned that if tests came up or papers were due and a practice or even a game had to be missed, that'll be fine with me. All I wanted them to do is inform me beforehand so I could plan accordingly.

During that meeting, I also praised and thanked President Nixon—a fellow that most of their parents had probably demonstrated against in their student days in the sixties—for what he did on June 23, 1972: that's the day he signed into law Title IX of the Higher Education Act. It seems I've been referring to Title IX often these days. And, of course, at the meeting I also reminded the athletes of all that the women's movement of the late sixties and early seventies had done in helping bring about Title IX. . . .

Thanks to Nixon and the women's movement, I stumbled into a coaching job that promises to be far more challenging and satisfying than coaching men's baseball would've been. There aren't many coaches who'd dare juxtapose Nixon and Steinem, but I did today.

Tomorrow is our first practice. I'll be out there—midwife of the program—directing feet, balls, and head shots. Should be a lot of fun. . . . One thing for sure: it's not going to be hard to achieve that goal that I playfully set up for the program i.e. to resist playing winning soccer.

After writing that diary entry, I walked to our College Hill house, two blocks from my office, and thought of my upcoming fifteen-hours-per-semester teaching schedule—busy for a college professor, but maybe not so busy at a time when three hundred other Ph.D.'s would have loved to have the job—the upcoming home and away games, a highly supportive wife and four kids, and the students from my upcoming classes who were likely to encounter poor teaching at its best because of my heavy schedule and copious limitations as a teacher.

I thought about my soaring literary career, which was destined to land me in the newest and most sensational who's who–type directory titled *Outstanding Mediocre Modern Men*. And I thought about *When She Went Men-Bashing*, my whimsical first novel with a strong-willed, witty, learned, feisty, creative, politically conservative octogenarian heroine who assaults government's intrusion into our private lives, a novel that the heroine, Gladys Princeton, claims "is an Eliotic ode in code in the spirit of *The Waste Land*, written especially for the literary boy scouts of academia." I wondered if selling the novel to a publisher was going to be harder than selling fish-flavored ice cream (with sprinkles) to the public.

I also thought about Lori and how disappointed she must be in not having a woman as the head coach for the soccer team. I thought about how a woman would relate to the soccer players far better than I could, how she would serve as a splendid role model for our players and others who might join the program in the years ahead.

Most of all, I thought about the meeting and all those players whose insecure and searching eyes had stared at me as I explained the soccer program: eyes that had smiled politely, even hesitantly, as I tried to sneak in a few comical asides; that had wandered around the room sizing up the team and the competition for positions; that had seemed perplexed by the uncertainties of the days ahead; that had looked at me as if to say, "Hey, fellow, we don't know you now, but we will by the end of the season—and we'd better like you then."

Moments before I arrived at my house, I began to think of my old football coach, a six-foot-plus hulk of a man and a relentless yeller. He would yell at us on the field during practice, on the sidelines during a game, in the locker room at halftime, on the bus back from a loss, in the classroom during film sessions. He would yell so often that many of us believed he was the only coach in the country who practiced, indeed perfected, the art of "retroactive yelling." This phrase, which we had frequently assigned to certain yelling streaks, helped us endure his behavior, his tirades. And what tirades some of them were! At times he would get so angry that we were sure we could light a cigarette off his bald head. (None dared try, however.) Poisoned with blasphemy and profanity, his tirades tried to motivate us to improve our play, to correct our mistakes, and to hit with greater passion and intensity. Even when those tirades worked—and the coach must have thought they worked often, for he had an impressive winning percentage—I detested them and the humiliation they heaped upon us.

On that walk home, I resolved never to raise my voice in anger during the practices or the games. If football coaches wished to yell at their players, that was their business; if men's basketball coaches wanted to yell and throw chairs à la Indiana's Bobby Knight, that, too, was their business. I felt that such behavior was inappropriate in women's sports and ill-advised in men's sports as well. I reasoned that if I could not motivate our players in a civil manner, I had no business being their coach. I vowed to treat the players much like I treated the students in my classroom: with the utmost courtesy and respect at all times.

It remained to be seen whether Geneva's women would like the soccer program and the ways of a scholar-coach, especially those of a laid-back English professor who fancied himself to be a comic writer of sorts. The following day was the first practice that would lead to other practices that would culminate with the opening game on September 7, less than two weeks away. Throughout those early practices, one thought curled up in my mind like the fortune in a Chinese cookie: Winners win, beginners undertake an adventure.

2

The Midwife Directs Feet, Balls, and Head Shots

"What do soccer coaches do before their first practice?" Rita asked.

"Wait for it to come," I said, glancing at my wife. "And that's not like waiting for Godot; practice will be here tomorrow."

"Sure will," my wife said.

"And you and I have a little project to do after the kids go to bed."

"Oh, we do?" she asked.

"What's that, Daddy?" asked ever curious Rita.

"We're going to design a soccer stationery that I might use. That's a special sheet of paper on which to write my athletic-related correspondence."

After dinner, I watched PBS's "MacNeil/Lehrer News-Hour," then the "CBS Evening News," and then played with the kids while occasionally glancing at the interruptions in CNN's "Crossfire." After the children went to bed, my wife and I designed a stationery with a bold, banner headline that read, "GENEVA'S GOLDEN TORNADOES," a nickname that I liked because of its paradoxical feel. Immediately below the headline to the left were the words "S. S. Hanna, Ph.D., Head Coach," and to the right, "Women's Soccer." An inch or so from the bottom of the page was a thin line; below it, the college's name, address, and telephone number were listed. We fiddled with a logo, but since the only artistic gifts both of us owned came by

35

way of Christmas presents, we decided against our strange-looking creations.

Throughout our creative fit, we had only one major disagreement: I wanted to leave out the Ph.D. title and to use the initials S. S. with Hanna. (I like the way initials neutralize gender identification and believe more people should use them.) But my wife suggested that I use the Ph.D. title or, better yet, what she labeled "your New Jersey pizza-parlor middle name, Sal," which she and the children liked far better than S. S. (Rita often popped open the initials and nicknamed me "Short Stop" Hanna. "In doing that, Dad," she would say, "I'm referring not to baseball but to the way you look when you stop.")

"If you remove the Ph.D. bit and use your initials," my wife said, "then people won't know whether to write you as Mr., Ms., Miss, or Mrs.—and I'm sure your goalie is going to have a lot of those. With the Ph.D. in there, the problem is solved; they'll call you Dr. Hanna, and the 'Dr.' is gender neutral."

"That it is," I said.

"Without the degree title and with the initials, people won't know whether you're a male, a female, or a flagship," she said with a straight face.

"But a coach is a coach," I said.

"True," she said, "but a coach can also be a Greyhound bus and a buss can be a kiss and we can go on forever with this wordplay."

"I remember from those football-coaching days in Kansas that no matter what you teach, no matter how many degrees you have, football players will still call you Coach."

"Yeah," she said, "but football players are jocks."

"But they hold scholarships, not jockships," I said.

"'Scholarships' might well be a misnomer, but I suspect Geneva's women athletes and others will have more respect for you and call you *Dr.* Hanna," she said, her eyes telegraphing a sinister "just kidding" smile.

"We'll see. Let's leave that Ph.D. bit in there, though I know that a coach can have more degrees than a thermometer, and a coach will always be a coach."

At eleven-thirty on the eve of the first practice, I went to the offices of the student newspaper, a weekly for which I served as faculty advisor, used the headline machine and light table, and produced a camera-ready page. The next morning I headed to the registrar's office, home of the best copy machine on campus, and copied the page fifty times on quality bond paper. When the first copy came out of the machine, I looked at it closely, pushed it away, then slowly brought it toward my eyes again and said, "Presto—it's done. Now if only our first victory comes this easily." I called my wife and arranged to meet her at DeAngelis for coffee and doughnuts.

She liked the stationery and told me to use it not only with athletic-related correspondence but also with literary matters. "You'll get more attention from the Doubledays of this world if you're not only an obscure college professor but an obscure women's soccer coach as well."

During my morning and afternoon classes that day, I announced to the students that I was coaching women's soccer and that I might have to miss an occasional class because of a road trip. I also told them to speak to me after class if they knew women students with or without soccer-playing experience who might be interested in joining the team.

Sure enough, after class I received the names of two students: one was a psychology major from a suburb of Pittsburgh who had played outdoor and indoor soccer throughout high school and on a strong club team during the summer; the other was a bright pre-med student from upstate New York who had played extensively before coming to Geneva, a former student in one of my advanced writing classes. I immediately met with both students, and though I implored, begged, and pleaded with them—and if that sounds redundant, that's the way I must have sounded to them—they turned me down for the simple reason that they wished to devote all their time to their studies. "Good graduate schools in psychology," the psychology major told me, "are tough nuts to crack, and one has to study and study, then do more study, to get in. Soccer will simply take too much time." And the pre-med student reminded me how tough medical school admission standards are. "Dr. Hanna," she noted, "you serve on the medical school admissions' committee; I don't need to tell you that." At one instance, I thought of asking them to show up and play in the games and forget about coming to practice, but I quickly dismissed that idea. Even if I had made that suggestion, I am sure that their sense of integrity and fair play would have led them to reject it, however much they loved, to use the words of the pre-med major, "game day of that wonderful game of soccer."

Geneva's first varsity game was ten days away. Our first practice was the afternoon of the first class day. At three o'clock, clipboard in hand, I headed down to the field house's equipment room and greeted the cheerful and ever helpful gentleman who attended it. I pulled out the ball bag, which resembled an old soccer goal net, counted the fifteen balls that he told me were in it, grabbed several red cones, some old shin guards, and a whistle, then waited outside the door for my player help to arrive. At about three-fifteen, four players—dressed in shorts, T-shirts, and sneakers, ready to practice soccer—arrived and began filling a bucket with water and ice while I got the first-aid kit from the trainer.

When I returned, we carried the assembled items and strolled across the football field, then walked up to College Avenue and down to the football practice field, slowing our pace as we headed to the periphery of the field and admired the hunks who played on the line and the wiry athletes who played in the backfields. Most players were either standing around or casually throwing passes, waiting for their practice to begin. The football players, dressed in their uniforms and shoulder pads—the occasional envy of European fashion designers—elicited sympathetic comments from the women soccer players heading to their own practice on this hot afternoon. As we passed the football team, goose bumps flowed down my arms like falling dominoes, for I remembered my happy football-coaching days at Sterling College. That particular afternoon, I found myself, in the words of T. S. Eliot, "mixing memory and desire." But as the days peeled off more practices and we repeated our trudge up and down those fields, my mind focused on the soccer team's immediate performances and virtually ignored the past.

The first practice was typical of all our other practices. On their own, the players would go through their muscle-stretching exercises. At three-thirty, with all the team members there, I would blow the whistle and ask the players to form a small circle. I would stand in the center of the circle, hold a clipboard—the insecure coach's baby blanket—and take roll; then I would inform the players of the schedule for the afternoon, specifying the various drills, the breaks, the scrimmages, and whatever material I had been able to gather about our forthcoming opponent.

One day, midway into the season, I ended the pre-practice announcements by saying, "Hope you like our table of contents for today."

"Sounds like *Finnegans Wake* to me," Angi said.

"What?" another player asked.

"Boring," Angi said.

"You mean, hard to get through?" I asked.

"That too, Coach," Angi said.

To be sure, several of the practices were hard to get through, but not that first one. At the end of the announcements on the first day, I asked if the players had any questions. They had none, so I told them to kindly back up and make a larger circle, then I whistled, an authoritative whistle that transformed a simple request into a command, metamorphosing the scholar's pipe-smoking gentleness into the coach's clipboard-slapping toughness. "That whistle," I later recorded into the "Soccer Season Diary," "footnoted in a manner that was puzzling to me and probably to most of the players all my previous comments on fun and enjoyment. Whatever, that was the whistle that signaled the beginning of the season in earnest."

Following that whistle, the players did calisthenics that I had demonstrated while standing in the center of the circle. They hopped on one foot, then the other; they skip-jumped with legs together then apart; they rotated their trunks in both directions; they ran on the spot with knees high; they jumped and twisted their bodies with their hands on their hips; they flicked the muscles of their arms and legs, loosening the feet for kicking; they sprinted forward, closing the circle, and backward, stretching it out once again. Then I demonstrated the various kicking categories: the inside of the foot, the inside of the instep, the full instep, the outside of the instep, the toe, and even the heel. That done, I demonstrated dribbling the ball: that is, the moving of the ball by means of a series of short kicks or, in more pedestrian language, running with the ball. From my position in the center of the circle, I kicked the ball to each player, asked her to dribble toward me then back to her position in the circle. Once at her position, I asked her to pass the ball to me using the inside of the foot.

We worked for a while on dribbling and passing techniques. Then came the welcomed five-minute break followed by the dribbling exercise. The players dribbled five laps around the women's soccer field, which was about twenty yards longer and ten yards wider than a football field. After that, we did more passing work, more dribbling using cones for markers, and more dribbling around the field for conditioning purposes.

At every practice I would introduce a new aspect of the game, work on it for a while, then go back and practice—again and again—techniques that had already been learned. By the first game, the players had been exposed to basic kicking techniques; passing categories; dribbling; trapping techniques with the foot, the thigh, and the stomach; heading the ball; kickoffs; free kicks; throw-ins; corner kicks; goal kicks; penalty kicks; and other concerns.

Those early practices introduced me to different dimensions of the team. I came to know, almost instantly, that I was to coach two teams: one was made up of beginners who struck me as being ineptness personified. Eager to learn, they worked hard and seldom complained about any aspect of the practices, save the sweltering heat of late August and early September, a heat made more oppressive by all the running that the players did with or without the ball.

As a caste, the beginners were high on desire and awkwardness; fortunately, their desire remained high as they began to chip away, ever so slowly, at their awkwardness. I would frequently tell them as I instructed them in the fundamentals of passing and dribbling and stopping the ball: "Practice does *not* make perfect; it makes permanent. Let's not pick up and be saddled permanently with bad habits. Let's do things right. One of the virtues of being a beginner is that you don't have any bad habits to unlearn." The beginners had numerous skills to learn and practice. These skills differed vastly from any that they might have acquired from their childhood days playing softball or basketball or volleyball, sports that rely more on the use of the hands and arms than the feet and legs, the limbs of soccer.

One beginner's athletic experience impressed me greatly. Suzanne Maslo, or Suzie, as she wished to be called, was the team's smallest player at four feet, eleven inches and 130 pounds. She refused to call herself "short," preferring instead "down-to-earth," or "close to the ground." She once told me, "My motto—and I know you can't say it fast—is: 'When you're on the ball, the tall will fall before the small.'" That was Suzie: she loved to play with words and to participate in different sports.

At her large Pittsburgh high school, Suzie had been captain of the swimming team for four years (Geneva didn't have a swimming team), a letter winner on the volleyball team, and a starting pitcher on the fast pitch softball team. She had pitched a no-hitter in a varsity softball game, an achievement that had caught my attention. I concluded that Suzie was a versatile athlete who would quickly pick up the techniques of soccer.

A business administration major with a four-point average (every grade she had received in her first three years in college was an A), Suzie participated in two musical groups at Geneva: one was the large college choir and the other was a small singing group that traveled around the country during the school year and especially during the college's periodic "long breaks."

She was also involved in the college's Haiti Mission Project. At the end of her junior year she had gone to Haiti with a group of students and faculty members to help build a house for orphans. She later wrote about her experience and published her reflections in the student newspaper and the yearbook. "Every day they were there to meet us," she wrote, referring to the orphans at the site of the building project, "and during lunch we were able to play with them. We took along some balls and things, and they taught our guys a few things about soccer."

Back in the United States for her senior year, Suzie came out to learn about Geneva-style soccer. Unlike the first-year students, who expected to develop their soccer skills in four years, Suzie joked, "As a senior, I expect to develop my skills instantly; maybe I should say 'mystically.'"

The most striking feature about Suzie was her hair. One day in practice when Angi was standing next to me and Suzie was dribbling the ball toward the goal, Angi said, "Coach, look at Suzie's quick, choppy strides as she dribbles that ball, and look at her disgustingly beautiful short, curly blond hair. Why, it looks like a bowl of coiled pasta! Doesn't it?"

"On hair," I said, "I make no comments."

"I can see why," Angi said. "Yours looks like an empty bowl."

We both laughed as Angi charged after a ball that had drifted to her area. She stopped it and passed it back to a group of beginners who were practicing and practicing the most fundamental of soccer moves: passing the ball with the instep.

Compared with the beginners, the experienced players seemed refreshing indeed. They knew how to pass and dribble and trap the ball and how to use their bodies and especially their heads to stop or advance the ball. In practice, I would often divide the team into beginners and experienced players. I would work with each unit, then I would assign an experienced player to work with two or three beginners. (No one could ever accuse me of being selfish, for I shared my frustrations.) The experienced players, in effect, took on the role of assistant coaches.

Four such players—Amy, Angi, Jill, and Barb—struck me as being particularly talented. Amy Widener, far and away, had the strongest leg on the team. Her punts from goal would go high and far, bringing a smile to the coach of the kicking game in men's football. Punts of forty or fifty yards, sizzling line-drive kicks, well-placed passes, dribbles laced with acute turns and dazzling footwork—all were part of Amy's kicking repertoire.

During idle moments in practice, I would occasionally glance at Amy, and she would be relaxing not by sprawling on the grass or heading to the water bucket but by flipping the ball from her foot to her thigh to her head and back to her foot, looking more like a professional juggler than a strong soccer player who had honed her talents by playing on a men's team in the macho state of Texas. At times, Amy would trap the ball between her insteps and jump up, yanking the ball to the height of her head and slightly in front of her; she would then whistle or grunt while driving her foot into the suspended ball, slashing her right leg toward her body, revealing a splendid example of a strong follow-through to a booming and creative punt that had never touched her hands. Not only could Amy flip and punt and shoot the ball with finesse and authority, but she could also drop-kick it, and she could use her right arm and body in throwing a long and accurate "baseball pass."

"My coach in Texas," Amy once told me as I watched her from the side of an improvised goal, fielding shots during practice, "didn't like the goalie to use the baseball pass, especially if the ball had to travel more than five yards. What about you, Coach? Do you object to me using the pass?"

"Not at all," I told her. "You be the judge of the wisdom of using it in a given situation. I've always loved that expression, 'the baseball pass.'"

"Oh," Amy said, as she reached over and blocked a shot with her right foot; a spirited Angi followed the blocked shot by dribbling the ball for a step or so, dipping her body in one direction, faking a shot, then sailing the ball in the opposite direction— and scoring. "That won't happen again," Amy said, embarrassed that she had fallen for Angi's fake.

"Good," I said.

"What is it about that baseball pass expression that you like so much, Coach?" Amy asked, fielding another shot, this time with her hands.

"It's one of those unique expressions in sports that alludes to no less than three sports at once."

"How so?" Amy asked, swatting the ball to the right of a plastic red cone that we used as a goal marker during those early practices.

"You associate the pass with basketball; that's one sport where it's used. You call it a 'baseball pass'; that's two sports. You associate the long pass with football; that's three sports. And then the long throw you also associate with baseball," I said, feeling slightly dissatisfied with what might have appeared to Amy, a communications major, to be some garbled rhetoric.

"Oh, you English teachers are all alike, always looking for meaning and association in phrases and expressions," she said, as she lunged to her right to deflect another of Angi's low, strong shots.

Angi Moyer, a five-foot, four-inch junior from Cumberland, Maryland, was another experienced player who had impressed me. I knew her well from English classes. She served as the grading assistant in my freshman composition classes, and as a writing major in a small college (Geneva has slightly more than a thousand students and four full-time English professors), Angi had taken so many of my courses that when people asked her what she was majoring in, she frequently said, with her sarcasm intact, "Hanna."

During practice and the games, Angi often wore one of those headbands that tennis players wear. She was a slender athlete, quick and shifty. She could dribble, weave, and pass the ball with remarkable skill. She could appear to be going in one direction with the ball, completely reverse that direction, cutting sharply to her right or left or turning around completely. She could dip her body one way and go in the opposite direction. She could pull a moving ball behind her with her spikes and pass it quickly with her heel, as quickly as she could with the other parts of her right foot.

Angi always wrapped a wide bandage on her right thigh. I never knew why she wore that bandage, and I never asked. (It wasn't a dark bandage, so I assumed that she wasn't protesting the death of a person, a pet, an idea, a cause, or a lifestyle; Angi was the type of person who'd protest the death of these and other matters, and she'd do it in her own style.) She played right wing, and as our goalie, Amy, often reminded me, "Angi's shots at goal are particularly effective because they are strong and low, lower than a foot in some cases."

Jill Weakland, a five-foot, six-inch 130-pound sophomore majoring in business administration, caught my attention with her steady performances in practice. She knew the fundamentals of the game, and she always yanked sighs and exclamations from the beginners when she head-stabbed the ball. I use the word *stabbed* advisedly in that Jill wouldn't wait for the ball to get to her head; she would lunge and attack the ball. She would often practice passing the ball with her head. Some team members would occasionally practice long corner kicks, with Angi or Barb kicking the ball high from the right or left corner of the field, and Jill, who played center forward, heading it into the goal. The drill was so enjoyable that Amy frequently left her goal position and joined Jill and Kristin Menningen and Sara Smith in taking head shots at the wide-open soccer goal.

In high school, Jill had lettered in track and soccer, and at Geneva she participated in both sports at the varsity level. At the intramural level, Jill joined Angi and Amy in playing "gym floor hockey," a version of ice hockey played with no skates but with vicious gusto. Floor hockey was an exceedingly popular sport at Geneva; more students and faculty members would often attend the women's hockey battles than would go to some men's basketball games, and basketball was a popular sport.

During our preseason soccer practices, I noted that Jill said the least and played the best. That, I also noted, could be an excellent quality in a team captain. One day in practice, I asked her from whom she had inherited her reserved personality. I expected her to say from her mother or father or grandparents or aunts. She answered, "From Solomon, son of David, king of Israel. How do you like that?" I smiled and she continued, "In Proverbs, Solomon says, 'Even a fool who keeps silent is considered wise; when he closes his lips, he is deemed intelligent.' Notice that Solomon, in his infinite wisdom," she added with a wink, "uses the masculine pronoun *he* to refer to a fool." We both smiled. "These days we paraphrase Solomon and say, 'It's better to keep your mouth shut and let people think you're stupid than open it and remove all doubts.' And as a professor, you probably know that some people can be pretty graceful at removing those doubts. Now, does that answer your question, Professor-Coach Hanna?"

"Before I tell you," I said, "let me say you just disproved Shakespeare's famous adage: 'Brevity is the soul of wit.' Anyway, that bit about your reserved personality—which now doesn't seem so reserved after all—was just small talk, a warm-up, as it were, to the real question, which is this: Would you consider serving the team as the captain for the entire season?"

"Well," she said, "let me think about it." After a pause, she added, "I just thought about it, and the answer is yes. Thanks for asking me."

I thanked her for accepting and told her that I would announce her appointment during an upcoming classroom meeting with the team.

Our left-footed left wing, Barb Schwettman, was the fourth experienced player to catch my attention during those early practice sessions. Barb was a shy eighteen-year-old freshman from Fairfield, Ohio, who had excelled in soccer in high school. She was the tallest player on our team at five feet, eleven inches, and she had long, strong legs and long arms (great assets for a person playing first base in softball or center in basketball, sports that Barb had played and lettered in during high school). Barb was recruited to play softball at Geneva, but she gladly came out for our team because soccer was played in the autumn and softball in the spring.

Barb's kicks featured a wide, sweeping follow-through. For a tall 145-pound player, she was fast; her long strides made her faster than most shorter players her age. Her ability to pass and shoot the ball impressed me, though we had to work on her sense of anticipation, that intangible quality that gets a player to move in a certain direction, to get in a position to go to—or be in—the right open spot at just the right time. Developing that sense would take time, particularly on a team with so many beginners. Barb on the left wing, Jill in the middle, and Angi on the right wing were to be our scoring punch. At least that's what I deduced from those early practice sessions.

After practice, several players and I always carried the water bucket, balls, shin guards, and other soccer gear past the football practice field. "There's a lot of standing around in these football practices, Coach," said one player who carried a stack of red marking cones.

"I'd say so," another player added.

"You know," I said, "I coached college football in Kansas, and that was always one of our biggest problems: how to prevent a lot of standing around."

"How did you guys solve it?" Angi asked.

"By standing around, pretty much as you see here," I said, pointing my chin. "When you've got four units, and you've got to coach and teach and execute and repeat—especially with that first unit—all that's bound to lead to standing around. And all that standing around robs a lot of athletes of opportunities to develop their gifts."

"I bet some of those players couldn't endure all the running and kicking that we go through," another said as we marched behind a line of football players who were watching a play in action.

"That's right," Angi agreed. "We do long-distance running in our laps before and after practice, and we do wind sprints and more wind sprints during the scrimmages, especially when we chase that ball, dribble it, pass it, go out for a pass, shoot it, chase it again."

"I know for sure—and I base this on my experiences as a football coach—that many of the guys who play the line on offense or defense and indeed many of those linebackers couldn't take all the running that you people do in soccer," I said.

"Sounds strange, but I bet it's true, Coach," a player said as we approached the sidewalk leading to the stadium's field.

"You bet it's true," I said. "I was there as a football coach, and I'm here now as a soccer coach. Believe me, it's an informed comparison that I'm making."

The soccer players' endurance levels and athletic skills (or lack of them) must have been entertaining, for frequently during practice, people would stand outside the high wire fence that surrounded the field, clutch some openings in the diamond-shaped lacing of the wire, and look in. Occasionally they would say "Good kick" or "Nice shot," or they would cheer at a head ball by Jill, our head-baller extraordinaire.

That kind of crowd—mostly older males and grade school boys on bikes—did not bother our players. What disturbed them, however, were all the truck drivers who traveled the main road of College Hill, Interstate 18, a highway that hugs the periphery of Geneva's campus. Those truck drivers and their rigs would appear practice after practice with the certainty of the colors and patterns in a revolving barber pole. They would first halt at a stop sign twenty yards from our goal. Then they would slowly climb College Hill, slowing even more at the sight of young women in shorts running on the lush green grass or chasing a ball, their long blond hair flapping in the breeze. At times—too many times, sad to say—the drivers would honk their horns, yell out some sexist remarks, and continue their climb or descent, as the case may be, of College Hill.

"I'd love to see that guy," I once told the players during practice, referring to an obnoxious horn-addicted, foul-mouthed sexist driver, "come down here and stand in that goal where Amy's standing. And I'd love to see Amy or Barb or Jill dribble toward him and take ten shots at him—hot, firm, vicious shots. And I'd love to see the shots not go through the goal—that'd be too easy—but smash him. They'd stun him; they'd get him to develop an instant respect for what it takes to play this game." Then I said silently to myself: It takes a heck of a lot more skill to play this game than to pull the horn of that massive rig of his.

•   •   •   •   •

One evening, we had a special classroom meeting during which I announced the name of the experienced player I had appointed as captain. "For a team captain this season," I said, "we need to have a woman who is a good athlete and who uses her head a lot. So I took the liberty of appointing Jill, and she accepted." The team members clapped, and several yelled, "Go, Jill, go, go!"

"Where should I go to?" Jill asked with a smile.

I also explained in detail the rules of the game, using the blackboard and handouts. Moreover, I announced that two players had left the team for personal reasons. (One was a beginner; the other had classified her experience as "more or less," but my evaluation notes had placed her in the "less" category. The beginner's career goal was to become a missionary; a knowledge of soccer, she had believed, would help in her work on the mission fields of Asia or Latin America, where she hoped to be assigned. "I discovered from our practices so far that I'm not really aggressive enough," she had told me privately.)

I discovered that I must not have been complimenting the players enough, for they asked: "How are we doing as a team?" "Do you think we're going to be competitive?" "Do you really think it's going to be possible to field a competitive team composed of half beginners and half experienced players?" "Are we picking up things quickly enough?"

"Speaking of picking up things," one player said, "that field has lots of stones in it, Coach, and you should ask maintenance to send a crew to pick them up. We keep tripping over them."

"Yeah," another agreed, "we look tipsy out there, not because we're uncoordinated but because of all those big pebbles."

"Stones, you mean," another said.

"Rocks," a third shouted.

"Until a few years ago," I said, "a cork factory was there. The factory moved, donated the buildings and land to Geneva, and Geneva had to tear down the buildings and haul the remains away. They just finished tearing down the joint, and they've tried to plant grass. You know, we're the first team ever to use that field for an athletic activity."

"We can believe that," a player said. Others nodded or hummed in agreement.

"From what I understand," I said in defense of Geneva, "a certain Dr. Merriman, a retired pediatrician, a wealthy and generous gentleman from College Hill, an exceptional athlete at Geneva in his day, and a big benefactor of the college, is planning to give Geneva lots of money to develop the women's soccer field and to improve the football practice field and the women's softball field, and the college plans to call the area down there 'The Merriman Athletic Complex.' All that, however, is a couple of years away."

"Isn't it ironic," Angi commented, "that a pediatrician would be interested in our program in that our program is a fetus of sorts?"

"I want to return to that tipsy bit," I said.

"Oh," one player said.

"And I want to do it via Joe Namath who—"

"As in Broadway Joe, the old football quarterback?" a player asked.

"Right," I said.

"He's not exactly the hero of our generation, Coach, but go ahead anyway," Angi said.

"I don't know how many of you know that Joe Namath is from Beaver Falls; this is his hometown; he played his high school football right down here in our stadium." The players appeared unimpressed, but I continued, "When Namath became instantly rich, thanks to his professional football contract, he's reputed to have bought a place with such thick carpeting that even a teetotaler would have appeared to be tipsy when strolling on it."

"There you go again, Coach," Angi said. "You're comparing our field to Joe Namath's living room. Is that sophistry at its best? Or is it the desperate irony of a jock-prof?"

"Whatever it is," I said, "we've got to do something about those stones. Maintenance is too busy this time of the year. Here it's our eighth day of practice, and we still don't have goalposts or nets."

"That's incredible in itself, isn't it?" Angi asked.

"It really is," Amy agreed, "especially when they knew in May about this soccer program and all that it would need."

"I bet it wouldn't be this way if we were a men's team," Angi said.

"Yes it would," I said. "Most of our problems here at the college result from cash flow. Geneva's cash flow, when it comes to certain programs—and not just women's sports—experiences a urinary tract infection, making it appear more like a dribble than a flow. You see, as a college, we're tuition-driven; the more students that we have in a given year, the more money we'll have to spend that year. But recruiting students is tough these days; it really is. Many other colleges are in the same bind. The higher-ups around here started our soccer program partly to recruit students and partly in response to Title IX. To save money, the school doesn't want to buy ready-made goals; they want to make their own, and that'll probably take a little while. As for now, we'll still have to make our own goals in practice by using those red plastic cones. Okay," I added, "now listen to this carefully: I've got an idea on what to do with all those stones on the field, and the idea deals with the cones that we currently use for goals."

"Try that again, Coach," one player said.

"Please don't," Angi said. "Just explain it."

"Okay, here's my explanation," I said. "You don't need to write this down, just remember it."

"There's no danger of that, Coach," Angi said.

"Danger of what?" another player asked. "Writing or remembering?"

"Writing" came the quick reply.

"Anyway," I said, "you know those dreaded dribbling laps, the five laps that we do *after* practice? I'll omit those from tomorrow's practice if all of us right here and now agree to do one thing before practice, and that is go up and down the field in single files, picking up the rocks and putting them into piles. If we go up and down that field half a dozen times or so, we'll have them all picked up in no time. How does that sound?"

"You've got a deal, Coach," Angi said.

"Sounds good to me," Amy said. Others nodded their agreement.

"We'll look like citizens who have volunteered to help law enforcement agencies by combing the fields in search of a missing body, but we'll get the job done." I looked around the room, stood up, and said, "Before we break up this meeting, we've got one more item to do, and you may blame Angi for it; she's a writing major, you know."

All the players looked at Angi, who had just put her head down and covered it with her arms, much as softball fans do when a fly ball comes their way and someone yells, "Heads up!" With her head down, Angi said, "You'll like this; you will—I *think*."

"I don't know if you will," I said, "but I have agreed to Angi's request. She wanted me to read to you something that I have written so that you might come to know me in a different context than a coach. Since I've only had as students in class the three writing majors, I don't know the rest of you, and you don't know me other than that fellow who blows the whistle and drives you to do all sorts of grueling exercises. Angi's reasoning went something like this: I'm not your typical jock-jock coach. And she's right: I'm what you might call a word-jock coach. To be brutally honest, I'm a certified failure as a writer; most people from my caste pursue a Ph.D. then take to teaching creative writing or other courses in English. And we teach with confidence that which we couldn't do, much as Little League baseball coaches who couldn't make it as baseball players teach with confidence the skills and moves of that sport. Unlike most English teachers, however, I've tried my hand at coaching football and now soccer and, in the future, baseball, I hope."

"Get to the point, Coach," Angi said. Her tone and choice of words might have shocked some players, but I thought to myself: In time, they'll learn to say what everyone who knows Angi says, "Well, that's Angi all right."

"Okay," I said, "I chose two very brief selections—"

"Good," someone sitting in the back of the room said. I didn't know if the "good" referred to the fact that there were two or that they were brief. I suspected the latter.

So I decided to read just one, the one that might invite the players to relax and laugh at me in my capacity as a struggling comic novelist. I began reading:

So You Want to Be a Writer?

Irritated by the caller's pleading, the editorial assistant put him on hold and consulted the senior editor who agreed to "take care of him for good."

"Hello," the editor said. "Aren't you glad I put the 'o' at the end of that; it's been that kind of day."

"Hello, Mr. Huntly. How are you, sir? Three months ago, I sent you a novel of mine, and I'm now making this *courtesy* call to inquire about its status, sir."

"Obviously, its status is low; otherwise I would have responded sooner."

"But you didn't respond at all, sir. I'm calling you to find out its status."

"What's the title?"

"Would you want the full title, sir?"

"Full of what?" A long pause followed. The writer-caller seemed shocked. "Are you still there? Hello, hell-o, hel-lo" the editor said.

"Yes."

"Go ahead , give me the full title."

"First, sir, let me explain my book. It's a novel on epistemology."

"Is it a first novel?"

"Yes."

"The kind that we invariably lose money on?" A long silence, the kind that a loaded coffin elicits, followed that question. Then the editor added, "How much money do you want us to lose on *your* first novel?"

"Sorry, sir, I'm just making this courtesy call to inquire about the status of the manuscript."

"And how quickly do you want us to lose it? Eh?"

"Okay, I'll give you that."

"Without reading the work, sir?"

"Well, I don't know. Maybe I read it. you haven't even given me its title."

"No, sir; sorry about that. Here's its short title: *When the Dog—*"

"Oh, no, not another dog—"

"No , sir, it's not another dog story; it's on epistemology."

"A pisswhat?"

"Epistemology."

"Does that have anything to do with urology?"

"No, sir, epistemology, though I see how you get the connection, sir."

"Is that a commercial novel?"

"No."

"Gothic, romance, fantasy?"

"No to all three."

"Mystery?"

"No, sir, not that either."

"What the hell is it? Sounds like a mystery to me."

"It's a philosophical novel, sir, probing philosophical questions, deep philosophical question."

"Is that deep as in profound or throat?"

"Profound."

"So you expect the novel to appeal to what crow?"

"To the readers of *The American Scholar*. That's the journal of the Phi Beta Kappa society, you know."

"No, I didn't know that; doesn't sound like a best-seller to me."

"But you haven't looked at it, sir."

"I don't need to. Your novel seems to have half of the bestseller formula; it appeals to the Phi Beta Kappa crowd."

"And the other half it needs to appeal to?"

"The readers of the *National Enquirer*. That's the journal of the Phi Beta Krappa crowd."

"The who?"

"You heard me right; I'm not going to repeat it. Hit both crowds and you've got the best-seller formula."

"Any topic that you suggest, sir?"

"Yeah, how about a book on astrology—not epistemology, now, but astrology, White House astrology and don't you dare lapse into a Southern accent when you pronounce that word."

"Good idea, sir. Thank you so much."

"Oh by the way," the editor stated, "what's your full title?"

"I'm a full professor of psycho—."

"No, no, I know you're full, professor. But the title of your novel?"

"Oh, that."

"Yes that. What is it? I don't have all day; I've got some more status calls on hold."

"It's probably logged under the first word I gave you, so you look it up and send it back. I've had it!"

The writer slammed the phone and shouted the irrigation word. The editor asked his assistant to look up the manuscript, cover it with the standard rejection slip, and pass it back to him for a quick comment.

"Sorry, not for us," the editor wrote ant took a peek at the rest of the title, which read: *"Takes the Question Mark Posture."*

"The last time I sent out this comic-short," I told the athletes before we broke up the meeting, "I sent it with a cover letter that read: 'The enclosed piece is guaranteed to make you laugh or bring your sense of humor back.' Well, the editors misinterpreted the guarantee and sent the manuscript back." I smiled and said, "See ya tomorrow at practice."

On the ninth day of practice, Geneva's women's soccer team began its workout by walking up and down the field collecting stones and placing them into four piles. This is the task for which the players had bartered their dribbling drills, and they seemed to enjoy the deal. In a diary entry for that day, I recorded a casual comment made by one of the players: "If this is what getting stoned is all about, I'm not missing much." I heard another say, "I can't believe we're doing this."

At noon on Friday, the last day of practice before the opening game that was to introduce a new varsity sport to Geneva College, I went to the faculty lunch table at the Brig, the snack bar in the student union. Questions about the team, the schedule, individual players, my outlook, and my personal goals as a coach hit me from all directions. I responded directly and honestly, never understating our strength, which, in any event, was a verbal and conceptual impossibility. Most faculty members seemed to enjoy my account of the ways of our beginners, many of whom, I noted, "are earnest and dedicated players who will often run up to the ball and do a kind of Kickapoo Indian dance around it until the ball is near their right feet—"

"Feet or foot?" one faculty member interrupted.

"Boy, you must really have extraordinary ballplayers if each has more than one right foot," another added.

"Don't laugh," I said. "Sometimes, many times, I wonder if a player thinks she has more than one right foot—but let me continue. Having gotten the ball just where she wants it in front of that right foot, she'll look at the ball again to make sure it's still there, then she'll look up, cock her foot, and swipe at the ball. This little ritual will usually lead to one of three things: one, she'll miss the ball entirely; two, she'll spin it in place; three—and this is worst of all—she'll see an experienced player take it away." After a pause, I added, "You know what Woody Hayes—"

"You'd better say the *late* Woody Hayes; he's now dead, you know," a faculty member cautioned me.

"Why should I say that?" I asked. "I never called him *early* when he was alive, but for the sake of peace, I'll say 'the dead Woody Hayes.' Is that acceptable? Anyway, here's what Woody used to say about the forward pass in football: 'Three things can happen to the pass, and two of them are bad.' Well, Coach Hanna says—"

"Who, by the way," a faculty member interrupted, "isn't exactly the Woody Hayes of women's soccer."

"Thanks for that inspired clarification," I said with a smile, "but I can still observe with confidence that to a beginning women's soccer player near the ball—and this could be at

Geneva, Yale, or Bloomsburg State—three things can happen to the ball, and all three are bad. I shudder to think what's going to happen to us tomorrow. We're going to start four players with heavy soccer experience, two players with light experience, and five players unburdened by experience."

"Beginners, in other words," a business professor said.

"'Beginners' is the word, raw beginners, if you will." I concluded my comments at the lunch table by saying, "If you don't know much about soccer, here's an analogy for you: you don't put beginning swimmers on your varsity swim team, do you? We're going to have to do that tomorrow."

As I walked toward my office, I thought that the analogy might be improper, perhaps a bit too harsh. To be sure, I reasoned, our beginners have a lot to learn about soccer, but in the first ten days of practice, they had picked up some—not a lot, but some—basic skills. On the other hand, I told myself, it might indeed be a proper analogy, and the beginners had not really picked up the skills but had been simply exposed to them. My thoughts drifted back to the analogy: Soccer—like swimming or tennis or ice skating or baseball—is performed best by college students who have been playing the sport from an early age, and ten days' worth of practice might well be equivalent to moving the arms in the free-style stroke while standing in shallow water.

When people say that a soccer team is good "because they have a lot of foreign students playing on it," what they're saying in effect is that many of the athletes on the team have been playing soccer throughout their lives. The frequent associations made between foreign students and fine soccer have led me to wonder if foreign students have inherited soccer genes. None of our experienced players were foreign, but all had played the sport in high school and even earlier, and their skill level showed that. Our beginners, however, were beginners. I kept reminding myself not to expect the beginners to have picked up in ten days of practice what the experienced players had developed in ten years.

In trying to help the beginners understand the concept and tactics of soccer, I often found myself referring to a sport they had known since childhood: basketball. "Like basketball," I would explain, "soccer requires you to dribble the ball, to pass it back and forth, to work it toward the opponents' goal area, to try to get a player as close to the goal as possible before taking a shot at the net. All along, of course, your opponents will try to prevent all that: to steal the passes, block the shots, dribble and work the ball toward your basket. You all know how hard it is to make a basket on the backboard by the garage, and you know it becomes harder when people are in your face. In soccer, getting a ball into the net would be easy if no one were guarding the net, for the ball is smaller than a basketball and the goal is much, much wider." Then I would usually switch sports: "But soccer, like hockey, has a goalie whose job is to prevent you from scoring. And like hockey, in which you pass the puck a great deal, you've got to pass and pass that ball in soccer.

"Dribbling and passing," I would inform the beginners, "are as crucial in soccer as they are in basketball. The only difference, of course, is in soccer, you've got to use your feet to dribble and pass, and you can't use your hands. If you use your hands in soccer, it's a penalty, and if you kick the ball in basketball, it's a turnover."

And so the beginners and I worked and worked on dribbling and passing during those first ten days of soccer practice. And much as Sal and his fifth grade basketball teammates at Saint Philomena School, under the superb coaching of Jake Pavlinich and Paul Long, tended to favor their right hands as they were learning to dribble and pass the basketball, so, too, our beginners dribbled and passed the ball with their right feet. Trying to get them to use their left feet, especially in passing the ball, was like trying to get little Sal to eat his spinach: difficult but not impossible, possible but not pleasant. Using their heads to pass a ball was even more unpleasant and unnatural than using their left feet. Still, they followed orders and used their heads, and every time they did, they cracked a smile. A wince and a smile.

The beginners tried hard. In their efforts they exhibited the typical awkwardness that besets players trying to learn a complex sport at an older age; that awkwardness was accentuated when juxtaposed with the fluency of our experienced players. Not far from where the beginners labored in practice, the experienced players strutted their stuff, maneuvering the ball on the dribble, exchanging quick passes, trapping kicked balls with their stomachs, coasting passes with their left feet, slashing kicks with the outside of the instep, lofting balls across the field, faking movement in a certain direction with their hips and bodies, only to go in the opposite direction. Instead of wincing when "heading" the soccer ball, the experienced players would attack it with courage and grunt-spiked pleasure. We would practice heading drills not just for the purpose of passing the ball but for controlling, deflecting, and shooting it, especially off high corner kicks.

If a single image from soccer lingers in the mind of a new spectator, it is likely to be that of a player rising and leaning into a moving ball, hitting it with her head as a pass to a teammate or a shot at goal. That image, distinct as a stretch limousine, is associated perhaps with no other sport but soccer. I often enjoyed seeing our beginners salute that image in their own way and our experienced players execute it in the proper way. All the players sensed my enjoyment and indeed shared it frequently, for there was seldom a practice when the heading drill was absent from the agenda.

There probably was no better player in western Pennsylvania to demonstrate heading to our beginners than our team captain, Jill. Her demonstrations featured a cheerful, enthusiastic, somewhat comical approach, borrowing a technique from Plato's *Republic*. Plato spends several pages telling his readers what justice is not before he finally explores what justice is. So, too, with Jill: she would first show the players how not to head a ball, exaggerating the faults just enough for some players to see their own mistakes (and to laugh at them); then she would demonstrate the proper technique. "And it's going to hurt a bit," Jill would add, "especially if you're heading a fast-moving ball."

"It won't hurt Coach Hanna," Angi once informed Jill and the assembled players during a demonstration practice session.

"Why's that?" Jill asked.

"Just look at him," Angi said.

"It certainly *would* hurt him," Amy interjected while slapping her right thigh, "if I kick that ball with all my might."

"No, it won't," Angi said. "There's no way it would hurt him; it simply would not. Understand?"

"What if Barb hit him?" a beginner asked, winking at a usually taciturn Barbara, whose strong kicks in practice had impressed all the players. "She'd certainly hurt him, wouldn't she?"

"Nope! Barb, like Amy, will do no damage, absolutely none," Angi said, her eyes focusing on me as she addressed the team.

A couple of players standing next to me snorted.

Finally I asked Angi, "Why wouldn't it hurt?"

"That's easy, Coach," she said, "because you're forever wearing your helmet. Understand?" I stroked my bald head and flashed a wince-free smile that ignited laughter among the players. (By associating my bald head with a helmet, Angi was alluding to a self-deprecating story I had occasionally used in my writing classes. Most players were unaware of the allusion, so they laughed; but I laughed at the appropriateness and timing of her remark, and especially at the way she set it up.)

Heading the soccer ball was admittedly a difficult, unnatural, even painful skill to learn, and I certainly did not expect our beginners to master it, not that first season anyway. But I did expect them, by season's end, to develop some confidence in their abilities to dribble and pass the ball with both their left and right feet, and not only when they were alone on the field but also when other players tried to take the ball away from them.

As coach, I practiced often with both the experienced players and the beginners, and the two groups often practiced together. After all, it was my job to try to mold all the players into a solid team, a team whose kicks were as appropriate, as well timed, and as nicely set up as Angi's remarks. What I suspected I would end up doing was assembling a team of sorts, one that would stutter through the season.

Friday evening, September 6, I wrote in the "Soccer Season Diary" a long entry that read in part:

What a delight it is to coach women who are witty, intelligent, cooperative. I hope they maintain their cheerful disposition when the losses begin to pile up in the weeks ahead. If the players do, they, in effect, would supply me with a good angle on the soccer book, an angle that'll celebrate the joys of sports in a small liberal arts college while at the same time satirizing that lust-to-win-at-all-cost mentality that tyrannizes most big-time college sports. . . . Another angle on the book could be a slice from the life of a scholar-coach, a coaching tradition that lives on in most of the nation's finest prep schools, but that seems to have died at most colleges and universities.

Both angles are fine. What's likely to get the book reviewed in the influential review forums (*Booklist, Choice, Publishers Weekly, Library Journal, The New York Times Book Review*) and thus bring it to the attention of a wide audience is the women's angle. Most books on sports fall into a win-and-tell-all category. Such books, directed at male readers, usually deal with male teams or with male heroes from major sports programs.

The book that I hope to write will be directed at both sexes, and it'll explore my coaching of a women's sports program at a small college. Given the fact that we're a new program, the book is likely to be a lose-and-tell-all book. My experiences thus far are telling me that coaching women can be challenging and rewarding and fun. I suspect, however, the nine-game season is too short for me to get to know the complex personalities of the women on the squad and to focus the book on them. If I end up coaching for several seasons, then the focus on the athletes will be a different matter. I'll just have to wait and see what develops.

Whatever angle I end up taking, this much I know: the book will *not* be written in my typical Ph.D. style. Too deadly. That style, footnote-strangled and jargon-crammed, is leading me to establish (at least in my comic fiction, and maybe I should do it in real life) Scholars Anonymous: a support group for scholars who used to write for narrow and uptight audiences. In writing the book, what I'll need to do is try to use this diary as a frame, and I'll need to weave the book's narrative while re-working and refining the diary's prose, reproducing conversations, profiling incidents, capturing tidbits of character, sketching scenes as they occur on the practice field, in the van on road trips, at home during varsity games, in the class-rooms with non–soccer players, at home with family members, in the Student Union with colleagues, in the office with some players. Chances are I'll end up presenting the book from my point of view.

A more engaging point of view—one that would certainly ap-peal to me—would be that of the players, and in time, several players might write about their experiences on Geneva's first season in var-sity soccer. It might be wise to ask the players to keep diaries of the entire season, then collect the diaries, read them, and weave some of their insights into the fabric of my book. But I don't feel right about asking them now to do that. Had I thought earlier and set up the soccer program in conjunction with a writing class, then whatever writing I required might have been justified and indeed cheerfully done. Still, I'm going to do all I can to reproduce in this diary a lot of what I hear the players say and see them do during the season.

Suffice it to say, my point of view is the one that I know best; it's the one with which I feel most comfortable; and I hope the sense of irony and self-deprecating humor that I enjoy so much will be part of the soccer season profile.

Saturday morning was the season's opener. The Highlanders of Houghton College from upstate New York were coming to the hills of western Pennsylvania, to Beaver Falls, a once dreary and productive mill town, now a notch on the country's rust belt, a good town that for over a century had served as the home of the Golden Tornadoes of Geneva College.

Part II

Houghton and Oberlin

3

Joe Namath and the Team
That Paraphrased Tolstoy

"We're in Joe Namath country," I told the Houghton College coach when she called from upstate New York on Thursday to confirm our Saturday game. "Namath grew up here, played his high school ball here, on Geneva's field, as a matter of fact. Soccer around here is a footnote to football."

"It's the opposite with us," she said. "We don't even have a football team. Soccer is it. It's our fall sport."

"How does the team look?" I asked, innocently enough.

"Great."

"Great, you say?" I asked, sheepishly.

"Great and ready," she said, snapping her words in a tone that exuded confidence. After a long pause, she added, "We lost our three All-Americans,"—I really can't recall, and my diary fails to note, whether she said "All-Americans" or "All-American candidates"—"but we've got a good group now. We're looking forward to playing you guys at Geneva."

"Geneva is a nice European name and you'd expect we'd have great soccer here," I said, "but this is only our first year in women's soccer, and I'll be honest: I don't think we're going to offer much competition."

We talked about other pregame matters, then I asked, "You sure you still want to come down and play us? Our talent is really limited at this stage."

"You bet. It's a scheduled NAIA varsity game, and we have no choice. It should be fun indeed," she said before we exchanged goodbyes.

I shoved the phone aside and looked around the office walls—some lined with books and others staggered with pictures of Hemingway, Kafka, Steinbeck, Orwell, Lawrence, Eliot, Stein, Ginsberg, Plath, Pound, Berryman, Sexton, Joyce, and Virginia Woolf. I rocked in my swivel chair, placed my feet on the corner of the desk, cupped my chin with my right hand, and stared ahead, thinking: It might well be that the Houghton coach hadn't intended to intimidate me in this brief conversation, and if that's the case, she's a master at achieving the inadvertent.

Whatever her intentions, no team intimidated us as much as Houghton, perhaps because Houghton was our first varsity game ever. On our schedule for the year were teams belonging to the National Association of Intercollegiate Athletics (NAIA Division II) and the National Collegiate Athletic Association (NCAA Division III).

Friday morning, while leaving my creative writing class in the Science and Engineering Hall, I came across that bright pre-med major from upstate New York, the student with the soccer-playing experience who declined to play for Geneva because she wished to devote all her time to academic pursuits. I told her about the upcoming Houghton game, and she said, "Oh, Dr. Hanna, I pity you. That's the soccer belt out there, you know."

"No, I didn't know that," I said. "Tell me more."

"I'll tell you one thing: those players are good." Her voice dipped as she slapped a southern accent on "good," stretching the word to make her point.

"Oh, don't tell me any more. That's enough; I get the point," I said, and changed the topic to her course work.

Friday afternoon, I stepped into the office of Geneva's vice president for business and finance, a friend whose B.A. degree was from Houghton. The vice president and his wife, also a Houghton graduate, played racquetball with my wife and me every Wednesday at noon. I suggested a change in our usual time, to which he agreed. "By the way," he said, "I hear your first game is tomorrow."

"Boy, Milt, the acoustics must be good in this office because what you hear is correct," I said with a smile. "And you know the team we're playing?"

"Sure do, and I trust you're ready."

"Ready?"

"I'm sure *they*'ll be ready," he said. "You know, there's no football at Houghton. Soccer to them is like football is to us here in the football-crazy Beaver Valley."

That was the second time in two days I had heard that football-soccer juxtaposition, and I had heard it from two different people. Saturday, the juxtaposition would wallop a special poignancy.

Our shoes had arrived Friday morning. (Other parts of our uniforms had arrived a few days before that.) After a light Friday afternoon workout, we headed to a classroom where I distributed soccer shoes and gave last-minute instructions relating to the next day's game, scheduled for ten in the morning. "Any questions before we break up?" I asked.

"Yeah, Coach," Angi said. "I'd like to make a comment and not ask a question. Is that all right?"

"That depends on the comment, but go ahead."

"My comment isn't a slam at you," she began, "but I can't believe we're actually going to play a varsity game tomorrow without ever having had a single shot at a goal, and I mean a real goal, one made out of wood and pipe and net, and not those phony goals of cones and stones that we use. If we were a men's team, I bet we'd have everything we need—and instantly."

"I doubt it. In a small college," I said, "athletics play a role, but it's not a dominant one. The men's resources around here aren't all that great either. But I see your implied point: we've got to fight for equity in sports."

"That we do," Angi said. "It's all politics, at a small college or a large university: men have the power and the resources, and that's got to change."

"And it's changing and will continue to change," I said. "Do you remember our first meeting in the classroom when I spoke to you about Title IX? Well, in the late eighties and the nineties, a huge point will be made by women and men who cherish equity in sports, and the point will be this: start obeying and enforcing Title IX or risk all sorts of legal challenges. Equity in sports is one of those rare issues that political conservatives, moderates, and liberals are likely to agree on, because people across the political spectrum have daughters who play sports, and people expect their daughters to be treated fairly. If they're not, they'll fight for such treatment. If schools fail to obey Title IX in the years ahead, you're going to see a lot of legal kicks in the gut. Notice I said 'gut,' not 'butt,' because a kick in the butt doesn't hurt."

"Coach, I had to leave that first meeting early," one player said, "and to be honest with you, I'm not familiar with Title IX. What is it?"

"It's the golden legacy of the Nixon administration," I said. "It's the law that President Nixon signed way back in 1972 that prohibits sex bias in athletics and other activities at all educational institutions that receive federal assistance. It's a law that, in effect, mandates gender equity in athletics. Having said all this, let me add that we've got to be patient with our hardworking, friendly, and dependable maintenance department in regard to our goals."

"Will we have those goals by next week?" Amy asked. "Are you planning to remind them of what we need?"

"I hope so. I'm going to call the shop and follow up my call with a memo. They really do excellent work down there, but I know they're busy, and we're an unanticipated burden, you see."

"I see," Amy said.

"Coach," another player said, "I see also but—"

"The three of you," Angi interrupted, "sound like optometrists or beer commercials to me."

Several players laughed, but one, a Maine resident, asked: "How do you get beer commercials in all of this?"

"The 'I see,'" Amy explained as she pointed to her eyes, "could also refer to Iron City, a famous beer around here. IC beer commercials are all over the idiot box, but leave it to our Dante—oops, I mean Angi—to see levels of meaning in them." Amy, sitting next to Angi, laughed and slapped Angi's shoulder. Both were beginning a friendship that, in time, would blossom and lead them to a joint trip to Europe.

"Okay, on that noble note—and assuming there're no more questions," I said, "let's call it a day. I'll see you tomorrow morning at Alex's at eight for our pregame breakfast. Remember, the game starts at ten."

When I went home that afternoon, I drove our family to the Kentucky Fried Chicken in the nearby town of Rochester. As our minivan was climbing College Hill on the way back, we looked out the window and saw a host of women soccer players in Geneva's football stadium, shooting long and short kicks at the football goal. "That's strange," I told my wife. "Why would our players be down there at this time without me? This makes me angry."

"Well, maybe the captain suggested it," she said, "by way of showing her leadership."

"And breaking in those brand-new shoes that I gave them this afternoon," I noted. I looked directly at her and said, "They really need to break those shoes in, don't you think?"

"They do," she agreed, adding, "I wouldn't feel threatened by their presence down there if I were you."

"I'm not th—"

"Yes, you are," she snapped.

"No, I'm not."

"Then where're you heading?"

"I'm going to drive down there," I said, and bit my lower lip. "I'm curious as to what's going on."

"Don't, please don't. You'll ruin it for them," she said. "I'm sure they don't mean ill by it."

"Maybe all they want to do is get a feel for a few shots at a goal, at something that resembles a soccer goal, with two posts and a crossbar," I said, trying to convince myself that their presence could be beneficial to the team, something that I should appreciate and not dispute. Then I added, "Admittedly, football goalposts are no soccer goals, but they beat those goals of cones and stones that we've been using in practice."

"Now your reasoning makes sense," my wife said.

"But practicing shots at goals, real or otherwise, won't be necessary," I said, "judging from what I *think* I know about Houghton and from what I *know* I know about us."

"Now your reasoning is back to nonsense because you seem to be conceding the game already, and I don't think that's good or healthy."

"But it's honest and realistic: remember, I'm coaching a soccer team and not running for public office."

We drove halfway up the hill, turned right, and parked on the road directly beyond the goalposts. We looked down at the players, and much to our surprise, they were not our players, but Houghton's. There must have been twenty or more, and they instantly struck me as being wiry, quick, relaxed, confident. Our entire family watched with interest. What registered in my mind were all those athletes running up to the ball, leaning to the left or the right, scooping it with their feet and lofting it to various parts of the football field. Their dribbling seemed quick, their cuts sharp, their passes often crisp and accurate. Even their head shots impressed me. They drifted in and out of routines and drills with precision and apparent ease, leading me to conclude that they were a well-coached team.

We watched them practice. We watched silently and intently. My eyes declared a moratorium on blinking.

"They look impressive," I told my wife and children. "And they're without their three All-Americans, who have graduated. Can you imagine what they'd look like with them?"

"Without them," my wife said, "they're impressive indeed."

"Look, look at that shot," I said as a Highlander slammed a line-drive kick just above the outstretched hands of the goalie. "Mighty impressive," I added as I saw a courageous player rise and head the ball.

"Wow," Paul said.

"That looks like a dolphin hitting the beach ball in the pool at Sea World," Sal added.

"Without a doubt," my wife said, "these players are good; I see now what America's soccer belt produces."

"I do, too," I said, "and I don't like it."

"What're you going to do, Daddy?" Rita asked.

"Show up and play them," I replied, then asked rhetorically, "What else can we do? These players aren't in town to clean the mirrors at the Beaver Valley Motel, that's for sure." I turned on the ignition and slowly drove away. "It seems that so far," I told my wife, "I've psyched myself up by cataloguing one intimidation tactic after another."

"I'm sure none are intended as such," she said.

"You're right, but my coach's insecurity files them as such."

Later that evening, when the Houghton coach called from their motel outside of town, she mentioned that she had tried and failed to reach me moments after arriving in Beaver Falls. So she had taken her team and searched for the women's soccer field on campus. She had failed to find it partly because the field was still a field, unlined and minus the goals. Undeterred, the Houghton coach had taken her players to the football field.

"That field is off limits to all two-legged creatures except football players—and that only on game day," I told her.

"Oh, I feel bad now," she said.

"Please don't. That place is only sacrosanct," I said, and quickly added, "but apparently nobody with authority saw you folks. If they had, they would've asked you to leave, I'm sure." I informed the coach about the visiting team's locker room facilities at the field house, and we said our goodbyes in fear and anticipation—hers being anticipation.

"Seven in the morning gets there in a hurry when you're not looking for it," I told my wife when we woke up Saturday morning. At eight, I met the players at Alex's. While eating breakfast, I tried to relax them with some light comments. I failed. The task before us was far too serious, in their minds at least, and it was too early in the morning, anyway. So I joined the players and ate in silence, reflecting on what to say to them after the meal. The team we're about to face, I thought, appeared strong, powerful, loaded with talented players. Amy, Angi, Jill, and Barb could start on the Houghton team, and if we had sixteen more players of that caliber, we could offer Houghton a good match. I considered what might be going through the minds of our beginners: agony, uncertainty, hesitancy, fear of flying by the seat of their pants. I also thought about our experienced players and wondered if they were looking forward to the game, much as skilled, competitive athletes relish the promises and challenges of game day. I wondered what kind of crowd was going to show up for the game: its size, character, and expectations.

At the end of breakfast, we prayed, asking God to spare both teams from injury during the upcoming game. Then I announced the starting lineup, which had five of the players with soccer-playing experience on the front line playing forwards and wings. They were to be our offense. The sixth player with experience, Amy, was to be our goalkeeper: the final line of defense. Two beginners were at fullback, playing in front of the goalie, and three other beginners were ahead of the fullbacks at the half-back positions.

"If an airplane pulling a Domino's Pizza banner," I told the players, "should circle the sky over our field, or if the Goodyear blimp should hover above like a giant cockroach in heaven—and, by the way, there's no danger of either happening; it wouldn't pay for them to do so, because our crowd won't be that large; but for fun let's assume that to be the case—and if the pilots of both should look down to see our positions on the field at the start of the game, then they should see us in a pyramid pattern, and Houghton will probably be in one as well. Maybe their coach calls their pattern a triangle; I like the pyramid metaphor. We associate collapse with a triangle, as in a folding carpenter's rule, and we associate strength with a pyramid. So let's go out there this morning and play strong ball for old Geneva."

"We might not win many games this year," Angi proclaimed with her sarcasm intact, "but we'll surely win the metaphor wars."

I told the players to meet at the field at nine-thirty, and I reminded those who wished to have their ankles taped to stop by
our house.

Four players—Amy, Angi, Jill, and Barb—stopped by to be
taped by my wife, who was to serve as our game day trainer.
While taping in our living room, she also directed Rita, Sal, Paul,
and Sam as they began to load our minivan with water contain-
ers, cups, ice, first-aid kits, oranges, balls, shin guards, and the
like. I watched the kids out of the corner of one eye and talked
to the players standing in our living room. We exchanged small
talk about the sunny morning and the joys of the approaching
Pennsylvania autumn, with leaves falling, footballs in the air, and
band music filtering through the campus. I cut the small talk by
asking what turned out to be a painful question: "How do you
think it's going to go today?"

"You want us to be honest, Coach, don't you?" Jill, the
team's captain, asked.

"Of course," I said.

"We're going to get killed," Jill said.

"Why do you say that?" I asked, watching my wife as she began to tape another ankle.

"I'm doing all this," my wife protested with a smile, "so that
you can go out there and get killed?" The four athletes in the
room smiled.

Paul, one of our five-year-old twin boys who happened to
hear the conversation, said, "Daddy, I think your soccer girls are
going to take it on the—you know what," he said, pointing to
his chin and smiling.

"Do all of you share Jill's pessimism?" I asked the other three
athletes.

"Most of us who've played before do, Coach," Angi said.

"But why?" I asked. All four players appeared to be in excellent physical condition, thanks in part to some soccer playing that
they had done in the summer on club teams in their hometowns.

"Why?" Jill repeated. She fiddled with her pigtails, joining
them together as if they were a basket handle. At that instant, I
thought to myself—though I did not share the thought with the

athletes—I hope this game is not going to turn our team or me into a basket case.

"Yes, why? Why are you so discouraged?" I persisted.

"It's tough," Jill said, "to play this game with beginners. There's so much passing involved in moving the ball downfield, and the passes have to be quick and instinctive and sharp, and our beginners, like all other beginners, have a tough time with that."

"Some of our beginners are playing soccer because it counts as a gym class," Angi said.

"So what?" I asked.

"So they've got no real interest in the sport," Angi said.

"Or talent," Amy added.

"Coach," Jill said, "I hate to put it so bluntly, but it's a fact: we're going to play with six people; six against eleven. Oh, we'll have eleven on the field, but I doubt if we'll do much today."

"There's *no* doubt about it," Angi added. "We're going to get trounced, Coach. Prepare yourself for a disaster."

"I know that as a coach," I said, looking at Angi, "I should be upbeat and positive, and part of my job is to try to get your confidence level up."

"And if you try, Coach," Angi said, "we'll see right through it."

" I don't know what we're going to have, but those Houghton players are going to have fun," Amy said.

"We will, too," a usually quiet Barb added.

"Listen to her," Amy said, pointing at Barb and laughing.

"I've heard of 'tell it like it is' rap sessions," I said, looking at Amy, "but this is really ridiculous. The more I think about it, the less I like this 'tell it like it is' conversation."

"Coach, this isn't 'tell it like it is,' not at all," Angi said. "This is tell it like it's *going* to be; it's conjugating the future tense— or should I say 'tension'?"

"Say nothing, Angi," my wife said. She gently slapped Jill's heel and shouted, "Next!" Angi stepped up to be taped.

"I know, I know," I said, and continued to watch my wife's taping techniques.

Jill looked at me and said, "Do you ever notice our beginners in practice?" She didn't wait for me to respond. "They get that ball and do all that they can to get it next to their right foot, but by the time they do that and try to pass it back or lead us with a pass, the ball is taken away. It's so, so frustrating, Coach."

"Yes, I know," I said.

"That's right, Coach," Angi said. "What Jill is saying is true."

"So you see absolutely no way for us to do well this morning?" I asked, desperately hoping to hear a cheerful note.

"That's right," Jill said.

"So, what do you think I should do?" I asked.

"There's not much that you can do, Coach," Amy said. "Not much this year, anyway."

"I'd recruit if I were you," Jill suggested. "And don't simply wait on our beginners to develop. Developing will take more than a year. Go down to the suburbs of Pittsburgh—"

"That's where women's soccer tends to be played, isn't it?" my wife asked.

"Right," Jill replied. "The girls in the inner cities tend to play basketball and run track; they play softball or volleyball on the playgrounds. Soccer is king in the suburbs and the small towns."

My wife stopped taping and looked up at Jill. "You'd better say soccer is 'queen' of the suburbs," she said.

"Don't misunderstand us, Coach," Jill said. "Our beginners are wonderful kids, nice and all. Well, you see them everyday in practice; they're so nice, they'll do—try to do—anything and everything that you tell them, but—"

"But in the words of my favorite athletic cliché," I said, "'Nice guys finish last.'"

"I don't like that expression anymore," my wife said. "We should have a modern version of it—"

"Like what?" Amy said.

"Like, 'Nice dudes do lose,'" Angi said.

"But we're dealing with dudesses in our Golden Tornadoes," I said, then added with a sigh, "I just hope we can keep it close this morning."

My wife continued to tape, the kids continued to load the van, and the experienced players continued their frank assessment of our beginners and our pending disaster. At one point, Jill asked about the pieces of abstract art in our living room. The question afforded me the opportunity to give a mini-lecture on our artistic taste.

"Some people," Amy said, "like art work that looks like something—a field, a tree, a fruit, a knee, a navel, a cathedral— but you obviously don't."

"That's right," my wife joked. "Our artistic tastes usually hang below magnets on refrigerator doors or make the cover of the *New Yorker* magazine."

"These two blue abstracts here look like Frisbees to me," Jill said.

"I think they're pies with some peculiar cuts in them," Amy added.

"More like a circle of cheese with a cut in it," Barb said.

"You know what I think they look like?" Angi asked as she reached down to touch her taped foot.

"What?" two of the players asked at once.

"The twenty-third-century boobies of male athletes." We all laughed as Angi added, "I suppose an art critic would see spatial intensity and negative spaces all wrapped up in these abstracts."

Our playful excursion into art relieved, ever so slightly, the tension I felt from the experienced players' relentless assault on our beginners. I continued the excursion by telling them an art-related story: "When I was in graduate school in the late sixties in Bloomington, Indiana, a friend of mine received his Ph.D. in English and began his search for a teaching position. Unable to locate one, he decided to go to Indianapolis and drive a cab. Before leaving, he held a moving sale. One of the items that he was selling was a painting that he had done with one purpose in mind: to cover up some obnoxious holes in the plaster of the old house where he lived. The way he did the painting was most unusual. He borrowed—really took—a square yard of mounted canvas from a former girlfriend of his, went down to K mart, bought several cans of spray paint, returned home, and quickly

sprayed different designs on the canvas. In less than three minutes, the painting was done—and signed. The instant painting,
which he titled 'Frozen Microwaves,' was priced at $5. Many
items around it—bookshelves, chairs, lamps, file cabinets, items
priced in the $10 to $20 range—moved rapidly, but the $5
painting remained. When I arrived at the sale, I told my friend,
'The only way you could sell that painting for $5 is if one con-
siders it an attractive nuisance, but if you raise the price to, say,
$125, then it'll go as art.' He raised the price to the suggested
amount, and the painting moved quickly. Bloomington, you see,
is a proper and sophisticated university town."

Angi said, "There's a moral in this tale, but I don't know
how that moral would relate to our upcoming adventure."

"I do," my wife offered. "It'll relate not so much to the game
but to the crowd. If your crowd is going to be just like the men's
soccer team crowd—and I know this from going over to those
games to see my brother play—then you're going to have very
few people there. Your games, like theirs, are free? Correct?"

"Yes, they are," I said.

"Charge a price," my wife said, "and watch your crowd grow."

"Obviously, Mrs. Hanna," Angi said, "you're a fortunate
lady in that you haven't seen our beginners play, but if you'd
seen them play—"

"*Perform* is the word, my dear," Amy said, lapsing into a
British accent spiked with a Texas drawl; her index finger and
thumb joined together to make a zero. She smiled, then burst
into laughter.

After my wife completed her "taping task," as she called it,
the four players—dressed in their gold shirts with white stripes,
gold shorts, black shoes, and light gold socks with black trim—
trotted to the field. The Hanna family, kids and all, jumped into
our van, and I began the short drive to the field as Muff, our
poodle, alternately barked his disapproval and good wishes.

"Do you have the checks?" my wife asked.

I said nothing. I drove around the block, parked in front of
the house, and laughed with the rest when Rita said, "Actions
speak louder than words." I jumped out of the car, went to the

study, greeted a confused Muff, fetched the two checks—fifty dollars each—that the women's athletic director had acquired from Geneva's business office. The director's note that accompanied the checks instructed me to "give the checks to the officials *before* the game starts."

When we arrived at the field, the children unloaded the van. Our team, under the guidance of Jill, was warming up on one end of the field, and Houghton used the other end. I introduced myself to the Houghton coach; we exchanged pleasantries regarding their trip to Beaver Falls, our respective schedules, the sunny day; then the two officials joined us. After some small talk, followed by the officials' explanation of the substitution rules and other matters, I handed them their checks and thanked them for agreeing to officiate the game.

As ten o'clock approached—and it was going to do that sooner or later, I thought to myself—the officials met at midfield with the captains of both teams, and members of both teams headed to their respective bench areas. Our players paced the area, and I have no idea what Houghton's players did. When our captain returned, she walked directly toward me and the rest of the players crowded around us. "Is there anything special that we need to be aware of, Jill?" I asked.

"Nope," she said.

"Okay, let's go out there and have fun," I said. "If any of you have parents here, please consider introducing them to me after the game; I'd like to thank them for coming to see us play. I guess we've got a decent crowd here because this is a historic game of sorts. Whatever, all of you will get to play, I can assure you. Let's break on what?" I asked, as we extended our arms so that they became spokes, our hands meeting to create the hub.

"Go, Geneva!" said Jill.

"Okay, on three, let's say 'Go, Geneva!'" I said, and counted, "One, two, three."

"Go, Geneva!" we all yelled at once. The players took their positions on the field. The official started the game by blowing the whistle. Four substitutes stood behind me. I turned and looked at them, then looked at the field where I saw a Houghton player dribbling the ball, weaving her way past our players as if they were cones; she reached the goal area, looked as if she were going to shoot it with her right foot, but suddenly she switched the ball to her left foot, then back to her right foot, and blasted it into the upper left-hand corner of the net. Her teammates mobbed her, jumped all over her, and she collapsed under their bodies. Several minutes later, she got up and repeated a similar feat, though not as quickly and with a bit more resistance from our players.

Most soccer games between evenly matched teams tend to be defensive struggles, ending in one-to-zero or two-to-one scores. After Houghton scored their second goal so early in the match, I sensed that the assembled spectators were going to be spared the agony of a defensive struggle. Standing on the sidelines, I remembered the words of an American sports reporter who detested the defensive nonbattles that choke many soccer games. "I have real trouble," the reporter wrote, "with the notion that a team took an insurmountable one-to-nothing lead." Our first game promised to be a slug fest, with Houghton doing the slugging and the feasting.

Throughout the first half, Houghton displayed a strong, basic, relentless attack that relied heavily on constant movement by the players as they initiated, responded, and advanced the soccer ball with sharp passes, sure dribbles, and occasional head shots. The Highlanders' quickness, their unselfish passing, their patience, their shot selection—coupled with our benign defense— led them to register several more goals in the first half. Midway in that half, I took Amy out of the goalie position—even though she had made some extraordinary saves—and replaced her with a player who had at one time played goalie. Our defense, composed of beginners, was so weak that I felt Amy's confidence might be damaged if Houghton's massive and versatile attack continued to charge her virtually unchallenged. As it turned out, the new goalie gave up six goals, which in addition to Amy's two gave Houghton an eight-point lead in the first half. If one to nothing was an insurmountable lead, I wondered what adjective our reporter friend would use to describe an eight-to-nothing lead.

At halftime, we went to one side of the field to talk over strategy for the second half. My children served the players water, ice, and oranges, and I made slight changes in positions. I asked Amy to play the entire second half at goalie, and I moved all the experienced players to defense, to the halfback and fullback spots, and placed the inexperienced ones on the offensive line, "where they could experience confusion from a different sphere," to borrow the words used in my long and detailed diary entry for the Houghton game.

Our disappointed crowd—admitted free or perhaps bribed by my wife—consisted of three dogs, all leashed, and about seventy people, among them college professors and administrators, parents of players, friends of my children and some of their parents, curious people living in houses near the soccer field, and adults on dog-walking (*pooping* is the more accurate word) assignments. To my surprise, most of the spectators and the three dogs stayed for the second half. The sunny morning, the gentle breeze, the low-seventies temperature, the opportunity to visit with friends—all must have kept the crowd at the field.

"Even though the game is free, the crowd isn't that bad," I told my wife just as the second half began. "It's much bigger than any crowd that I've seen at a Geneva men's game, and I trust they're pleased to have seen and are continuing to see history in the making."

"Be quiet," she told me, "and pay attention to the game. Hey, you're the coach now; pay attention and don't visit with me."

"You know what I'm referring to when I say they've already seen something historic?" I asked.

"Yes, I do," she said. "Please pay attention to the game you're currently coaching."

"I'm paying attention," I said, smiling. "And I really don't think a goal has ever been scored more quickly than that first one. I'm sure it's a record," I told my wife and yelled encouragement at our hardworking captain and other players. "The other historic aspect, of course, is that this is Geneva's first varsity women's game, and that might explain why we have such a large—put large in quotes—crowd for a soccer game."

"That might be," she said, and walked toward our kids, who were playing behind our bench, kicking a soccer ball with several of their friends and classmates.

Houghton continued to dominate the game, but our players offered stronger resistance in the second period. They crossed into Houghton's side of the field several times during the game, but we failed to take a single shot at goal. Indeed, we failed to come close to the goal. Their goalie, I thought to myself during the second half, could have made a dent in *Gone With the Wind* or *War and Peace*, given all the idle time she had.

Minutes before the end of the game, Rita and Sal ran up to me. Rita said, "Daddy, their goalie could've had a pizza and a Pepsi while this game was going on."

"I'd say she could've gone to Pizza Joe or Domino's for a pizza and a Coke," Sal added.

"She surely wouldn't have needed goal service," Rita said, smiling.

My wife heard that exchange and laughed. "Kids can be cruel to each other and to their soccer coach dad," she said, leaning over and embracing the kids. She landed a soft kiss on their foreheads and continued to watch the fading moments of the game.

All fifteen of our players played in the two forty-five-minute periods. When the final whistle blew and the game's official scorekeeper announced the final score—"Houghton twelve, Geneva zero"—I told myself: Not a bad period; we cut our losses in half. I walked over and congratulated the Houghton coach with an apology: "Sorry we couldn't offer you a more challenging match. Have a safe trip home."

Our players gathered near our bench. "Thank you all for playing so hard," I told them. "Have a cheerful weekend, and we'll meet again at practice Monday." As our players headed to their dorms to shower, I mingled with the crowd, met and thanked the parents of our players, and promised other spectators better soccer in the days ahead. "Maybe not winning soccer," I said, "but interesting soccer, better than what you saw today."

After the Geneva football game that day, when people asked me how the women's soccer team did against Houghton, I replied, "Houghton beat us by two touchdowns."

Saturday afternoon, two beginning players called and volunteered to watch the children if my wife and I wished to go out to dinner. We took them up on their offer.

At first we thought of going to a Chinese restaurant on the outskirts of Pittsburgh, some thirty miles away from Beaver Falls, but we decided against that and went to a place on College Hill several blocks from our house.

Signs in restaurants located near colleges often advertise events at the colleges; the signs usually hang near the cash register or on windows or bulletin boards. Then there are other signs that the management places on the walls. One such sign caught my attention moments after we claimed a booth. It read: T-BONE $1.95; that was the big print that gave it to you. The small print that took it away noted, WITH MEAT $11.95. I directed my wife's attention to it, and she laughed, then laughed some more when she directed my attention to another sign near the cash register. It featured large black plastic letters on a white background and advertised a PUBLIC LECTURE AT GENEVA. Someone had popped and pocketed the letter *L* from "public."

"I bet a student did that," my wife said. "Many of them, you know, come here late at night to drink coffee and study."

"Probably," I said.

"Sounds like it might be an interesting lecture," she added.

"Sounds to me like someone wants to hear a good old-fashioned lecture on Queen Victoria's period or—"

"Dot in mathematics," she said, alluding to the subtitles in the Third World film that we had discussed once upon a time.

"Seriously," she said, "it might be fun to go and hear that lecture." I glanced at the gap in the lecture sign, a gap that reminded me of David Letterman's teeth, and listened to her ask: "You going to order one of your beloved bagels? This place has great bagels, you know."

"Oh, I know it does," I said. "And even though they look like doughnuts dipped in cement, I can't resist eating those bagels."

"A bagel would sure beat that clump of bread they call a dinner roll in this place," she said.

Soccer—and not the joys of bagels or the hyphen in Letterman's teeth or the lectures at Geneva—dominated our conversation the evening of our first slaughter. "If I were you," my wife advised me, "I'd invite the two beginners baby-sitting our kids out for lunch on Monday and get their reactions to the Houghton game. If they're down, encourage them; and if their spirits are up after that loss, then you're in deep, deep trouble, deeper trouble than I had thought." She stretched the word *deep*.

"But I told them even before the season had started that winning isn't our concern," I said.

"Still, playing well is—or should be."

"And they didn't really play well today, did they?"

"No. In fact, playing well seemed to be against their religion," she said.

"And the beginners seemed to be exceptionally devout," I added just as the table attendant gave us two glasses of water and menus. I took a deep breath and said, "Other than everything, what else do we need to work on as a team?"

"I don't know, but there must be something that you could do that'll make them improve their play," she said.

"I know of something."

"What?"

"Ignite the coach."

"They're *not* going to fire you this early in the season," she said. "You're it, buddy. You're stuck with the job like a fly on a suicide strip."

We exchanged more comments laced with comic remarks about our inaugural disaster. We ordered our food and coffee, and when they arrived, we found ourselves at a more serious juncture in the conversation.

"Let's assume," my wife said, "you're still the coach for the next game at Oberlin and for the remaining games of the season."

"A fair enough assumption, I'm afraid," I said, and looked around the sparsely populated restaurant.

"As coach," she leaned forward and asked, "what're you going to do about the tension between the beginners and the experienced players? You know, the tension that came out this morning in our living room. You recall what tension I'm referring to, don't you?"

"I sure do," I said, "and I really don't like that tension. I don't think it's healthy, but I suppose it's to be expected." I paused, fiddled with a napkin, then added, "Some frustrations were bound to surface, but I didn't expect them this early."

"I'll tell you one thing," she said. "The players that I taped this morning were honest; they didn't mince words. They spoke their minds, and you've got to admire them for that."

"I do." I hesitated, took a long swig of coffee, and added, "I *think* I do."

"Too bad there's not much that you can do about things at this stage," she said.

"It really is too bad," I said. "It's so, so very difficult to play a reasonably good game of soccer with vastly uneven talent. We've got solid players out there in Amy, Barb, Angi, and Jill; we really do. And we've got beginners with potential: some with more potential than others."

"Yeah," she said, laughing. "Some of those 'others' are something, aren't they?"

"They are," I quickly agreed. "You know how in basketball they have a shot called 'air ball'? That's a ball that one shoots with absolute care in the hopes of sinking a basket, but the result is that the shot hits absolutely nothing: it misses the backboard, the rim, the net; it misses everything. Well, we have the equivalent of that in soccer."

"Oh, you do?" she said, reaching for her coffee.

"We do," I said, "and you saw that equivalent brilliantly illustrated—or should I say 'choreographed'—by several beginners in this morning's game."

"How so?" she said.

"By their kicking techniques," I said. An uncharacteristic bit of anger permeated my voice as I added, "Several times during the game, those beginners would come up to a ball, kick it with all their might, and miss it entirely, kicking nothing but air. Sometimes I wondered if they were doing a magic show out there! Anyway, it's that kind of kick that I think is equivalent to the air ball in basketball; I call it an 'air kick.'"

"And that's the difference between you and me," my wife said. She looked up at me, drank some coffee, then added, "What you call an air kick I call an 'excellent demonstration of the follow-through in kicking.'" She raised her voice slightly when she said, "Hey, Coach, come on, lighten up! What do you expect? It's only a game and you got trounced, and you're going to get trounced again and again as the season goes along."

"I'm afraid so," I said, and reached for my coffee. A lot of coffee, I thought to myself, would have to fortify me through the season.

"Looking at the entire program from a woman's perspective," she said, "I think the college is to be applauded for starting a program, but I think they might have made a mistake in starting the program so quickly and without the urgently needed resources." I kept eating as she continued. "They should've hired a real coach and paid her/him a decent salary; they should've appointed an assistant coach; they should've designated a team trainer; they should've made sure that good fields were ready; they should've bought portable goals with nets and pipes and all, instead of making their own with those super heavy four-by-fours and two-by-fours; they should've bought the players gym bags and provided them with locker room facilities. The men have all of these for their team, don't they? Why shouldn't the women? I know Geneva is a fair place and in due time—maybe even in the near future, like next year—the women's soccer team will get their due. But to do so, they'll probably need a coach who is a stronger fighter than you. A woman making forceful demands would help. Sometimes that's the only language people understand." She reached over and covered my hands with her palms and said, "At least you helped them start the program; it had to start someplace, and if I were you, I wouldn't feel bad about the program: many women's programs all over the country start with such poverty of resources and personnel. But it shouldn't be this way, you see. If the funding for the women's programs that should be there is there, then that won't be the case."

"I'd say 'amen' to that, sister."

"Who says women can't preach?" she said, laughing.

"Seriously, I couldn't agree more; funding for women's programs is crucial," I said. "In the context of Geneva, better resources might have helped our team's morale but not their poor performance. I don't want to blame what happened this morning on lack of resources. I'm responsible for what happened and for how well we were prepared; after all, I'm the coach. And I can truthfully say our first game was horrible. You and I have tried to filter its horror through humor, and that helps, but that only goes so far."

"You're right on that," she said.

We spent the remainder of our dinner not so much dissecting the loss and the program but charting strategies to improve the team. The results: Be patient with the beginners, encourage them at every turn, work with them on fundamentals, continue to de-emphasize winning, much as professors who can't publish de-emphasize research and writing. Pursue the physical plant people and try to make sure that the goals are on their way and that the practice field is lined for soccer. We failed to come up with a game plan to handle the experienced players; we left our wooden booth trusting that the experienced players' love of the game—not their love of victories—would keep their interests high in soccer Geneva style.

Given our first performance as a team, a victory seemed far away; to attain it, our beginners needed to improve greatly and our opponents needed to be considerably weaker than Houghton. "In fact, what you need," my wife said as we stood near the cash register, waiting to pay, "is a weaker opponent, an improved bunch of beginners, and stronger coaching on your part."

When we returned home, I followed my wife's advice and scheduled a lunch date with the two players who had baby-sat our children. The date was for Monday at twelve-thirty in the same College Hill restaurant with the peculiar signs.

That evening I also wrote a detailed entry in the "Soccer Season Diary," recording the activities at the team's breakfast, the ankle-taping session in our living room, the game proper, and our dinner. The entry also had an unusually long addendum concerning Leo Tolstoy, Geneva's athletic czar, and a bizarre spectator who informed the crowd of his bowel movement or, more precisely, lack of it. The addendum stated:

Count Leo Tolstoy, the Russian literary giant, of all people, drifted in and out of my thoughts at dinner with my wife. While we reflected on our first loss and the promises of many more, the opening words of *Anna Karenina* flashed before me: "Happy families are all alike; every unhappy family is unhappy in its own way."

I saw those words in their original form, and I also saw them in a slightly paraphrased form that read: "Winning teams are all alike; every losing team loses in its own way."

At the end of our first loss, Geneva's athletic czar, "Chick," that handsome and creative vice president who hired me to establish and coach the team, came over and spoke to the team; he encouraged and assured us that "the college is fully supportive of this brand-new soccer program and women's sports in general." He promised that "all the resources that the men's team has would be forthcoming to the women's squad," and looking at me, he added with a wink, "All the resources—and then some. Right, Coach?" Chick's final words to the team: "We're definitely committed to gender equity here at Geneva; and our commitment is not only in words but deeds as well. Mark my words and follow our performance in the days and seasons ahead."

Our first loss was witnessed by a select crowd punctuated by, let's say, an odd spectator. In that crowd were faculty members, administrators, soccer field neighbors, dog-pooping monitors, students, parents, and friends of players. During the course of the game, I yelled a civilized command at our players. "Think out there," I said, and clapped my hands and paced the sidelines.

"They stink," someone standing behind me said.

"Say, watch it; he's the coach," I heard another person tell the bespectacled spectator with a full beard.

"I don't give a shit," the spectator announced.

"No person is requesting you to do so," I mumbled to myself, "so there: your objection is academic."

If I learned a quick lesson from that incident, the lesson is this: when the stands have sixty thousand fans in them, then maybe the coach does not really hear the crowd; but when the crowd is small (more like sixty persons), then the angry fans are certainly heard, and what they say can hurt the coach and hurt deeply, though the unwritten rule requires the coach to ignore all comments and to pay undivided attention to coaching the team. Referees might be able to ignore the angry comments of the fans; secure and confident coaches might also; but insecure coaches (who probably think they can hear the burps of the ants) will recoil into a ball of anger and hurt.

At the end of this first game, I feel terribly insecure, but I hope I'm not coming across that way to the players. Ambiguity and humor should cover my insecurity. If someone should ask me now, "How's it going, Coach?" my response would have to be: "Can't kick."

I would often listen to folk music on public radio on Saturday nights and write long entries in the diary. The diary, like the pope, formed an audience of one; and like those world leaders who visit the pope, I would visit the diary and speak my mind, confessing my frustrations, fears, and failures.

On Monday I arrived at the restaurant three minutes before the two beginning players and three hours before the first practice following the Houghton defeat. After we placed our orders, we volleyed the obligatory small talk about the weather then delved into our topic proper: soccer.

"I trust," I began, "you found our Houghton game to be slightly disappointing."

"Discouraging," one player said.

"Depressing," the other added.

I smiled, then laughed out loud. The players seemed puzzled by my laughter. "What's funny, Coach?" one of them asked.

"I'm sorry to laugh," I replied, "but our disappointing-discouraging-depressing progression reminds me of this crazy piece of fiction that I'm working on. In the piece, one of the characters starts a company that manufactures disposable dog diapers."

"Diapers for dog?" one of the players said, disbelief all over her face.

"Yep," I said as our drinks arrived.

"Anyway, please continue, Coach," the other player said.

"Well, the character calls the company 3D—a name made memorable by 3M—and she devises for it a television, radio, and print media slogan that invites potential buyers to 'SEE YOUR DOG IN 3D.' Of course, the biggest market for the product is *not* the wide-open fields of Texas, where the dogs roam at will, but the nation's big cities, such as New York, where the pooper-scooper laws are on the books and are enforced."

The players giggled; their giggles ballooned into laughter that ended with one saying, "My uncle in Queens could use one of those."

"You mean your uncle's dog?" the other said, laughing.

Now, I thought to myself, how do you get out of this? How do you get them to think about soccer, to think *seriously* about soccer? You don't, I quickly reasoned. So, we volleyed more small talk until our food arrived.

While we ate, the "D" words formed the theme of our conversation. The players noted how disappointed they were not only by their performance but by the lack of support and positive reinforcement from the experienced players. They pointed out how discouraged they—and indeed the other beginners—felt in learning how to play soccer. "All the sports that we've played so far," one player said, "rely so heavily on eye-hand coordination—sports like softball, basketball, volleyball, tennis, and racquetball—but not soccer. Soccer relies on eye-foot coordination; it's so difficult to make the adjustment; it's much too discouraging at times."

"To say downright depressing, Coach, might be overstating the case, but depressing is close," the other player added.

"Coach, it doesn't take much to notice that we're having problems developing smooth passes and kicks with our natural right feet," the first player said, "but you want us to use our unnatural left feet as well."

"That I do," I said, and bit into my hamburger.

"But that's hard, Coach," the player responded, "really hard."

"Very hard. Boy, is that hard," her friend added.

"If you find that hard," I asked them, "then what do you think of all those head shots that we practice regularly?"

"Oh, those," one said. "They're impossible—"

"But fun," the other added.

"Yeah, impossible and fun at the same time," one said.

"Like charging hell with a bucket," the other added.

"Impossible and fun," I said. "Impossible and fun, eh?"

"And hard on the head, too," one said, smiling.

"Frankly," I said, "I don't expect you to perfect any of those skills at this stage of your career."

"And please, don't worry, Coach," one said. "You're looking at two players—and I'm sure you know others—who won't ruin your expectations."

Before we left the restaurant, the players asked me to look for and accentuate, throughout the week's practice, the positive aspects of the Houghton game. They urged me to pump them, over and over, with positive feedback in the hope that the experienced players would follow my lead, and they begged me to continue to be patient with them, to continue to practice and to repeat the various kicking techniques, however basic and dull they might appear to me or to the experienced players. "Forget about strategies and plays," one player told me as we were about to part ways. "We've got to learn to walk before we can run. It's that simple, Coach."

At Monday's practice, I followed the recommendations of the two beginners, and the practice went well. At our family dinner that evening, the conversation drifted to the Houghton game. "Sorry, Dad," Rita said. "That was a rough way to start the season."

"Sure was," Sal said.

"I wouldn't say your players were exactly awful, Dad," Rita said, "but I can honestly say that I didn't know soccer could be played like that."

"Is that like when Mom burns the chicken?" Sal asked. "We never tell her, 'This is awful stuff, Mom'; we say instead, 'We didn't know chicken could be cooked like this.'"

"I guess so," Rita said, then asked, "Who's going to win your 'Advil Player of the Game' award?"

"The what award?" Paul asked.

"The Advil Player of the Game," Sam said.

"Yes, Advil," Rita said. "That's the award he's going to give to the player who gives him the biggest headache each game."

"That's not why they give them on TV," Sam said.

"Don't give individual awards, Dad," Sal said. "Soccer isn't golf or fishing: it's a team sport. Coaches and broadcasters blow it when they give out these awards. Some coaches even give players stickers for their helmets."

"Well, then, give it to the team," Rita said.

"Don't worry," I told the family. "There's no such award; Rita's using her imagination again. I'll take the blame for that first game, and I think a paraphrase of a famous quote from Tolstoy might well frame our team's exploits so far."

"And the quote?" Rita said.

"Winning teams are all alike; every losing team loses in its own way."

"I like Rita's quote better," Sal said. "'I didn't know soccer could be played like that.'"

"Or chicken cooked like this," Rita said, referring to the food in front of her.

"Okay," I said, "when it comes to quotes, kids stay with kids, and literature professors stay with famous writers."

"Maybe literature professors should stay out of coaching," Rita said.

"Please, let's not go over that game now," my wife said. "This is beginning to sound like football coaching days in Kansas, though then you won a lot more than you lost. But I can still remember the dismal mood at those postgame meals after a loss."

"Let's not," I agreed. "But I can assure you all—I'll guarantee you, in fact—that things will be different next Saturday at Oberlin."

"I hope so," Sal said.

"I hope so," Paul added.

"I hope so," Rita said.

"I hope so," Sam said.

These successive remarks reminded me of the "good night," "good night," "good night" dribbles in *The Waste Land* of T. S. Eliot.

4

Princeton, Henry Aaron, Ginsberg, and Amy's Feat

Having successfully coached the Golden Tornadoes to their first resounding defeat on a Saturday morning and through their first practice after that defeat on a Monday afternoon, I decided to forget—insofar as it was possible—about soccer for Monday evening. Instead, I turned to my literary pursuits and entered into the word processor several poems that I had written and revised before the soccer season began, preparing them for submission to potential publishers.

To accompany the poems, I first wrote a gentle and conventional cover letter that went something like this: "Please consider reviewing the enclosed poems for publication. I hold a Ph.D. in literature . . . and my works have appeared in . . ." Aware that poetry magazines and journals receive thousands of unsolicited poems a month, I crumpled that letter and took a lesson from Gladys Princeton, star of *When She Went Men-Bashing*.

In the novel, Lady Princeton had tried to find ways to get her literary works isolated from the publishers' huge slush piles and to have them read—rejected—ahead of the rest. She reasoned:

Sending in works on perfumed paper . . . won't do it, for that just shows bad taste; fancy headings, justified lines, neat type won't do it, for that just shows that the writer has access to word processing or desktop publishing equipment; an appeal from a friend of a friend won't do it, for that just shows that the writer attends parties where insignificant people gossip about important folks; institutional letterhead from such places as Harvard, Stanford, St. Elizabeth's Hospital, U.S. Senate, Attica Prison might occasionally work, for some institutions speak louder than others. What, I suspect, will work in getting potential slush pile manuscripts read at once is a strange cover: the stranger the cover letter appears, the quicker the reading response is likely to be.

Lady Princeton's advice led me to write a quirky cover letter that I typed on the soccer letterhead of Geneva's Golden Tornadoes, stationery that Lady Princeton (and my wife, for that matter) would feel speaks louder than that of the college's English department. The letter—which I thought of forwarding to *Field*, a distinguished poetry magazine published at, of all places, Oberlin College—stated:

Dear Editor:
My mother doesn't write poetry, but I don't know of any other person who doesn't. My mother, however, does read the stuff. Please consider the enclosed for her sake.

Sincerely,
S. S. Hanna

This letter, I told myself before preparing for bed, should bring some kind of attention to the enclosed manuscript, and that attention will be a good and necessary first step, even if it resembles the attention given to a patient who has just received an appendix transplant.

On Tuesday evening the head of the education department came to the house for a visit. On his not-too-hidden agenda was a discussion of the Houghton game, which he had not seen but had heard about from various people. "That was a game heard round the campus," he began by paraphrasing Emerson, and staying with Emerson he added, "If women's soccer is an institution and if an institution is but the lengthened shadow of a single man—what a sexist claim!—then you're it, brother. But you don't want it to be a losing institution, do you?"

"Oh, no," I said. "Losing certainly is a foolish proposition, and what I want to do—to stay with Emerson this Tuesday evening—is avoid being consistent at it, for 'a foolish consistency is but the hobgoblin of little minds.' Right?"

"Right," he said, yanking his goatee slightly as if to pop out another witticism. "Consider this: if 'but' is a coordinating conjunction and if you as an English teacher do teach about all those coordinating conjunctions, what is it that led you to trip and fall on yours last Saturday? Now, Coach, please be specific in your defense."

"Come on, Dave," I fired back. "We weren't that bad. Given all the earnest beginners—and I mean beginners, as in 'unable to play,' 'never played before'—that we have, we did a good job, but we still need to do a lot more work. We'll coordinate this program yet, though I don't know if we'll ever get to the level where we'll be kicking coordinating conjunctions, as it were."

Practice on Wednesday afternoon started on two good notes. We arrived and found our field lined for soccer and our netless homemade goals in place. Both matters cheered us. I worked hard on accentuating (not to mention locating) the positive aspects of the Houghton game while focusing the players' thoughts on Oberlin. "That's a great music school out there in Ohio," I said, "and they'd probably love to see what it feels like to orchestrate a Golden Tornado. Our job will be to show them that it's not easy. Again, winning is not our concern; we want to go out there and enjoy the sport of soccer."

All week in practice, we worked and worked on the fundamentals of passing, dribbling, shooting, and playing defense. The experienced players appeared to be getting sharper and the beginners showed signs of improving. We were fortunate in that all fifteen of our players had escaped injury in the Houghton game and stayed healthy throughout the hard week of practice.

Friday's practice was, by far, the easiest. We went through basic passing and dribbling drills. Near the end of practice, I gathered the team in a circle and asked, "Does the name Antoinette Brown mean anything to any of you?"

No one said a word. I looked around, and finally a player asked, "Who was that again?"

"Antoinette Brown," I repeated. Hearing no response, I added, "Remember now, I'm speaking in the context of Oberlin."

"We give up," one player said.

"Would any of you like to venture a guess?" I asked.

"Sure, I'll try," Angi said. "Is she the Oberlin Yeomen's—oops, I better say Yeo*persons*'—best player?" That remark triggered other comments.

"Their highest scorer?" Amy said.

"Did you get a detailed scouting report on them, Coach?" Jill asked.

These three comments came in such rapid succession that I failed to respond to them. "I bet," Angi added, "she's my counterpart: their hot-shooting right wing. Right, Coach?"

"No," I said.

"Their goalie?" Amy asked.

"Negative again," I said.

"Say the name again please, Coach," Angi said.

"Antoinette Brown."

"She's obviously a woman of color," Angi said. "Now, having said that, is she their star player from Ireland or England?"

"Nope again," I said. "Give up?" Most of the players nodded, and some relaxed on the grass, sensing a little lecture of sorts. "Okay," I said, "you'll find her in the history books. Oberlin, as you probably all know, was the first coeducational college in our country. It was the first college to grant degrees to women, and it did it two centuries plus one year after Harvard College was founded; that makes it, what—1837. Now, our friend Antoinette—love that first name—"

"Beats the one that you once told us in class you planned to give to one of your boys," Angi said, "but your wife—a very smart lady, I might add—vetoed your choice."

"What was that name, Coach?" several players asked in unison.

"You don't really want to know," I said.

"Sure do," several players said.

"Well, I wanted to name one of our twin boys 'However' so that when he'd go on the football field to kick a field goal or an extra point, the announcer would say, 'Onto the field goes However Hanna.' Now, tell me, doesn't that sound sharp?"

"What's even sharper," Angi said, "is if the announcer also says, 'The kick is up and the kick is good.'" Some of the players laughed; they must have recalled the "kick in the gut" motif that we had discussed the previous week and during our first classroom meeting, the "legal kick" stimulated by Title IX that the women's movement was about to level at men's sports.

Amy, who was sitting on the grass, flipped back, locked her fingers together, used her palms as a pillow, looked up at the cloudless sky, and asked, "What name were you going to give the other twin, Coach?"

Before I could offer a response, Angi manufactured one: "Hyphen."

"Hyphen Hanna," Jill added, leading the roar of laughter.

When I stopped laughing, I returned to Antoinette Brown, who in 1850 received a theological degree from Oberlin and three years later—after numerous difficulties—was ordained into the Christian ministry. I tried to impress upon our soccer players Oberlin's place in our history, pointing to the early and historic strides that the college had made in the education of women and its crucial role in the Underground Railroad. I informed the students that Geneva—which was established in 1848 in Northwood, Ohio, and moved to Pennsylvania in 1880—had also played an active role in the Underground Railroad of the pre–Civil War era, thanks to the firm antislavery stance and the courageous and relentless crusades of the college's founders, the Reformed Presbyterians of North America, whose motto was: "No union with slaveholders, political or ecclesiastical." Several Geneva professors and administrators, I told the student-athletes, served as conductors on the railroad, hiding fugitive slaves in caves, houses, churches, and hay wagons, then escorting them as far north as Sandusky, Ohio, before their final escape to freedom in Canada.

Beyond their commitment to free the slaves, those professors and administrators during the early years of Geneva exhibited a deep-seated desire to minister to the needs of the liberated slaves. After the Civil War, there were periods when nearly half of Geneva's student body was composed of former slaves. And, like Oberlin, Geneva was among the earliest colleges to admit women, graduating its first black woman in 1866. "And in case you're wondering," I said with a smile, "the name of that Golden Tornado, whose parents used what today seems like an original first name, was Ophelia Hall Nesbit. Ophelia went on to become a teacher in Cincinnati."

Turning again to Oberlin, I remarked that Charles Finney, one of the greatest preachers in the United States during the nineteenth century—his emphasis on conversion and revival may be compared to that of Billy Graham—was president of Oberlin in its early years. I spoke about Oberlin's fine conservatory of music and some of the magnificent stone buildings on campus. I even mentioned the Memorial Arch erected in 1903 in behalf of the daughters and sons of Oberlin, the Christian missionaries who had died in the Boxer Rebellion in China in 1900. "It should be a fun and educational road trip," I told our players, "and I trust we'll give a good account of our athletic ability." I emphasized how far we had come as a team just by having another week of practice. "Let's meet tomorrow morning at nine in Old Main circle," I said at the end of practice. "I'll have the college van, and we'll be ready to roll a few minutes past nine. I'll try to bring with me either However or Hyphen. How's that?"

"Sounds good, Coach," a voice said as the players broke the circle and started to walk up College Hill to their dorms to shower. Several volunteers, the team captain, Jill, and I collected the first-aid kit, balls, cones, water buckets, and unclaimed shin guards, and we hiked up to the equipment room in the field house. The volunteers walked several yards ahead of Jill and me. On the way, I asked Jill to point out any issues that needed to be addressed, to give me a feel for her reading of the team's morale, to suggest changes or additions that she or others might like to see done. This informal chat with the captain became part of my coaching routine, a helpful and often illuminating visit, for Jill was a frank, shrewd, and insightful woman, a talented player, respected by her peers and admired by the fans.

Saturday morning at seven, I woke up little Sami, younger of the twins (by eight minutes), who had asked to accompany the team on the first road trip. Sami and I picked up the college van, filled it with gas, recorded the appropriate mileage at departure, and headed to the field house to load up the soccer-related gear. Then we met the players in front of Old Main circle. The captain told me that all were present. The players loaded their gear onto the van, and we took off.

Sami, a gentle and delicate left-hander, often loved to tilt his diminutive body, wind up, and show off his precocious athletic development (not uncommon for left-handers, it seems) by throwing what he called "a tight sthpiral with an adult football." Sami was his given name, but because he was so tiny and delicate, we called him Sam, a name one might associate with a strong and gruff steelworker or a beer-bellied coal miner from western Pennsylvania. As I drove, I occasionally turned my head and told Debbie and Barb, the two players between whom Sam sat, all about our family's thinking in nicknaming him.

"Had he not been fortunate and gotten the name Sam," Debbie asked, "would he have been the 'However Hanna' of the family?"

"Or the Hyphen?" Barb asked, smiling.

"The Hyphen," I answered.

"Did you know your dad was planning to do that, Sam?" Debbie asked him.

"Do what?" Sam said.

"Name you Hyphen or However," Debbie said.

"I didn't know about Hyphen, but Mommy and Daddy told us about However," Sam said.

"What would *you* have liked?" Debbie continued as she gently poked Sam in the chest.

"I like Sami," he said, lacing his "s" with that distinctive "th" sound that a missing tooth frequently invites.

"Not Sam?" she asked.

"No, Sami, but everyone calls me Sam."

"We'll call you Sami," both players said and hugged him at once. He smiled, contentedly.

Debbie Schaefer, a junior writing major and a soccer player with light experience, had enrolled in many of my classes and seemed to be an introspective person: imaginative, skillful, somewhat shy, highly sensitive. She entertained Sam by telling him stories that her parents used to tell her when she was a child. Sam loved the role of an engaged and enchanted listener.

Other players sat in the long van that accommodated all fifteen of them; occasionally, players sitting in the middle or rear of the van would direct Angi, who had claimed the bucket seat to my right, to pick up and fine-tune some music on the radio and deliver it to them via the rear speakers. As I drove on, stations faded in and out, keeping Angi busy. Besides that, she and I talked about all sorts of topics.

Early in the trip, Angi pulled out a half-pint carton of milk from a brown bag that she had packed before breakfast in Geneva's cafeteria. "That little carton of milk there, Angi," I said as her thumbs dug into the carton's jugular, "reminds me of an incident I once witnessed in Milwaukee when I was a boy."

Her thumbs and index fingers ripped the top of the carton, then she tenderly popped out a spout, dipped in a straw, and asked, "Is it a funny incident, Coach?"

"Well, let's put it this way: it's an unusual one," I said.

"Dealing with what?"

"Baseball."

"My favorite sport," Angi said.

"Indeed, the sport of America's literary elite—"

"My former favorite sport," Angi quickly added with a smile.

"And the star of the incident is none other than Henry Aaron—"

"*The* Henry Aaron," she interrupted, twitching the fenders of her dainty nose, "the Babe Ruth of our generation."

"Right. And the supporting cast is a substance and a drunk," I said.

"And the substance is what?"

"Milk."

"Milk?" Angi said, moving the carton in her hand in my direction.

"Right, milk. So, we've got Henry Aaron, milk, and a drunk as—"

"Henry Aaron, milk, and a drunk," she said, punctuating her remarks by popping her eyebrows.

"And if you stop repeating after me, I'll tell you all about Aaron and his celebrated public love affair with milk and how that love affair was saluted and slapped by the wisdom of a drunk before my very own eyes."

"Okay, Coach, you're on," Angi said, leaning over and turning on the air-conditioning unit. "With this thing on and with the radio and the noise in the back, you've got to talk a little louder, Coach."

"What?" I shouted

"Not that loud," Angi said, laughing.

"Anyway, the incident took place," I said in a normal voice, "in the late fifties in Milwaukee, the place where Aaron had forged his home run heroics. In those years, the Braves had beaten the famed and powerful New York Yankees in the World Series. Aaron was the most brilliant player on the Braves' star-studded lineup; he was what today we'd call a superstar, the kind that would make an ideal product pimp, and he was certainly used for that." I glanced, the flat lands framing the Ohio Turnpike. "Wisconsin, as you well know, is America's dairy land; that's what their license plates boast, and they do make a lot of milk and cheese and other dairy products up there."

"But it's also America's beer land, Coach, isn't it? Old Milwaukee and Miller and many other beers come from there, don't they?"

"They sure do, but I reckon the milk folks got Aaron before the 'kiss of the hops' boys got to him," I said.

"I see," Angi said, fiddling with the radio knob, fine-tuning Bob Dylan's voice.

"And when they did, they devised a simple slogan: 'Make Mine Milk.' The ad folks plastered Aaron's picture all over the city—on billboards atop buildings, on highway billboards, on the outside, inside, and backs of buses, on grocery store windows, on the sides of vacant and occupied buildings. Under the huge picture of Aaron dressed in his Braves uniform, flashing his boyish, toothy smile, were the words MAKE MINE MILK printed in dark, bold letters. There was no way to escape the milk campaign. Wherever you went, there were MAKE MINE MILK signs. All those signs, no doubt, pleased the young Milwaukee mothers who had tried to get their children to drink milk, but they must have irritated some of the drunks about town, and one of those drunks once confronted Aaron. I was there when that confrontation took place."

Angi seemed to be attentive, but I waited a good while before speaking again. The other soccer players in the van slept, read, or conversed with each other while listening to whatever music Angi was able to tune and send via the van's rear speakers. I intended to continue to talk to Angi about Aaron, milk, and the drunk. Indeed, she invited me to continue in her own way: "Well, Coach, are you going to fill me in on that confrontation, or do I have to score a goal to hear the rest of it?"

"Oh, no, I'd rather finish the story now and not wait until next season," I said.

"Boy, Coach, I love the confidence you have in me."

"Anyway, to go on: the confrontation took place at Milwaukee County Stadium. I was sitting in the right-field bleachers in one of the seventy-five-cent seats; they were that cheap then. Home plate was a good ways away, but Aaron, the right fielder, was only a few yards away, and the bull pen was only a few yards to our right. The Brooklyn Dodgers—Dem Bums,' as their nickname had it—were in town, the Dodgers of Gil Hodges, Duke Snider, Pee Wee Reese, Carl Furillo, Don Newcombe, and Johnny Padres, the pride of Flatbush that Roger Kahn immortalized in *The Boys of Summer.*"

"Okay, got that much, Coach," Angi said as she twisted her body so that her back rested against the van's door. Her brown hair—an unruly mass of corrugated strands—dangled to the lower reaches of her neck, flaring off her narrow shoulders.

"In those days," I continued, "I'd go to almost all of the Braves' home games; I worked in the YMCA and made a dollar-ten an hour, so the seventy-five-cent bleacher seats were affordable and the ballpark was not all that far from our house. In the late fifties, the Dodgers and the Braves were always involved, it seemed, in the pennant chase. And the day that Aaron was chastised by the drunk took place during one of those tense, decisive games. If memory serves me right, the game was in the eighth inning, and the score was one to one—"

"In the Dodgers' favor?" Angi asked with a smile.

"Yeah, right," I replied, and continued, "—and the packed stadium was hoping to see Aaron hit a home run or two. Instead, he struck out twice and hit a high fly ball in the infield. At the top of the eighth, one Dodger reached first on a walk, then another smashed a single to right. Aaron charged the ball and leaned forward to scoop it so as to throw it back to the infield in order to keep the lead runner on second, but unfortunately, the ball slipped between his legs and scooted all the way to the right-field fence. The runners dashed around the bases as Aaron waved away the center fielder who was running toward him to back up the play. Aaron scampered to the fence, leaned over, picked up the ball and whipped it to the cutoff man. While this was happening, the man sitting next to me—sporting a massive beer belly and wearing a white T-shirt, and a blue Milwaukee Braves baseball cap—sprang to his feet, hoisted his genuine plastic beer glass, pounded his right fist in the air, and shouted at a disgusted Aaron, 'Drink *more* milk!'"

"Well, that was a sober bit of advice," Angi said, smiling and turning slightly so that her body rhymed more comfortably with the contours of the bucket seat. Then she asked, "Who won the game?"

"The Dodgers. Thanks to Aaron, a routine single took on the punch of a run-scoring triple, giving the Dodgers a two-to-one victory," I said.

"I wonder," she said, "if Aaron took the drunk's advice."

"I really don't know, but wouldn't it be nice if that milk formula works for our team?" I asked.

"It sure would," Angi said. "We've got a lot of milk-drinking athletes in this van, Coach." She finished her milk, tucked the carton into her little brown bag, and continued to listen.

"But to get us on the winning ways, we're going to need a lot more than milk," I said. "We're a young team; we need to grow and grow and grow." I took a deep breath and added, "You know, there ought to be a way to use that incident in our creative writing class."

"That's right, Coach," Angi said. "If I were you, I'd relate the incident to the students, then I'd ask them to expand on it, transforming it from an incident into a story. You know how students are good at writing incidents but have real problems in writing *stories* with conflict, tension, crisis, climax, resolution, character, and theme."

"That's an idea, a good idea," I said.

"Maybe," Angi added, "we could have Aaron calling for a time-out and replying to the drunk, who would reply back; or maybe Aaron could climb the fence, charge the stands, and flatten the drunk. Have the drunk press charges, et cetera. The thing could really take off, you know."

Angi, not unlike other players on the team, crusaded for women's rights and longed to see women's athletics receive the same kind of attention and financial support as men's sports. However, she refused to see soccer as an all-consuming activity, a perspective that a hard-core jock might bring to the sport. Indeed, none of our players seemed to fall into that category. Some, especially among the beginners, saw soccer as a gym class, an outlet for supervised and intense exercise. Angi saw it as a competitive sport that, to use her words, "connected the participants with especial feelings of joy and accomplishment by winning." As we chatted in the van about the topic of winning, Angi told me, "If we fail to win—and it looks like that's going to be the case—then our joy would have to come from weaving the Geneva soccer experience into our prose or poetry."

Angi had selected writing as a major because she wanted to write short stories, novels, poems, and plays, but she knew and believed the pithy wisdom of the writer who noted that "one can make a fortune off of writing, but it's impossible to make a living off of it."

After Geneva, Angi hoped to land a writing-editing job, preferably with a magazine, book publisher, or newspaper. She believed such a job would guarantee her a steady income while she, in her words, "pursued the muse." She loved the poets of the Beat generation; occasionally, she would come to class dressed in dark, tight apparel as well as glasses and hats that one might associate with those poets of the late fifties and early sixties. I always felt that a copy of Allen Ginsberg's *Howl*, the little square version of Lawrence Ferlinghetti's City Lights Books, cowered in one of the big pockets of the bulky overcoat she often wore during those cool evenings of late autumn and the snappy days of winter.

Angi occasionally acted in unusual and unpredictable ways. I always feared that on a soccer road trip she might turn around in her bucket seat, call the players to attention, whip out a copy of *Howl*, and begin reading. And if I knew Angi, she would first read the last line of William Carlos Williams's Introduction to *Howl*, in which Williams says, "Hold back the edges of your gowns, Ladies, we are going through hell." Then, of course, she would begin with energy and flair:

> I saw the best minds of my generation destroyed by madness,
> starving hysterical naked, . . .

The other players on the team respected Angi's soccer-playing abilities so much that they would forgive her such an idiosyncratic act, chalking it up to the generic explanation, "Well, that's Angi."

On that initial road trip to Oberlin, Angi did not read from Ginsberg's poetry, but she did flash a measure of her wit on several occasions. Midway into the trip, I turned off the radio for an instant and entertained suggestions regarding a rest stop. An unexpected mini-dispute erupted, leading one player in the back of the van to preface her remark with the quaint rhetoric of parliamentary procedure encountered, no doubt, in a political science or a speech class. "Coach," the player shouted rhythmically, "may I speak to this matter from the rear?"

"You may speak from anywhere you can," Angi quickly responded in a soft voice that only I could hear.

"Ang," I said.

"What, Coach?" she said, smiling.

I smiled and told the player, "Please do."

And so, on the long drive to Oberlin, one writing major, Debbie, occupied Sam; another, Angi, conversed with me about all sorts of topics; and a third, Sharon Hasek, who shared my initials—we often called each other by those initials—sat somewhere in the middle of the van, drumming up support for Geneva's literary magazine with which she was involved, occasionally singing along with the artists on the radio, and constantly reminding Angi to fine-tune the reception or to find another station. At times I would sail a lighthearted remark to Sharon, and she would quickly whip one back, as if my remark were a Frisbee. My diary for the Oberlin game notes that I paid an inordinate amount of attention to the writing majors, and that might well be, because I knew them better—much better, thanks to frequent contact in class—than any of the other players on the team. As the season progressed, however, my knowledge of and interaction with all the other players increased.

Once we passed the road sign that proclaimed Oberlin to be "A NUCLEAR WEAPONS FREE ZONE," we felt we were in Oberlin proper. We drove around to get a feel for the town and the college. The huge and attractive stone structures, the Memorial Arch, the spacious lawns, the towers, the Finney Memorial Chapel—all impressed our players. Angi took particular interest in the appearance of the students strolling in front of the academic buildings and the library. "Look," she told me. "Some of these male students with long hair, sandals, and beads around their necks and the females in casual dresses with leather purses, unshaven legs, and no bras remind me of the era of Kerouac and Ginsberg. Oberlin is like the sixties all over again."

"How quaint," another student added. "Look at that." We all looked to our right and saw nothing special.

"Look at what?" someone asked.

"Right there," the amused student responded.

"Stop, Coach," another player said.

I stopped the van and also asked, "Look at what?" Then I noticed a person riding a Vespa, one of those motorcycles that make the rider appear as if he's sitting on a toilet stool. But I didn't think the cycle or the rider was strange or extraordinary, so I said, "There seems to be nothing special out there; it's just a corner, a street corner in a small town, a college town, historic Oberlin no less."

The player who had deflected then arrested our attention spoke up again: "Lots of college or university towns have a college or university avenue, but when was the last time you've seen a street named Professor? Here's one."

"And Professor-Coach Hanna," Jill said, lapsing into an authoritative captain's voice, "you'd better get us to the field and the locker rooms. We'll need all the remaining time to get ready for today's game. Sight-seeing will have to wait for another day."

The time was about twelve-thirty, and game time was at two. I followed Jill's advice and headed toward the field, urging the players to walk around it and see whether it had lumps or stones or other features that might require some caution.

As the players surveyed the field, Sam and I introduced ourselves to a passerby, an Oberlin soccer player, as chance would have it. She pointed out to us the locker room reserved for visiting female teams. I, in turn, pointed it out to our team when they returned from their walk.

While the players were getting dressed and taping each other's ankles, Sam and I exchanged small talk. At one instance, I found myself telling him, "When I coached football in Kansas, most of the nervous freshmen would form—just before the game was about to start—a big, long line to the urinals. They'd get so nervous, they'd want to go to the bathroom. I wonder if that happens with the women soccer players."

"Daddy," he said, "I want to go to the bathroom."

When I heard that request, I kicked myself. I knew that using the word had been a bad idea. But ideas have consequences, so we walked the campus in search of a bathroom. I hope finding a bathroom at Oberlin, I told myself as we walked, is going to be easier than finding a Chinese restaurant that serves bread. It was.

When we entered, Sam headed to a compartment and closed the door; I stepped away and used a urinal. We were the only ones in a large room with a high ceiling that had enough urinals, sinks, and toilets in it to furnish numerous bathrooms. I was reminded of the "Leach Index," that is, the number of bathrooms the rich and famous have in their houses. In the television program "Lifestyles of the Rich and Famous," Robin Leach, the host, strokes his narrative so that it reaches its climax when he announces the number of bathrooms in a given house. The filthy rich have many bathrooms. (Wouldn't it be nice, I always ask myself when I see that show, if Leach would do a feature on the house of a college professor, not a humble associate professor/ soccer coach, but a full professor? Chances are, Leach would note that the full professor, despite his status, is likely to have no more than two bathrooms and a bottle of Pepto-Bismol.) When Sam heard me urinate (bathroom acoustics in nineteenth-century stone buildings are unimpeachably excellent), he asked, "Daddy, are you nervous?"

"No, Sam, just hurry."

"I *am.*"

"Should I wait outside for you?"

"No, stay here; I'm hurrying, Daddy."

"Okay, I'll stay."

"Daddy, Daddy, you've got to come and see this! Oh, Daddy, you won't believe this!"

"What is it, Sam?"

"You won't believe it, Daddy."

"Tell me just what it is that you're seeing, and I'll tell you whether I believe it or not, Sam."

"I just know you won't believe it."

"What *is* it, Sam?" I asked, raising my voice.

"Dad," Sam said, speaking more calmly, "it's a picture of a big, *big* crayon."

I laughed. "Hurry, Sam, we've got to meet the players and go to the field pretty soon."

When our players finished dressing and trotted to the field more or less as a unit, an Oberlin player walked up to me and asked, "Is that your team?"

"Yes."

"Where're the rest?" she asked.

"That's it. We have fifteen players."

"So that's your traveling squad?"

"That's our home *and* traveling squad," I said. "Ours is a new program and we simply don't have that many players out for the team."

"Have you won many games?" she asked.

"No. How many players do you people have?" I asked.

"In the thirties, but probably twenty-four or -five will show up today," she said, adding, "Soccer is a big sport around here; people love to play it."

"What position do you play?" I asked.

"I get put in on defense; I don't start, but maybe I'll play a lot today. I hope so," she said, winked, and tousled Sam's long, dark hair. "I just love his large brown eyes and olive-colored skin," she said, pinching Sam's right cheek. "Bye, sweetheart," she told him, and walked in the direction of the Oberlin gym.

"She seems like a splendid person," I whispered to myself, "but I hope she doesn't get to play a lot today. Oh," I added, taking a deep breath, the kind they want for a chest X ray, "I don't expect we'll win this thing, but I just hope—oh, I hope— we play well. I hope our players see progress in the team, and I hope they experience satisfaction in their individual efforts."

"What does the back of her shirt say, Daddy?" Sam asked, referring to the Oberlin player as she pulled open the gym's door.

"It says, 'IT HURTS TO WIN.'"

"I don't understand," Sam said.

"And I'm not in the mood to explain."

• • • • •

Before the start of the game, I gave our team final instructions. I advised Angi and Barb, the two wings, and Jill, the center
forward, to run back as often as possible and help with the defense. "Now, those of you playing at the halfback/fullback
spots," I said while standing in the center of the circle, "listen to
Amy; she'll direct you while the game is in progress. Also, listen
to Jill's voice and mine." Then I offered words of encouragement: "We had a good, a very good, week of practice back home
in Pennsylvania, so let's go out there and show these Ohio folks
what we can do. Let's try to enjoy the game and see what improvements we've made individually and as a team." Before the
players took their positions on the field, I said, "All of you will
play, and you'll play a great deal. We'll try to keep the experienced players in for the entire match, and we'll make appropriate
substitutions as the game goes on. If—"

"Excuse me, Coach," Angi interrupted. "To whom do you
refer when you say 'we,' or is that just rhetorical?"

"That's just rhetorical," I said.

"Well, I thought you might be referring to Hanna and his
Hyphen," Angi said, pulling Sam closer to her.

"If some of you want to come out of the game for whatever
reason," I continued to address the players, "please let me know.
And if you're on the sidelines with me, please pay attention to
the action on the field. If you notice some adjustments we could
make that would help our performance on the field, please suggest them to me." I looked at the faces that surrounded me,
smiled, and added, "Asking to go in for someone, however, is
not one such adjustment." Most of the players smiled. "Please let
me make the substitution decisions, but let me assure you once
again: *All* of you will play, and you'll play for a good while."

The Golden Tornadoes roared as we broke up the circle and
the starters headed to their positions on the field.

Early in the game, the ball remained near the center of the
field. Oberlin would advance it twenty yards or so, and our players would return it to the center of the field, and on occasion, we

would penetrate Oberlin's side of the field. Several times, Angi, Anne, and Jill or Kristin, Barb, and Jill worked the ball downfield and looked as if they might be heading to take a shot at goal, only to have the Oberlin defense derail their efforts. I smiled when I saw Lori, a beginner who played at right fullback, slow down a strong kick by an Oberlin player and pass the ball to Amy, who had come out of her goal position and requested the ball. (I smiled because a beginner's instinct, I assumed, was to advance the ball forward, not backward.) Amy punted the ball to midfield, and Oberlin began another drive toward our goal. As the game progressed, Oberlin's drives took on a vigorous and determined tone. Oberlin's players hurled all sorts of shots at our goal, and Amy stopped—in some instances with spectacular moves—all of them.

At the twenty-eight-minute mark of the first half, Oberlin's strong center forward dribbled downfield, faked out a couple of our defenders, then slammed a wicked low shot past the out-stretched arms of a diving Amy. A cheer went out from the Oberlin bench and the moderately populated bleachers and side-lines. A disappointed Amy stood up, took a deep breath, pulled the ball from under the net, and threw it disconsolately toward the center of the field. She put her hands on her knees and looked down at the grass. She perked up again at the sound of the whistle.

When Sam heard the Oberlin crowd cheer for that first goal, he asked, "Is it over, Daddy?"

I felt like saying, "That's a loaded question, son," but I didn't. I said, "No, we've got a long way to go. Too bad there're no swing sets for you to play on; I know you're going to get bored."

Oberlin scored two more goals in the first period. At half-time, I congratulated the players on their efforts. "That first game," I told them, "we gave up our first goal in less than eight seconds. A national record, no doubt. But in this game, we played for twenty-eight minutes before giving up that first goal."

In the first half, Sam had paced our bench area and occasion-ally visited with the four substitute players on the sidelines. In the second half, he did the same, though at one point he drifted toward the center of the sidelines, where the official scorer's table was set, and struck up a conversation with the two Oberlin women charged with recording substitutions, goals, blocked shots, and the like. Midway in the second half, I went over to get him, and the Oberlin scorekeepers pleaded, "Please let him stay; he's not bothering us."

"Call me if he becomes a nuisance," I told them and headed back to our bench area. With about ten minutes remaining in the game, and as Amy continued to block more and more shots, much to the joy and applause of the Oberlin fans, I went to the scorer's table and asked, "How many blocked shots does our goalie have?"

"A huge sum," both women said at once it seemed. "We've never seen anything like this." They counted and came up with thirty-four.

"Our goalie, Amy, is tough," I said. "She's got the physical attributes, the courage, the quickness, the timing, the instincts that a good goalie needs. She also has had lots of experience playing on a men's team in Texas, no less. But she can't do it all herself; we'll need to work on strengthening the supporting cast, I'm afraid." Moments after I said that, Oberlin scored their fourth goal. "That goal is as superfluous as salt and pepper at an authentic Indian dinner at the Calcutta Cafe in London," I said with a smile. The scorekeepers laughed. I asked them to kindly inform me of Amy's final total of blocked shots. "I'm thinking of doing a feature article on Amy, with her performance here as the springboard to the piece."

"You don't sound like a typical athletic coach," one of them told me.

"Frankly, I'm not; I teach English at Geneva."

"How fine," one of them said.

"You'll like this," I said, tapping my index finger on a paperback copy of James Joyce's *A Portrait of the Artist as a Young Man* that one of the scorekeepers had near her ledger. "We're now reading this in Modern Literature; part of Joyce's literary style resembles our style of soccer," I said.

"How so?" one of the women asked.

"We play a kind of a stream-of-consciousness brand of soccer with our mixture of beginners and experienced players, don't we?" She smiled as I walked away.

When the final whistle blew, the Oberlin coach shook my hand and told me that he had done everything to play all his players. I thanked him for a splendid match. By playing everyone, he thought he might have helped me out a bit, but what actually happened was that he had a constant onslaught of fresh and obviously experienced troops—hungry troops that wanted to draw blood, score points, hear applause, and exchange high fives and low tens—while we had only four substitutes who were beginners. I substituted those beginners for other beginners on the field, only to hear an unusual complaint from the experienced players: too much playing time. They wanted less playing time and more rest time.

After the players showered and boarded the van for a drive to our postgame meal, I congratulated them on their performance, noted specific improvements at various positions, then focused on the high point of the match, the thirty-nine blocked shots by the goalie from the Lone Star State. I shared with the players my twofold plan: to call the NAIA office in Kansas City on Monday to find out if Amy's performance was a national record and to write a feature article on that performance and send it out for publication in a variety of places.

After we left Oberlin and drove for about thirty minutes, we found a large family restaurant not too far from the Ohio Turnpike. As we stood in the restaurant's lobby waiting to be seated, one of the players noticed a menu, placed near the cash register, which featured several vegetarian dishes. She rejoiced, announcing that she was a vegetarian. Her claim surprised us, for she appeared to be one of the strongest players on the team. "How do you get all your strength being a vegetarian?" someone asked.

"I get it just like the elephants do. They don't eat puppies, do they? They're vegetarians, too, you know."

Along with the players who had heard that exchange, I laughed at what sounded like a strange and sensible response. Those same players and I drifted toward a magazine rack that had a number of popular magazines, among them *Time, Newsweek*, the *Atlantic*, the *New Yorker*, the *Village Voice, Sports Illustrated*, and *VLS*, with its big, dark, bold letters. When Angi spotted the letters on top of the magazine, she told the vegetarian player and the rest of us within earshot: "Look at this place; they serve vegetarian dishes and carry the magazine of the Vegetable Liberation Society. That's like serving the flesh of dead animals and carrying the magazine of the Animal Liberation Society." Some laughed; others wondered what was funny. I reached over, pulled out a copy of the *Voice Literary Supplement*, paid for it, and followed the team members to our seats in the dining area. I asked the table attendant to put all the players' meals on one check and give it to me.

The team divided into groups of three, four, or five to a table or a booth. Angi joined Sam and me at our nicely padded, authentic vinyl booth. She sat for a moment, then she went over to the cash register and brought back some crayons and a small drawing pad to occupy Sam. Angi and I ordered Mexican dinners, and Sam asked for a hamburger with french fries.

"What's that, Daddy?" Sam asked when he saw my refried beans.

"Oh, these," I said, pointing to the beans with my fork, "they're Mexican refried beans."

"Are they good?" he asked.

I tasted them and said, "Yes."

"Were they bad before?" he said.

"No."

"Then why did they refry them?" he said.

"I always thought that was a strange redundancy," Angi said. We began to eat and talk over the match and the sixties and the Oberlin ambience. "Did you get any writing ideas out of this trip, Coach?" Angi asked.

"You mean other than a feature story on Amy's sterling performance?" I asked before crunching my taco.

"Yes."

"We'll have to wait and see," I said. "What about you? What're your impressions of this place, and will they find expression in your prose?"

"I tell you, Coach," Angi said, chewing her taco, "I'd love to come back here on my own and spend more time and really get a feel for Oberlin. You know, a couple of their players asked us if we wanted to go party with them this evening after the game."

"No, I didn't know that. I'm curious: When did they ask?"

"While the game was in progress," she said, "when some of those strong Oberlin players were belting all those shots at Amy."

"And what did you say?" I asked.

"I said, 'No way. We've got an old-fogy coach who's more conservative than all our fathers put together.'"

"Seriously," I said.

"That was serious."

"Come on."

"I would've loved to go, Coach. They sounded like really intriguing people, intelligent and all, but I knew that with one van and all, it would've been impractical," Angi said while twirling her fork in the refried beans.

"They were intriguing, weren't they?"

"They sure were," she said. "Just imagine what those Oberlin players would do to that old Victorian sensibility that once classified women as ladies dressed in corsets that cinched the waist, making them appear dainty, delicate, and petite. Imagine what they'd do to those in our culture who see women as sweet ladies, the sugar-and-spice types who invariably stay home and bake cookies."

"Are you suggesting," I asked, "that participation in sports is freeing women from those images?"

"You better believe it," Angi said.

"I do, I do," I said. "I wouldn't be coaching if I didn't believe in the educational, social, psychological, and confidence-building values of sports for women *and* men."

"That's good to hear," Angi said, "and I know you believe that, Coach." Then she picked up her stride in assessing the Oberlin squad: "Those players out there this afternoon were anything but frail and passive ladies; they were strong, vigorous, muscular, fast, and some played with reckless abandon. Some had hair on their legs and they peppered their language with 'shits' and 'damns' and no telling what else." Sam stopped eating for a second, looked up at Angi, then reached for a french fry. Angi glanced at him, then looked at me and added, "Our Jill really excels in heading the ball; the rest of us work at it. Oberlin has a dozen or so players who could head the ball with courage and do a heck of a lot more. And that one center forward, the one their fans kept cheering for, was scrappy and strong. Boy, was she quick."

Angi's tribute to the athletic excellence of the Oberlin squad was earnest and sound. It made me reflect on whether our team—or a future Geneva team—could ever scale such heights of excellence. If it weren't for Amy's extraordinary performance at goalie, we would have been crushed for the second straight week. To be sure, we were defeated, but it was an honorable defeat, I thought, made more bearable by Amy's performance and by the Oberlin fans' appreciation of that performance.

I told Angi, "I would've loved to work in their library, to explore their 'Little' and literary magazine collection," I said, "but all that'll have to wait for another day. Oberlin, as you well know, is a great academic institution. It's not just a good small college; it's one of the nation's best. I'm sure, for example, there's emphasis on good teaching here, but I'm equally sure the faculty members are expected to publish. In large universities," I added, "the cliché is if you don't publish, you perish. In most small colleges, if you don't publish, you languish. But I suspect—indeed I know—that's *not* the case at Oberlin."

"I trust Hyphen had a good time," Angi said, reaching down to hug Sam. She carried on a delightful conversation with "Hot Sam," as she occasionally called him, while the three of us continued to eat.

On the way home, several players slept in the van, others listened to the radio, still others did homework, Debbie told Sam more stories, and I kept to myself—replaying the Oberlin game, thinking about our upcoming game with Wheeling Jesuit College of West Virginia, and trying to assess the fate of *When She Went Men-Bashing* and whether it would lead me to join the ranks of the newly rich or keep me among the established poor. Marketing a first novel, I always believed, was like buying a lottery ticket: both can make one instantly wealthy. (The comparison, however, has other uncomfortable dimensions.) I also thought about my family and classes, my student-advising responsibilities, and all the time and energy that soccer was consuming. I reminded myself that I needed to listen to Sam tell his brothers and sister and mother all about the trip and to record the details of his perspective in the "Soccer Season Diary."

When we arrived in Beaver Falls at about eight in the evening, the Geneva–Washington and Jefferson football game was in progress. I thought of going up to the press box and asking the stadium's public address announcer, a student of mine who took a strong interest in women's soccer, to announce the following: "Geneva's women's soccer team just returned from Oberlin College, where they played earlier in the afternoon. The final score of that game was Oberlin, six."

Most of the players thought that such an announcement might be appropriate for an English professor and a team with three writing majors. "If read with the proper intonation," Angi said, "the announcement, however long, might still sound like an introductory dependent clause; an incomplete thought, as it were; a fragment, if you will."

"A kind of a run-on fragment, you mean," another player said.

"Right," I said. "Whatever that is."

"Coach, don't," Amy said.

"Do," Angi said, "and make them announce all the saves that Amy made."

"Coach, don't," Amy repeated.

"Okay, I won't ask to have the saves announced," I said. "I'll simply ask them to say, 'The score was Oberlin, six.'"

"You see," Angi said, turning to face the rest of the players in the van, "by not mentioning what the rest of the score was, the people in the stands will begin to ask each other: 'What was the second part of that score?' 'Did the announcer mention it?' 'Are we supposed to stay in suspense?' 'That sounded strange, didn't it?' 'Do we really have a women's soccer team now?' 'Did they really play at Oberlin?' You see," Angi continued, pointing her index finger upward, "a crazy, incomplete-sounding announcement like that will get people talking about our team. An announcement that gives both parts of the score arouses no suspense, no curiosity. It's a dead-end announcement. As we say in creative writing: if you suggest, you create; if you state, you destroy."

Jill, the thoughtful and often serious team captain, seemed unimpressed, unamused, and perhaps too tired to respond to any of the comments. She simply urged me not to make the announcement. I respected her view and did not make the announcement. In a manner of speaking, though, I did, but I made it as an entry in the diary for September 14, the day of the Oberlin game. That entry stated in part:

> Amy's brilliant performance at goalie reminds me of my failures as a writer. Several months ago, I sent out for publication several manuscripts with a Lady Princeton–like cover letter that read:
>
> > Dear Editor:
> > Every good writer should have a manuscript file entitled "WE'RE BACK." I certainly do. Please don't nominate the enclosed manuscript for that file.
> >
> > Sincerely,
> > S. S. Hanna

In a manner of speaking, that was the way it was this afternoon at Oberlin. Amy would stop a shot at goal; she'd hug the ball, look around at her teammates, and then she'd decide to punt it— football style. . . . Thanks to her strong leg and exceedingly fine punting skills, she'd sail the ball about forty or fifty yards down field, only to see the Oberlin players get a hold of it, pass it to each other with ease—if our beginners were in the area—or with considerable difficulty when our experienced players challenged them. And Oberlin was challenged often today.

In any event, Amy's punts (like my manuscripts) continued to come back. And just as her success could be compared to my failure, so too her "failure" could be compared to my success in that a few shots at our goal by Oberlin did get through and the Yeofolks did score. . . . A few of my manuscripts did "get in" several forums among them *Publishers Weekly*.

This evening for relaxation I watched two of my favorite T.V. shows: reruns of "Green Acres" (just love those farmers and their ways) and new productions of the wrestling spectaculars of the WWF, truly *the* opulent opera of the lower class. Too bad attaining a soccer victory is not as easy as staging one in wrestling. . . .

Also tried to fine-tune that segment of *Men-Bashing* that explores Lady Princeton's fear of the *National Enquirer* discovering her beloved Kafka. In the novel, she feels sorry for all those actors and politicians and T.V. evangelists and athletes whose hormones make headlines in the *National Enquirer*. From day to day, she lives with the fear that the *Enquirer* might, just might, go after her Franz. Her fear is as real to her as defeat is unreal to our team. We lost, but the women had a good time. Sam and I did also.

On Monday morning I called the NAIA office in Kansas City and talked to the person at the women's soccer desk. I informed her of our goalie's achievement and noted that the match's official scorer, supplied by Oberlin College, had tabulated what I felt might be a national record. "Unfortunately," the woman told me, "we don't keep national records on individual games, only on national tournaments."

I began the Monday afternoon practice by once again congratulating our athletes on an extraordinary performance at Oberlin, and then I passed on the sad news about how national records were tabulated. I assured the players that "in the next few days, I plan to write a feature article on Amy's performance at Oberlin and circulate it to numerous newspapers in the eastern Ohio–western Pennsylvania region. Some enlightened editors might find such a story refreshing, especially when juxtaposed with all these trite stories on football players that fill the papers this time of the year."

"Oh, Coach," a modest Amy said, "you don't need to do that."

"Do it, Coach, do it," several players insisted.

"You bet I will," I said. "Blocking thirty-nine shots at goal—and what vicious shots some of them were—remains an incredible achievement in our book. Right?"

A big roar, mingled with applause, began the Monday practice, the one that launched us into preparation for the third game against those folks from that wild and wonderful state of West Virginia: the women Cardinals of Wheeling Jesuit.

Geneva College's 1986 varsity soccer team. Front (*left to right*): Wendy Pillsbury, Suzanne Maslo, Sheryl Yost, Sue Zawislak. Back (*left to right*): Anne Stine, Jill Weakland, Angi Moyer, Sharon Hasek, Barb Schwettman, Amy Widener, Kristin Menningen, Anna Fawthrop, Sara Smith, Kathy Schwartz, Andrea Zook, S. S. Hanna. (Photo by David Stadler.)

This photograph is a reflection of our early days, with one experienced player kicking the ball, only to see the follow-through of her foot traveling up to a teammate's "coordinating conjunction." (This picture appeared in the 1986 Geneva yearbook.)

Suzanne Maslo dribbles and Anne Stine pursues her.
(Photo by David Stadler.)

Barb Schwettman (26) and Sue Zawislak during practice. (Photo by David Stadler.)

Jill Weakland, our team captain, dribbles ahead of Andrea Zook, one of our halfbacks. (Photo by David Stadler.)

Angi Moyer, the right wing. (This picture appeared in
the 1986 Geneva yearbook.)

Anne Stine, one of our forwards, followed by Sara Smith, a player who showed solid progress during the first season. (Photo by David Stadler.)

THE HAITI CREW

Geneva College's Haiti Mission Crew. One of our players, Suzanne Maslo (*front row, far right*), went on this trip and wrote about it for the newspaper and the yearbook.

Amy Widener, our strong and courageous goalie, diving after a shot in front of the homemade, netless goals that we used during practice. Amy made thirty-nine saves in the Oberlin-Geneva game. (Photo by David Stadler.)

Suzanne Maslo, class salutatorian, reflects the academic pursuits of our student-athletes. (Thomas Stein was the valedictorian.)

Sharon Hasek and Angi Moyer worked on *The Chimes,* Geneva's literary magazine. Sharon is reading and Angi (*at right, with hat*) is meditating. The photo composition—chimes of light, shadow, and thought—is by Sharon Hasek. (Photo by David Stadler.)

Eight players from the first-year team joined the second-year team, pictured here. Front (*left to right*): Carol Buckley, Tamara Hemphill, Deborah Schaefer, Wendy Pillsbury. Middle (*left to right*): Sara Smith, Tara Ledrick, Lori Toth, Jill Weakland, Janet Elliot. Back (*left to right*): manager/assistant coach James Locke, Andrea Zook, Colleen Neary, Barb Schwettman, Amy Widener, Debbie Genz, Yvonne Nienhuis, head coach David Mohr. (This picture appeared in the 1987 Geneva yearbook.)

Part III

Wheeling Jesuit and Slippery Rock

5

College Sports and Militant Urologists

Our first defeat was Saturday morning at home. Our second defeat was Saturday afternoon on the road. Both defeats were shutouts. Having successfully coached the Golden Tornadoes to two convincing defeats, I knew—better than any other soul alive—all the areas we needed to strengthen. All week in practice, I led the team in our now standard drills, emphasizing the fundamentals of dribbling, passing, shooting, and defense, defense, and more defense. "We've got to stop Wheeling from scoring" was my constant chant in practice.

Newspaper coverage of the soccer team came immediately after the Oberlin game. The Geneva College *Cabinet*, a weekly newspaper edited by a Spanish major who was a strong supporter of women's athletics in general and women's soccer in particular, published the following news story:

Lady Tornadoes Downed
Geneva's women's soccer team suffered its second loss of the season at Oberlin College last Saturday.

"It was a good loss, a very good loss," said Dr. Hanna, head coach of the soccer team. "At our first loss against Houghton College," Dr. Hanna added, "Houghton scored in the first minute of play. Oberlin's first score came at the twenty-eight minute mark." The final score of the Oberlin game was 6–0.

"Some athletes participate in athletic matches," Dr. Hanna said, "but our women's soccer team participates in adventures." On a more serious note, Dr. Hanna stated that the program is developing, and the players are acquiring the skills of the game.

Coach Hanna cites the playing abilities of Jill Weakland, the team's captain, Kristin Menningen, Barb Schwettman, and Angi Moyer as being impressive. He is also pleased with the development of several Lady Tornadoes among them Sara Smith, Anne Stine, and Wendy Pillsbury.

Goalie Amy Widener received the highest words of praise from Coach Hanna. In the Oberlin game, Widener had 39 saves.

After reading the article, I called the editor, a former student in my English composition class, thanked her for the coverage, and asked for the name of the person charged with writing headlines for sports stories. I then called that person and questioned the use of the word *lady* in the headline of the soccer story. I argued that *lady* was equivalent to *gentleman,* and much as the football coach doesn't refer to his players as "young gentlemen," so, too, women soccer players shouldn't be referred to as "ladies" or "young ladies."

"What would you use instead?" the headline writer asked.

"*Woman.*"

"Why?"

"Because *lady* has that gentle, delicate connotation, and our players are strong and tough athletes," I said.

"Yeah, but if enough people started referring to your athletes as 'ladies,'" she said, "then the connotation might change. Words do change their meaning, you know."

"I know," I said, "but people don't use it that way, so *women* might be better."

"Oh, no, Dr. Hanna," she said. "You'd never catch me using *women* for *ladies.*"

"Why?"

"Stop and think about it," she said. "The very word *lady* shows more independence than *woman* or *female.*"

"How so?"

"*Woman* depends on the word *man* to be complete; *female* depends on the word *male* to carry its meaning. So I stay with *lady,* which can stand on its own without reference to *man* or *male.*"

I thanked her for her explanation, concluded the conversation, looked at the receiver in my hand, then placed the receiver on the hook. Her reasoning impressed and perplexed me; I wondered if she were serious, or if she had found a creative way to tell me "None of your business, Coach." I wondered if I should start using *ladies* instead of *women* in referring to the soccer players; I wondered if *lady* would appear in future headlines pertaining to the soccer team. Time would tell.

While preparing the team for the third match, I questioned whether we were destined to win a game all season, especially with Slippery Rock University and Denison of Ohio coming up after Wheeling Jesuit. Indeed, I began to doubt my abilities and wisdom as a coach.

One day, as I was walking into the third floor bathroom of the science and engineering building, another man was leaving, a mathematics professor with whom I'd had enjoyable conversations and who was well known for the wit and irony he sprang in unexpected places. Paul raised his hand and arm in the right-angle court-swearing salute, said hello, then declared, "Well, at last we meet in the one place where all Geneva professors know what they're doing." I stood near the urinal and stared ahead, addressing the wall: "I wish that were the case. Do I know what I'm doing coaching soccer? Do the players think I know what I'm doing?" I flushed the urinal, washed my hands, and laughed again at Paul's greeting as I exited the washroom and headed to class.

There I handed out a test, and while the students worked, I pulled out a clipboard with a long legal yellow pad attached and began to go over the "shallow chart." When I played and coached football, we usually had over eighty players out for the team, and the chart with the players' names was called the "depth chart." I hummed to myself, as I thought about football and dealt with soccer.

After class, I met Angi in my office at her request. "Coach," she said, plopping on an easy chair, setting her green book bag on the carpet, and kicking the door shut, "I've got to talk to you about next week's game against Wheeling."

"Fine."

"No, it's not, Coach; you're not going to like what you're going to hear," Angi said. She sniffed and looked around the office.

"Oh."

"I'll get to the point right away," Angi said. "Two players and I are going up to Toronto and then Stratford to see several Shakespeare plays. We're going up Friday morning and coming back Sunday evening."

"What?"

"You heard me right, Coach. We already have the tickets and all," Angi said, pushing her fingers through the coils of her hair.

"Who are the other two players?" I asked. She named two beginners who had started and played poorly in the Houghton and Oberlin games.

"At least you're not taking Amy and Jill with you; that would've been a disaster," I said. "Still, Angi, how could you do this to me?"

"Well, Coach, remember your first speech to the team, how you emphasized the have-fun aspect and de-emphasized winning, how you stressed the importance of academics and, I trust by extension, culture?"

"I do."

"Well, we took you at your word and went ahead and committed ourselves to the trip. We did it under the theory that it's easier to ask for forgiveness than permission." She winked as she said, "We really want to go, Coach."

"Good," I said, "I hope you have a great time. We'll miss you, though. Oh, believe me, we'll miss you. With you here, we're having a hard time scoring; with you gone, it'll be impossible. Our goal output so far is not exactly overwhelming. The only time we score, it seems, is in practice; we're like that nation whose only war it wins is a civil war," I spoke slowly.

"Coach," Angi said, looking me straight in the eye, "you don't seem to be happy about all this. You seem worried, disturbed, upset. Are you?"

"I'll tell you frankly," I said. "Half of me is extremely pleased for you, but the other half is furious at you. If I were a 'jock jock'–type coach, to use your phrase, then I'd be thoroughly upset. But since I'm a so-called scholar-jock coach, I've got to learn to live with such inconveniences."

Before Angi left, we talked about Kenneth Patchen and the Beat generation. She borrowed several "Little" magazines from the collection in my office and dumped them into her book bag. She also borrowed Hemingway's *A Moveable Feast*, saying, "I'll be going to Paris before long, and I want to reread this book." Then she opened the book and added, "For now, I've got to read you my two absolute favorite passages from this." She turned to the title page and read the book's epigraph, words that Hemingway wrote to a friend in 1950:

If you are lucky enough to have lived in Paris as a young man, then wherever you go for the rest of your life, it stays with you, for Paris is a moveable feast.

Then she continued, "I also love the book's last paragraph." She turned to it and read it in a soft voice laced by long pauses:

There is never any ending to Paris and the memory of each person who has lived in it differs from that of any other. We always returned to it no matter who we were or how it was changed or with what difficulties, or ease, it could be reached. Paris was always worth it and you received return for whatever you brought to it. But this is how Paris was in the early days when we were very poor and very happy.

"Well," I said, "in terms of soccer victories, we're very poor all right, but I'm not so sure we're also very happy."

"Cheer up, Coach," she said, turned toward the door, and added, "See ya at practice in a bit."

"Most teams lose some players to injuries," I spoke out loud to myself, "but we lose ours to a Shakespeare festival." Their departure, I calculated, would leave us with twelve players for the

Wheeling game. That would be bad enough. What made my predicament even worse were the complaints about playing time that I expected to hear from the other players. This kind of complaint was a problem that beset most coaches—except that our players would complain not about lack of playing time but about *too much* of it.

I remained in my office and created several lineups with players at various positions. "If Wheeling turns out to be a powerful offensive team similar to Houghton or Oberlin," I spoke out loud again, "then we'll need to play our best players in the halfback and fullback spots. If, on the other hand, they seem average or weak on offense, then we'd better have our best players on the front line attacking their defense."

In the end, I kept four different lineups that integrated all twelve available players. I shared the lineups with the players, and throughout practice that week, all players played different positions. I even had our outstanding goalie, Amy—a natural soccer player who often begged me, before or after practice, to shoot hard and high, vicious and low shots while she defended the goal—slotted on an offensive and a defensive alignment. That pleased Amy, for although she wanted to play other positions, she hesitated to ask me, fearing that I might misinterpret her request and see her as intruding into my coaching domain.

Eager to show off what I felt was our improved soccer team, I went to the faculty lunch table at the Brig in the student center and talked about the team. I boasted about our defeat at Oberlin and the great work of our goalie. I warned, "Even though we're sending three players up north to Canada to get some culture, we plan to give a good account of ourselves against the Cardinals of Wheeling Jesuit come Saturday."

"Notice he didn't say, ' get a win,'" one faculty member said, "but 'give a good account.'"

"What's a 'good account'?" another faculty member asked.

"Whatever you envision that to be, I suppose," another said, looking directly at me.

"You know how your extraordinarily corrupt politicians," a faculty member interjected, comparing me to one, "always defend themselves when they're attacked?"

"No," I said, and looked up at my colleagues.

"How?" another faculty member asked.

"Oh, they always say, 'My record speaks for itself.' And it usually does."

"You'd never hear me saying that about our team, not at this stage anyway," I said. "No, sir."

"That's my point," he said. "You use another cliché: the 'give a good account' cliché."

"Look at it this way," a business professor added. "That's a whole lot better than a bad account."

When one of the assistant football coaches joined us at the table, the conversation shifted to the football team, which, like the women's soccer team, had two losses and no wins. Its second loss was to the Presidents of Washington and Jefferson College, a loss that the coach found himself explaining to a faculty that took its football seriously and its women's soccer lightly, thanks in part to the tone I was giving to the soccer program.

That tone carried over into my classroom work. Frequently, I would urge my students to "come out and see the women's soccer team, a nice blend of experienced players and beginners participating in an intricate sport, playing against far more seasoned teams. Most teams play athletic matches as such, but because of our makeup and, most importantly, perhaps, because of my coaching competence or lack of it, we undertake an adventure of sorts."

"Yeah," one of the football players shouted, "you guys really took it on the chin those first two games."

"As a matter of fact you fell flat on your—you know what," another football player added.

"Come on, man, say it. Go ahead and say it. On what? I dare you to say it," a third student said.

"Okay, I'll say it," the second player said, flashing a special measure of courage that came his way. "Fell flat on your donkey."

"Well," I responded, "it's not often when the word *donkey* is used as a euphemism, but it is today."

"And," another student added, "it's also used as a euphemism in the framework of the Democratic Party."

"Before we begin a political war," I said, "let's go on to today's lecture, but before doing that, let me please invite you, one more time, to come out and see our Golden Tornadoes go after Wheeling Jesuit of West Virginia this Saturday at four—P.M., that is—at the soccer field on Thirty-third Street. Come and compare us to the men's team; see who plays the more entertaining brand of soccer and why."

Those who came Saturday—and, my wife assured me, there were no more than sixty people in the stands at one time—witnessed another shutout. Both teams started slow or strong, depending on one's point of view. For about ten minutes, the ball was kicked all over the field. There was no score. Few shots at goal. As the game progressed, I began to get the feeling that we could indeed score a goal or two before the end of the first forty-five-minute period. Accordingly, I shed off my typically reserved, pacing-the-sidelines, visiting-with-the-spectators posture and began to shout encouragement and directions at our players. At one instance, I yelled, "Cut out those desultory kicks."

A spectator standing behind me yelled back at me, "Coach, they don't know what that is."

I turned around and told the protesting gentleman, "Yes, they do. They're smart athletes, believe me."

After thirty-three minutes had elapsed, Barb, our freshman left-footed left wing, took charge of the match. Barb had grown up playing soccer in Fairfield, Ohio. She had come to Geneva on a softball scholarship. Her height (five feet, eleven inches), her long arms, and her left-handedness made her "a natural first baseperson," she once told me, her ever ready smile framed by short, wavy blond hair. After seeing our soccer signs during registration, she had come to the first meeting and expressed enthusiastic interest in joining the team. As I came to know her, she turned out to be every bit as polite as Angi was blunt (and every bit as likable). On the field, Barb was Angi's counterpart, and I knew they would complement each other well if I could only get the other players—especially the beginners—to contribute to the flow of the offense instead of disrupting it by creating their own unorthodox, unmistakably beginners' flow (or is it dribble?). Barb had the ability to run with the ball faster than other players could run without it. She could pass it with accuracy, slam it into the net with power, and dribble it with vigor, zigzagging in and out of traffic.

That sunny afternoon in late September when Barb took charge of the Wheeling game, our right wing scoring punch, Angi, was in Canada. Our experienced players at forward, all too aware of Angi's absence and the limitations of the beginner who had replaced her in the starting lineup, knew that they would have to set up and feed Barb if we were to score. Accordingly, at the thirty-two-minute mark of the first half, Barb anticipated a pass by running to an open area of the field. When the pass arrived, she dribbled the ball past the first Wheeling defender, around a second, set it up to the comfort range of her left foot, then slammed it with the tip of her instep, following through as the ball soared past the lunging Wheeling goalie into the upper corner of the net.

On the field, the Golden Tornadoes exploded in utter joy, jumping around and hugging each other. People in the stands congratulated one another, and as I turned around and looked at the gate, I saw Geneva's president, a great supporter of both female and male sports, striding into the soccer park. "You just missed Barb's historic shot, the first goal of the year," I said.

"No, no, I didn't miss it; I saw it just as I walked in," he replied, and shook my hand.

"Good," I said, pumping his arm.

"Congratulations," he said.

"And look at them," I said. "They're still celebrating." All the team members continued to hug each other and exchange high fives. The referee's whistle that signaled the continuation of play brought the Tornadoes back to earth.

"They deserve it," the president said.

"Well, after playing their hearts out and coming up with two shutout losses," I said, "it sure is wonderful, very wonderful indeed, to score a goal. Boy, it feels good to get one."

The president mingled with the other Geneva dignitaries at the game, among them the vice president for business and finance, the chairperson of an academic department, my wife, a local pastor, and others. I turned around and paid attention to the game, only to see Barb dribbling the ball, passing it, getting in position to receive another pass, more dribbling, then the setup, followed by her powerful, leg-swooping motion—a kick that scored another goal. At the end of the first period, the score was Geneva, two, Wheeling Jesuit, zero.

At halftime, I took the team to one side of the field, and while my kids served them water, ice, and oranges, I talked to them. "Okay," I said, "we've never been in this position before, but boy it's a good position to be in. You know that famous saying of Yogi Berra, 'It ain't over till it's over'? Well, that saying can be nonsense or wisdom depending on the situation. In the Houghton and Oberlin games, the games were over for us from the winning-losing perspective after the first goal was scored. To claim otherwise would have been sheer nonsense, given the strength and character of those teams. Now, in terms of our game today, it's good to invoke the wisdom of that old Yankee catcher. This Wheeling team could come back. If it weren't for Amy stopping several hard shots at goal, we could be down three or even four to two at this stage."

The team members, sitting or sprawling on the grass, shouted, "Yea, Amy!"

"But we're up," I added, "and we've got to work hard to stay up. Thirty more minutes and we'll—"

"Coach," Jill interrupted, "permit me to remind you that the halves in soccer are forty-five minutes; you're thinking football again." All the players—tense, tired, sweaty, and happy—laughed. So did I.

"Jill's right," I said. "Forty-five more minutes and we'll bag our first victory as a varsity team. Those players at the Shakespeare festival in Canada aren't going to believe this. Whatever we're doing, it's right. So just keep it up. Stay at it. Our offense is strong. We've got to keep setting up Barb. She obviously has the hot foot now." Then, turning to Barbara, I said, "And you, Barb, don't wait for the pass. Anticipate it by running to the open spot, and the ball should be there, just as we did in practice." Addressing the team once again, I added, "Our defense is strong, and you women in the back move up with the flow of the action. Don't just stay back there to keep Amy company. Move up, even cross the midfield line if our attack gets to a consistent and dominant level."

Sure enough, in the second period, our attack did reach that level. Barb scored a third goal early in the period, and it was greeted by moderate applause, as if goals were becoming routine achievements for us. Oh, how quickly we forget, I thought to myself.

Midway in the period, things changed radically. Anna, one of our beginners, penetrated Wheeling's defense as she dribbled the ball. She passed it to Wendy, another beginner who was playing in Angi's position at right wing. Wendy fielded the ball, dribbled it, then passed it back to Anna, a perfect pass that rolled slowly in front of Anna's right foot. Anna kicked it as hard as she could, resulting into an exceedingly low kick that zoomed past the Wheeling goalie, who failed to reach it with her outstretched right foot.

Anna's feat ignited a huge celebration, especially among the beginners, for after all, a member of their caste had scored a goal. On the celebration meter's scale of one to ten, with one being a funeral director on maneuvers, our beginners would have scored a strong ten.

With less than nine minutes remaining in the game, Anne Stine ("Stine" is what we called her), a player with light soccer experience, fielded a pass from Wendy, dribbled it, passed it to Jill in the middle of the field. Jill dribbled it until she was fifteen yards or so away from Wheeling's goal, then she passed it to Stine, leading her just a bit with the pass. Stine, one of the quickest players on the team, dashed toward the ball, dribbled it slightly and took a shot at goal. The goalie deflected it with her right hand, but the kick was so strong that it fell into the goal. The celebration meter might have registered a six after Stine's goal, which, as it turned out, was the final one of the match, making the outcome Geneva, five, Wheeling Jesuit, zero.

After thanking our athletes for playing such a strong game, I invited them to a Wednesday evening dinner at our house. (I had cleared the invitation with my wife during the waning moments of the game.) "Look, let's be realistic," I said. "Next week we go to Slippery Rock, then Denison comes in; both are powerful teams. This might be our only win for a while, so let's enjoy it. By the way, we finish the season against Wheeling, down there."

An upbeat, happy mood hit our house the evening of our first soccer victory. My wife sensed it. Our kids sensed it. I suggested a dinner trip to Chi-Chi's in nearby Boardman, Ohio, where, as little Sam would say, "the beans had to be refried to be good."

"Will we go to Chi-Chi's after every win, Dad?" Sal asked as I drove down the Ohio Turnpike.

"I hope *not*," Rita said.

"Why?" I asked Rita. "I thought you liked eating at Chi-Chi's."

"Oh, I do, and because I like it so much, I'd much rather go there after every loss," Rita answered.

"I get it," Sal said. "We'll go there more often if we go after losses."

My wife, sitting in the seat to my right, whispered to me, "You've got perceptive kids, I'm afraid."

"Perceptive and calculating," I said.

When we returned to Beaver Falls late in the evening, we tucked the kids into bed. My wife read from her favorite medical magazines and journals, and because there were no nature programs on PBS that evening, I wrote a feature on our goalie's Oberlin performance in which I referred to the Wheeling Jesuit game and made a comment or two on women's soccer in general. For a byline, I used Anna H. Liahus, a pen name I had used in graduate school at Indiana University in the late sixties, when an experimental literary mode was part of the cultural scene in

Bloomington. The pen name permitted me to quote myself at will. "If a newspaper," I told my wife, "would want to publish the article and send me a little check for it—an unlikely possibility, to be sure—then I'd have to write, 'Pay to the order of S. S. Hanna,' and sign the check 'Anna H. Liahus,' and since I'm not going to turn around and sue myself, all will be well in the Hanna house."

Our student newspaper photographer was kind enough to print thirty pictures of Amy in action. Accordingly, I printed the article thirty times and sent it to thirty newspapers, one of which was in Oberlin, Ohio. I don't know if any newspaper published the piece; newspapers seldom forward tear sheets for unsolicited material. I do know, however, that the Geneva yearbook, in its account of the college's first year in women's soccer, published a shorter version of the article.

At first I had titled the article, "There's a Feat in Defeat"; I later rejected that title as being too cute. I tried several others, and in time "murdered those darlings." I finally sent the article with a bland title and a conventional cover letter. The article stated:

Amy Widener and Intercollegiate Women's Soccer
by
Anna H. Liahus

Her coach calls it "A remarkable individual achievement, equivalent perhaps to a running back amassing three hundred yards rushing in a single football game, or to a player scoring seventy points in a basketball game, or to a batter hitting four home runs in a baseball game."

The coach's reference is to Amy Widener's recent achievement in a varsity soccer game between the Yeomen (Yeopersons) of Oberlin College in Ohio and the Golden Tornadoes of Geneva College in Beaver Falls, Pennsylvania. Widener, the five-foot ten-inch Geneva goalie, stopped thirty-nine shots at goal, according to the match's official scorekeeper.

"Most goalies seldom stop thirty-nine shots in a season," S. S. Hanna, Geneva's head soccer coach, notes, "but Amy did it in a single game at Oberlin. That, of course, says two things: either our defense is extra mild or Oberlin's offense is Jalopeno hot." Oberlin won the game six to zero.

Coach Hanna remembers a shot in the first half when, in his words, "Amy lunged high and far to her right and swatted a fast moving ball to the right of the goalpost. The lunge was too far and the ball was traveling way too fast for her to catch it, but she did the next best thing. That, of course, led to an Oberlin corner kick that Amy fielded; then she punted the ball—fifty yards or so—, leading Oberlin to make yet another drive, or should I say assault, on our goal."

Oberlin's crowd impressed Coach Hanna a great deal. "Once the crowd realized that our offense wasn't going to mount an attack and beat Oberlin," he says, "the crowd focused their attention on Amy's one-woman show; they began to cheer and applaud her daring moves and booming punts." He adds, "One of our substitutes, surprised but pleased by all the cheering that Amy was receiving from Oberlin's crowd, told me while the game was in progress, 'Coach, all this cheering for Amy makes it feel as if we're playing at home.'"

Following the Oberlin game, Geneva played Wheeling Jesuit College of West Virginia. Widener blocked all nine shots at Geneva's goal as the Golden Tornadoes won five to zero. Barb Schwettman led Geneva with three goals. In the Wheeling Jesuit game, Geneva played without three of its regulars who went to a Shakespeare Festival in Canada.

"I was proud of our athletes," Coach Hanna notes, "for they sent three players up north to get some culture, and the rest went out and played well enough to beat the visiting team from West Virginia."

For a variety of reasons, the crowd at Geneva's women's soccer games tends to be small. "Our home crowd at the Wheeling game," Hanna says, "had an emphasis on quality, not quantity. I glanced back from the sidelines," he adds, "and saw a college president and his wife, a Harvard MBA, a chairperson of a department, a full professor (even though our field has no concession stands), a farmer's wife, an Englishman, a steelworker, an author, a fellow reading a newspaper, a pastor, and all sorts of students and my four kids." Coach Hanna, who holds a Ph.D. in literature and doubles as an English professor, cautions that "Soccer hoodlums and exceedingly refined soccer skills are British phenomena. We're relatively free of both."

Geneva College and a number of other colleges in Pennsylvania, Ohio, and West Virginia have recently introduced women's soccer as a varsity sport. Among the other colleges participating at the varsity level are Ohio Wesleyan, Allegheny, Denison, Wheeling Jesuit, Case Western Reserve, Wilmington, Bethany, Seton Hill, Mercyhurst, and the College of Wooster.

"The Geneva women playing at the varsity level appear to be enjoying the sport," Coach Hanna observes; "in fact, they enjoy it so much that when we lose, I often wonder if we have just played an athletic match or undertaken an adventure."

Hanna feels his own team needs to grow, and to do so, it needs to recruit from the numerous high schools in suburban America that have introduced women's soccer into their athletic programs. Widener, Geneva's sophomore goalie, transferred to the western Pennsylvania school from a small college in Texas where she played on a men's "club" team.

And so, I successfully coached—and wrote about, for that matter—the Golden Tornadoes to their third straight shutout, but this time instead of being the "shutoutee," we were the "shutouter," a more enjoyable state even to a coach who, presumably, cared little about winning.

When the team gathered at our house for dinner, the players continued to enjoy the residue of the win over Wheeling. Before the meal, they talked about the game, the joys of scoring, the team spirit, and even the other fall sports on campus. At one point a player said, "Send Angi away, Coach, and see what happens?"

"We've got to send her away again, Coach," another player added.

Rita, who happened to overhear the comment and who also happened to enjoy robbing adults of their sense of irony, said, "I don't think that'd be wise, Daddy. You need Angi."

The players filled their plates with food and spread out to different parts of the house. Players sat on couches, chairs, benches, chests, and carpets. My wife mingled with one group, and I tried to visit with another, then after a trip for seconds, I visited with a third. The groups did not divide into beginners and experienced players but into a nice mixture. Sal and the twins (Paul and Sam, known to the players as However and Hyphen) teased the players and served them their drinks.

After getting their desserts, all the players gathered in the spacious living room and began to talk about athletic politics at Geneva. At one point in the discussion, the issue of scholarships came up. "The men's teams around here seem to get a lot more scholarship money than we do," a player said.

"None of us gets a penny from athletic scholarships. Isn't that right, Coach?" a player asked.

"That's right. No one here is on a soccer scholarship, though the college does offer scholarships for basketball and other women's sports," I said.

"But I bet they're not as generous scholarships as the guys get in football or basketball," a player added.

"That's right," a couple of players said at once.

"Will we be getting scholarships next year?" a beginner asked.

"Yeah, will we, Coach?" Lori, another beginner, added.

"To be frank with you, I don't know," I said. "But I do indeed know that the college wants to build the program and use it as a recruiting tool, a tool to get students. At least that's what they told me in my coaching appointment letter."

"So," Angi said, "we're here, we're recruited and all, and they don't need to get us to come to dear old Geneva. What you're saying, Coach—and please correct me if I'm wrong—is if the college gives out scholarships in women's soccer, then those scholarships will go to outside experienced players from high school: potential recruits, that is. Correct?"

"Oh, no," Lori said, dropping a fork on her plate. "They'd come here and *replace* us."

"That, my dear," Angi said, lapsing into a British accent, "is what James Joyce would call an epiphany—a baby epiphany, to be sure, but an epiphany just the same."

"Well, yes," I said, looking in Lori's direction. "In a manner of speaking, that's precisely what'll happen." Then I glanced at Angi and spoke slowly, "A baby epiphany." A smile trailed my remark.

"This college," another beginner added, "is winner-conscious; they want to win and get their name in the paper and all."

"I'd hate to coach football or basketball around here. The pressure to win must be tremendous on those coaches," another player added.

"I bet Evans and Sullivan must really feel the pressure to win," Barb said, referring to the basketball and football coaches.

"But do you think that's proper?" a player asked. "Do we really need an emphasis on winning in a small college like Geneva?"

"Whether or not we do is besides the point; it sure felt great to get that first win Saturday," a player said.

That remark led us to relive aspects of the Wheeling Jesuit game. A player turned to me and asked, "Coach, what do you think? Is winning overemphasized around here?"

"I'd rather not speak to that," I said. "The coaches have their own philosophies, but if I were running the sports programs around here, here's what I'd do—especially in the minor sports like men's soccer and baseball, women's soccer, softball, and volleyba—"

"This ought to be good," Angi interrupted in a tone tinged with sarcasm.

"I'm not trying to be funny," I said. "I'm serious about this. I'd recruit a lot of players, and I'd assure them all—and I mean *all*—of substantial playing time. I'd further assure them—and I know this sounds ironic in light of what we're celebrating today—that we don't care about winning but that we do care about seeing all the players *participating* in the sport of their choice. For example, instead of having nine baseball players play the entire game and leave fifteen on the bench game in and game out, why not play each player for three innings, or why not play nine players one game and then nine other players in another game, rotating the players so that all will get substantial experience and pleasure out of playing? After all, those are the reasons most players go out for the team at a small liberal arts college like ours. We're not like those major universities whose football and basketball programs serve as the minor leagues for the pro teams. We're little Geneva, a small college, and we ought to be different from those large universities. Right?"

"Right," Jill said, "but that's your perfect recipe for nonwinning teams."

"Yeah, but fully involved teams," Lori said.

"True," I agreed with both, "we might not win that way, but we'll have more students fully involved in the program and fewer students who are merely a part of it, an addendum to it."

"But wouldn't a lot of players drop the sport if the team kept losing?" Jill asked.

"Maybe," I said, "but I suspect if all the recruits are made aware of the coach's 'participation philosophy' and the likelihood of it leading to losing productivity—"

"Watch it, Coach," Angi interrupted again. "You're beginning to sound like an oxymoron-conscious economics professor."

"A what?" someone asked.

"Be that as it may," I continued, "losing will *not* lead thoughtful athletes to quit the team. Now, please don't misunderstand me: I'm not suggesting that a team should strive to lose, but a team—especially one that's used as a tool to recruit students in colleges like ours—should involve all the recruits and do so on an extensive basis. If they're involved, if they're contributing to the losses and the wins, they'll stay at the college. They'll enjoy the thrill of participating in varsity sports. Retention of students will go up. I always feel sorry for those basketball 'minute men,' the ones who usually get in during the last minute of a game if their team is winning or losing in a big way. I'm not speaking about our team but teams in general, for most teams have them. Imagine those guys trying to explain their athletic experience with pride to their grandkids."

Lori started to laugh out loud. We all looked at her, and she said, "The reason I'm laughing is because your reference to 'minute men' reminded me of an unusual name for those guys that I heard the other day." She started to giggle.

"Well," Angi addressed Lori, "are we going to have the pleasure of hearing this unusual name?"

Lori replied, "Sure. The fellow, who was a sub in high school and doesn't even play for Geneva, said that in high school the last-minute subs used to refer to each other as the 'sliver studs,' and that was because they got so many slivers from sitting on the bench."

Anna, a beginner who was apparently baffled by my "make-sure-they-play" philosophy, asked, "How does your play philosophy differ from intramurals, Coach?"

"That's a fair enough question," I said, setting my dessert plate on the mantel. "Intramurals in a small liberal arts college tend to spring up in the two major sports: football and basketball. These are really the fan-supported sports, the money-makers, if you will—though in the context of Geneva, you should put money-makers in quotes. But all the other sports—men's baseball, women's softball, soccer for both, et cetera—have little fan support; moreover, not enough students are interested in those sports to form a network of intramural teams. However— and this is important to note—enough serious student-athletes want to play organized ball at the college level where genuine coaching and learning and growing take place. It is in these sports that my participation principle applies, and frankly, if I had my way, I'd even apply it to varsity football and basketball. All the players that I recruit *will* play—and extensively."

"Yeah, look at us," Lori said. "We all play."

"Sometimes I think too much," Angi said cryptically.

It was unclear whether Angi's comment alluded to the lack of rest time that the experienced players often complained about or to the beginners' ineptness. (It may even be that Angi's comment referred to the fact that she was experiencing a thought overdose.) To quickly cover up her poignant if not purposeful ambiguity, Angi said, "Coach, why don't you read us one of your comic prose pieces?"

"Oh, no," Rita protested.

"Come on, please don't," Sal added.

"Better yet," Rita said, "I'll recite you one of his poems." Then she asked the group, "Are you ready for this?"

"Yeah," the players said in staggered unison.

"Okay, here we go," Rita said, and recited: "'Now I lay me down to sleep, and get up when I hear a beep.'"

"Oh, Rita," I said.

"That's all, folks," Rita added.

"And that's a metaphor to his class lectures, I suppose," my wife said as the students clapped and laughed. From that little scene I smuggled the clue that listening to my creative stuff was not exactly what those happy players wanted to do on a balmy Wednesday evening in autumn.

Most of the players had arrived for dinner at five-thirty, and all but Angi left at seven. Angi stayed to help us clean the house and wash the dishes. I washed, she dried, and we both talked about our soccer team and sports in general.

"Well," I told her as I squeezed some soap on the sponge, "did the results of the Wheeling game surprise you?"

"Not really," she said.

"Say that again."

"Not really."

"That's what I thought you said," I told her. After a slight pause, I added, "Let me tell you, I was surprised to see us win. Frankly, I knew we'd have fun practicing and playing soccer—I was determined to make our experiences as much fun as possible—but I didn't expect we'd win a single game all season."

"Coach," Angi said, tapping me with her right elbow and smiling, "the reason I say I wasn't really surprised is because 'surprised' is not a strong enough word." She rubbed a white dish towel on a large plate. "There *are* words," she said, "that express my feelings."

"Among these words are . . . ?"

"Stunned. Shocked. Overwhelmed." Angi spoke slowly and emphatically.

"Okay, I see what you're saying," I said. "You know, Wheeling is in the same boat as we are, just starting their program and all. I didn't know that until after my postgame visit with their coach."

"It seems a lot of colleges are starting women's programs these days."

"That sure is the case," I said. "Women's soccer is going to take off nationally at the college level in the late eighties and early nineties. And I hope that as it grows it doesn't degenerate into one of those sports that, if you win, you're someone special, but if you don't win, you're a loser."

"Coach, that's a big-time college sports phenomenon, common to male teams coached by dumb male jocks," Angi said.

"I think you're right; indeed, I hope you are. I'd hate to think that such an attitude is rampant in small-college sports," I said.

Sal brought us several dessert plates from the living room. Angi thanked him, then said to me, "You know, after our defeats by Oberlin and Houghton, I, like you, figured that we wouldn't win a single game this season, but it was still fun to be out there playing. Competition makes exercise fun, regardless of whether we win or lose. There's a lot of fun in playing in those varsity games, but many of us find a great deal of pleasure in the practices, the drills, the scrimmages, and, if Oberlin is a typical example, the road trips."

"That Oberlin trip was pleasant, wasn't it?" I asked. "I really enjoyed it."

"So did I," Angi said, watching me scrub the insides of a dark iron skillet. "You're doing a good job, Coach."

"Are you referring to coaching or dish washing?"

"You really want to know?"

"No. You do know that our last road game is at Wheeling," I said, "and it would be nice if we could win again, so if I don't coach next year, I could say, 'I went out a winner.'"

"You mean you're thinking of not doing this again next year?"

"Yeah—thinking."

"Why?"

"All sorts of reasons: one of them is time. This year we have a nine-game schedule, and I like it this way. It's good to have a week to prepare for a game, to try to plan out strategies, to practice different things, to experiment. As you say," I continued, handing Angi dishes to dry, "there's a lot of fun in the practices, in the exercises, in just playing soccer as part of the college experience. But even a nine-game season takes way too much time, especially in view of my class load—typical for a Geneva professor—of fifteen hours a semester."

"That's high, isn't it?" Angi said.

"Very high indeed," I said, "especially when you add to that advising students, advising administrators—we call that committee work—writing articles or books, et cetera. When a college is as tuition-driven as ours is, and when the college wants to keep the tuition as low as possible, then there's no room for lighter loads to go with coaching, at least not for coaching a minor sport that takes a major chunk of your time."

"So why did you take on this added coaching load in the first place?" Angi asked.

"Not for the money, that's for sure," I said.

"But for . . . ?"

"The writing potential. Given my heavy teaching and advising responsibilities, there's no way I could be rummaging in archives, doing research, or reading detailed critical studies in my academic fields, so I do engaging—unusual—things and then write about them. In so doing, aspects of my lifework would, in effect, be my research. That's one way a professor in a small college could make time to do research. Of course, in a large university, the opposite is common. Administrators there want their faculty members to do research and publish; they grant them time and money to research and write. I doubt if they'd want to see them dabbling in other areas such as coaching. It would be unheard of for a person like me to get a coaching job at a major

Division I college, even in a minor sport." I washed and rinsed another plate and handed it to Angi. "Speaking of Division I," I added, "it's amazing—and sad—to see all this emphasis on sports and the exploitation of athletes in our culture. I'm not one who longs for that romantic notion of 'the good old days,' but in sports I think I do."

"In what sense, Coach?"

"In a variety of senses," I said. "Oh, I don't think colleges will ever go back to the tradition of the scholar-coach, to a time when coaches taught in academic disciplines other than physical education. Knute Rockne, you know, once taught chemistry and coached football at Notre Dame."

"Is that a fact?" Angi said.

"Sure is."

"What a strange formula," Angi said, poking me with her elbow. "It sure sounds strange for this day and age."

"These days, many coaches in the country's finest prep schools double up as scholar-coaches, but few do it at small colleges, and none that I know do it at large Division I universities. Imagine a major college football or basketball coach teaching ethics in the philosophy department: that might well be your strange formula," I told Angi. I passed her another wet plate and continued speaking, "When I was in college—and this wasn't all that long ago—freshmen weren't eligible to play varsity ball because the colleges wanted the student-athletes to succeed in making the difficult transition from high school to college. Without the pressure of varsity participation, those who received the full 'jockships' could devote themselves to scholarship, to trying to ease the transition from high school to college."

"In a sense," Angi said, "you've got that now, because most freshmen at those athletic factories don't play; they get redshirted, don't they?"

"They do, but they still go to all those practices and meetings, and some do play. That's why you occasionally hear an announcer say that a player is a 'true' freshman."

"And when the redshirted players play the next year," Angi asked, "do they refer to them as 'false' freshmen?"

I smiled and said, "Another thing: schedules. The schedules these days are way too long. Seven or eight football games a season should be plenty; fourteen basketball games should suffice. Too many schools play long and demanding schedules: ten to twelve football games, twenty-seven to thirty varsity basketball games. I think, by the way, that Geneva plays twenty-seven games this year. Last year, we played nearly fifty baseball games. In high school, you often hear the expression 'Keep the athletes busy, and you'll keep them out of trouble.' In college, the expression might well be 'Keep the athletes busy, and you'll keep them away from their studies.' Those long and exhausting schedules and all the practice sessions leading up to the games are just too much to ask of unpaid student-athletes. Don't you think?"

"I think, Coach, and I agree."

"Still another thing," I continued, "when I was in college in the sixties, many colleges were not permitted to play varsity games during the two weeks before the final examinations. These days, however, schools play games in the week when final exams are in progress. And this sad routine goes on in big-time college sports and even at some—maybe I should say many— small colleges."

"Here's another cup, Dad," Sam said as he walked into the kitchen. He handed me a coffee cup and smiled as Angi lightly poked his chest with her index finger.

"Yeah," I said, taking a deep breath and letting go a mini-sermon of sorts: "There are many concerns from our recent past that we might have done well to conserve: freshmen ineligibility, fewer games, appropriately scheduled games that take note of final examinations—these three come to mind. I'm sure there are many others. We live in a time when the tyranny of television strangles big-time college sports. Let's face it—and I don't think I'm overstating the case—many of our larger academic institutions have lost their innocence; nowadays, they conveniently overlook the student-athletes' academic welfare and consistently lust for wins and cash and TV exposure. Freshmen play in varsity games; and if TV dictates it, they play during exam week, even on exam day. Lots of teams will do whatever it takes, devious or otherwise, to become number one. All—"

"All I can say," Angi said, "is that there's a bit of the preacher in all of us."

"There is," I said, "and I'm sure you're aware that my little sermon isn't original: sportswriters and academicians have preached it before. And, of course, it applies mostly to the big schools; we play to a different tune here at Geneva."

"Only slightly different," Angi said.

"We certainly do so in our women's soccer program; at least I hope so."

"Keep hoping," Angi said, stacking another plate in the dish rack. She shifted the conversation slightly by adding, "Your maximum participation idea surprised several of the players."

"I sensed that," I said.

"I'd even go so far as to say it blew away a couple of them."

"Oh."

"And you're serious, Coach, about those ideas, aren't you? You weren't simply playing the devil's advocate, were you?"

"You bet I'm serious: in fact, I firmly believe that if a radical reformation of college sports is ever going to take place at both the small college and the large university levels, such a reformation might well begin with the maximum participation principle I suggested. If sports are to be meaningful to all athletes, women or men, then substantial participation of all the athletes is an urgent ingredient. I'd love to get an opportunity to speak at an athletic conference and sketch the full participation idea. If nothing else, it would be interesting to see what reception it received."

"Too bad you're not head-coaching football here," Angi said.

"Why do you say that?"

"Because their heads need a lot of coaching."

"Come on, Ang."

"Okay, because you can experiment with your idea, given all the players who go out for the team here."

"You're right about that. I'd love to experiment with the idea. I really believe it has potential for good in college sports."

Angi dried and stacked another plate and took the conversation back to the Wheeling Jesuit game: "I'm sure you'd agree with me, Coach, when I say that all our players really enjoyed that win. And I, too, enjoyed it, even though I didn't play in it. Shakespeare took me away. I'm really happy for all the players. Let's face it, Coach: it would've been utterly depressing for us to have gone an entire season without a single win."

"That it would," I said, and we continued to talk about the Wheeling Jesuit game and our upcoming schedule.

We finished the dishes, and Angi stayed and visited with our family.

After Angi left, I went to the study, relaxed in an easy chair (one that had taken me years to break in but that my wife felt should have been thrown out years before), and thought about the team's discussion of sports in general and Geneva's programs in particular. The maximum participation principle, which perplexed some players, had been brewing in my mind since the late seventies, when I had coached football at that little college on the Kansas prairies. I felt that the principle—or a variation of it—could well serve as a framework in reforming college sports, but I had never shared its basic features with anyone until the dinner with the soccer players.

The other ideas about changes in big-time college sports that I had mentioned—really preached—to Angi seemed to be tired homilies. Many other (much wiser and more influential) people have crusaded for those and similar ideas, but college sports remain in the same sad shape. Even if those ideas were realized, they might only patch the outworn garments. What college sports urgently needs are new garments, tailored to a new style of play, to a system of participation that will involve all the athletes in all the contests for all their years in college.

I sat in the study and thought: If the NCAA or the NAIA asked interested college professors to suggest ways to reform college sports, what would I say? Having played and coached football and soccer at the college level, I suspect my response would refer to those two sports as well as to basketball and base-ball, two other team sports in which I have a strong interest.

In my response, I would probably trot out the experiences of a talented friend, a young man who was a high school football quarterback, a star who was heavily recruited by major universi-ties, among them Notre Dame, Ohio State, Texas, Penn State, Nebraska, Miami, and Alabama. He ended up at a major univer-sity, was redshirted as a freshman, and was one of six candidates fighting for the starting job his first "unredshirted" year. He won the job, started the first two games, then lost the job to an-other talented quarterback. My friend watched his replacement lead the team for the following four years, as did three of the other heavily recruited quarterbacks; the fourth one transferred to a small college, where he shared the quarterback duties during his senior year.

My friend, who had stayed healthy throughout his college football career, went to all the practices, worked hard, cooperat-ed with the coaches and the players, excelled in his pre-med pro-gram, and made all the road trips but failed to see action in a single varsity game after a mediocre performance in his first two games. For four long years, he sat on the bench, a gifted backup quarterback. "I felt," he told me, "like that doughnut spare tire that they put in cars these days: the coaches knew I was there, but they hoped not to use me." My friend felt bitter, abused, and exploited, but he never expressed his bitterness to the coaches. "Had I done that," he said, "I probably would've gone down in the depth chart from second string to third or fourth. Now I have to live the rest of my life not knowing what kind of college quarterback I would've become had I been given a decent chance to play."

He was not alone in his predicament. His team had over nine-ty players; all were high school stars, big stars, but more than half of them watched the games from the sidelines. "The only differ-ence between us and the fans," he said, "was that we watched the games in uniforms." Many other colleges subject their student-athletes to the same treatment: the coaches recruit them heavily, the players attend all the practices, but they seldom play. If they do play, it's in the "mop-up" roles, finishing a game that could not be won or lost in the remaining two or three minutes.

This happens not only at the large football factories but also at many small colleges. When I served as an assistant football coach at Sterling College, we would recruit more than eighty student-athletes, issue them uniforms, and use the players in the practices, but during the games, they would become more students than athletes. Seldom would we use more than twenty-four players. If key players from the defensive unit were injured during a game, we sometimes went to their backups if the game was out of reach; but in a tight game, we would ask versatile offensive players to replace the injured players on defense. In other words, some players would go both ways, while other players would go neither way. After that happened a few times, I cringed, knowing that we were treating the backup players improperly. It was just another example of the pursuit of a win blinding us to our neglect of patient and long-suffering student-athletes.

Coaches want to win and win often. Winning to them is an irrepressible urge. As a result, only the very best, the most gifted athletes play in games or situations that matter. Other players who have some gifts—even substantial gifts, as in my friend's case—and would love to nurture them seldom get an opportunity to do so. They feel, to quote my friend, "cheated, ripped off." Team sports often become competitive matches between a select few from one team and a select few from another. This happens not only in football but in basketball, baseball, and soccer. The entire members of one team are seldom pitted against the entire members of another team. Maximum participation by all the athletes on both teams should be the central concern of any bold, radical, innovative, and meaningful system of reform in college sports. All the athletes would then get a chance to develop their talents, contribute to the wins and the losses, feel the competitive thrill, learn and grow from participation, and bond with the players, the coaches, and the fans.

The system that now exists in U.S. team sports is what might be labeled the Partial Participation system, and it prevents many student-athletes from developing their talents.

What we desperately need is a Full Participation system, one that will get all the players involved in all the contests for all their years in college. This system could borrow its pattern from the relay team in track, wherein the coach develops not just one runner but all four who compose the relay team.

The Full Participation system in team sports would differ slightly from the track model in that it would feature not four units (or runners) but three. All three units should be developed in a team, and all three should play against the three units of another team. Each unit should play for a third of the time. The system would require all team sports to make minor adjustments. College basketball, for example, might be changed from twenty-minute halves to three fifteen-minute periods. For a given game, team members would be assigned to a unit, and they must play with that unit only. Each unit would play for an entire period. Because a team unit would be required to play for an entire period instead of an entire game, the level of intense play in that period would be high, and the fatigue factor that usually contributes to sluggish play would virtually vanish. A pool of substitutes, drawn from team members not assigned to a unit, could be designated, and appropriate substitution rules could be devised.

Football could be divided into three twenty-minute periods, with three defensive units and three offensive units, and each unit would have to play a period. Better yet, football could be radically changed by having the players play offense and defense for an entire period, harkening back to the days of John Heisman, when the football players were more versatile athletes than they are today.

Soccer could easily be divided into three thirty-minute periods, and baseball games could be expanded to twelve innings, with each unit playing four innings. (This is no big deal, for most college games tend to be double headers anyway.)

The Full Participation system, then, would have all the students who go out for the sport and make the team actually involved in playing the sport and not simply involved in watching it in uniform. There would be no standing around on the sidelines or sitting on the benches game after game, year after year.

Except for a few substitutes, everyone who makes the team and practices must play in the varsity games. Of course, if a player is hurt, a substitute will be used. The makeup of the substitute list and of the various units could be changed from game to game at the coaches' discretion, but once the lineups are announced for a given game, they must stay intact for that game. This setup would motivate the players to work hard in practice and in effect move up from the substitute list to one of the starting units. If the coaches wished to win, they would be forced to develop all the players on their squad, not just a select few. Such development would help build a genuine—not a phony—camaraderie. All the players, much as in a relay team, would take credit for a victory or share in a loss.

Moreover, the Full Participation system would force the coaches to develop complex strategies for winning. Heroes would usually be all the team members, not one or two players. If it is difficult enough now to select the winner of the Heisman Trophy, the award given to the athlete voted as the best college football player in the country, it would be nearly impossible to select that player under this system. It might even launch the award into a merited oblivion.

Under the Full Participation system, sport competition at the unpaid college level would be less about the survival of the fittest and the best (that's the domain of the paid professional athlete) and more about the pleasure of the interested and—oh, yes—the athletically gifted. It must be remembered that not all college players who go out for a sport—or who are recruited by coaches—have the same gifts, but all certainly yearn to nurture whatever gifts they have. The current system that governs sports in the United States seems to rob many athletes of the opportunity to develop their gifts.

The abbreviation for Partial Participation is PP, a favorite expression of militant urologists, and appropriately so, for the system pisses off many athletes and their parents. Another such expression is RM, which stands for Rip-off Model. Like my friend, many gifted athletes feel that the current system of participation is a rip-off, plain and simple. What should replace the

PP system is the FP (Full Participation) system, and to that system one might add another RM, for Relay Model, which is patterned after the relay team in track in which all the athletes are developed and all participate. And participation for athletes—like winning for coaches—is an irrepressible urge.

I rose and stood near a shelf in the study; I stroked the spines of several books, looked out the window, and wondered if the Full Participation Relay Model (FPRM) would sound sensible to people in athletics: coaches, professors, administrators, athletes, reporters, spectators, and parents of athletes. I wondered if the day would ever come when enough college presidents would band together and establish a new association for sports, the Full Participation Athletic Association, which would rival the NCAA and the NAIA, both of which use the Partial Participation Rip-off Model (PPRM). Most of all, I wondered if women's sports would be wise enough to steer away from the Rip-off Model, common to male sports, and move in the direction of the Relay Model.

Could it be that the key to reforming college sports is in the pocket of the track coach? Could it be that the scandal in college sports isn't that a few good players don't get paid but that many good players don't get to play?

From the shelf beside me, I pulled out the "Soccer Season Diary" and wrote an entry that combined the affairs of the Wheeling Jesuit game of Saturday and the Wednesday evening dinner party. A segment of the entry noted:

When our team finally scored, the players erupted into a celebration extravaganza. The most touching aspect of the celebration came when some of the athletes maneuvered their hands and fingers into the pistol pattern and pounded them into the air above their heads. "Look at them," my wife said to me, "love those index fingers raised into the number one salute." I looked at her and replied, "No, no, they're not boasting of being number one; what they're doing is telling us and the world at large that 'That's our first goal, first goal—ever.' "

That first goal was good enough to snatch our first win. But would our one-game winning streak continue? To find out, we had to travel and negotiate its status with the Rockets of Slippery Rock University.

6

Sports, Cows, and Sex

"Where do you play next?" Milt, a colleague of mine, asked as he joined my wife and me. We were waiting for his wife to arrive so that we could play our Wednesday racquetball match.

"Slippery Rock," I said.

"Oh, they'll be tough," Milt said.

"Lots of physical education majors study at Slippery Rock," my wife said. "Christie knows; she went to graduate school out there." Christie was Milt's wife.

"Oh, I know, I know," Milt said.

"I do, too," I said. "Boy, do I?"

"You're not exactly loaded with those majors, are you?" Milt said, laughing and dribbling, ever so softly, the blue ball on his racquet.

"We've got a grand total of zero physical education majors," I said, leaning over to tighten the laces on my tennis shoes.

"You don't even have a physical education coach," my wife said in my behalf, "but a gypsy-scholar-comic-writer-English-teacher coach."

When Christie arrived and learned of our upcoming tilt with Slippery Rock, she said, "I remember when we were at the University of Michigan in Ann Arbor, the public address announcer would announce the scores of the national powers like Notre Dame, Southern Cal, Ohio State, Nebraska, or Oklahoma, then he'd *always* slip in the Slippery Rock score. Big cheers would go up if Slippery Rock was winning, moans and groans if they were losing."

"Good luck," Milt said, "but luck or otherwise, I suspect there'll be moans and groans at the Hanna house after the Slippery Rock game."

"I tell you what," I said. "There will be no video of our Slippery Rock game." I was alluding to our "Grandchildren Video," as we called it, a tape of the four of us playing racquetball. It was being filmed by David Stadler, the student editor of Geneva's video yearbook, *Memories in Motion*, and it reflected our desire to own a concrete slice of our energetic and athletic days, a slice to share with our grandchildren thirty or forty years down the line when they visited us, on their spring break, in the nation's geriatric ward: Florida. Implicit in my "no video" pronouncement was the assumption that we were going to lose the match to Slippery Rock. (My wife and I lost the racquetball match that day, though David was kind enough to end the taping when the score of the hard-fought match was tied.)

While preparing our players for the Slippery Rock game, I told them one afternoon before practice, "Why I scheduled this game, I really don't know. It wasn't on the schedule that was made out by the women's athletic director. This game is my own doing, I'll confess. I added it just before the season began. Those of you who are from Maryland, New York, Maine, Texas, Ohio, or other states probably don't believe there even is a Slippery Rock. But indeed there is, and it's home to Slippery Rock University, once Slippery Rock State Teachers College, and before that, going all the way back to its founding in 1889, Slippery Rock State Normal School."

Glancing at the clipboard in my hand, I continued, "Just for fun, I went out and did a little research on Slippery Rock University for you non-Pennsylvanians. The town and the university received their name by way of a 1779 expedition commissioned by George Washington and led by Daniel Brodhead. The troops in the Brodhead expedition crossed a stream lined with large, smooth, level rocks, causing the horse of John Ward to slip and fall and seriously injure the rider. This incident gave the town's creek its name. The town originally was named Centreville, but there was a nearby town also called Centreville. The name gave rise to confusion in postal deliveries, leading one Centreville to change its name to Slippery Rock. Later, when the state normal school was established, it took on the town's name: Slippery Rock. So if it weren't for that horse slipping and for an easily confused mailman, we'd be playing in Centreville University, not as classy-sounding a name as Slippery Rock. You'll find this tidbit in *History of Butler County*—that's Jill's stamping grounds, you know—written by C. Hale Sipe."

This prepractice information session was beginning to sound like a classroom lecture, so I changed course: "We might as well be playing at Jock U. Just listen to these figures: In 1973, Slippery Rock had 5,086 undergraduates; of these 1,266 were physical education majors. That's almost one-fourth of the school. I didn't look hard for more recent data than this. But if the character of the school hasn't changed much since the early seventies, the figures might still be the same or at least similar. Right?"

"Coach," a player from Pennsylvania added, "Slippery Rock now has over seven thousand students. I know that for a fact. I considered going there, and a couple of my best friends from high school go there, and they do so partly because of the cute name."

"You mean they think it's really cool to have a degree from Slippery Rock?" Angi asked.

"Exactly," the player said.

"That's like going to Tufts University in Massachusetts," Angi said, "so that you can say, 'I've got a tough degree,' or—"

"Ball State, to say you've had a ball," the player interrupted.

"That's not exactly what I was going to say, but that's just as funny," Angi responded.

Both women were booed by the rest of the team. "But seriously, Coach," the same player continued, "my friends tell me that many other students go there just for that reason, and when my friends go down to Florida on spring break or somewhere on vacation wearing their Slippery Rock T-shirts, everyone wants to trade with them."

"That I can believe," I said. "The Slippery Rock bookstore does a booming business in T-shirts, sweat shirts, and other memorabilia. A couple of sources that I came across quoted the bookstore manager, who says that the Slippery Rock merchandise is shipped to every state in the union and many foreign countries. You won't believe these figures that I came across. Every year the bookstore, through its mail-order catalog, sells about nine thousand T-shirts and ten thousand sweatshirts."

"What do you know about the team that we'll be playing, Coach?" Jill asked impatiently.

"Several things," I said, "and frankly, they make me uneasy. This will be by far the toughest team we'll play all year. They're not a varsity team as such, but a club team, and that's what scares me. On a club team, anyone can play. You don't have to meet grade-point requirements, class standing, or whatever. Some foreign students who are doing graduate study might be on the team. Graduate assistants who have played varsity elsewhere might be on it. There's no telling. I guarantee you that all—or almost all—will be well-conditioned physical education majors, and they'll be tough. Houghton or Oberlin or those women Cardinals of Wheeling Jesuit would be considered mild compared to Slippery Rock. But we've got to go up there. I scheduled the game. And we've got to play our very best if we're to have a chance at winning. We might even have to play rough to have fun."

Amy heard the reference to "rough," rubbed her hands together as if she were washing them with soap, then clapped them once, and said, "Oh, boy, this sounds good, Coach."

"Sounds very good," Barb said, her performance in the Wheeling game still fresh in the minds of the team members. "I'm really looking forward to facing those Rockets of Slippery Rock."

"The rougher they are, the tougher they fall," Jill added, pumping her clenched right fist and smiling. "It sure sounds like it's going to be mighty interesting."

One beginner said "Okay" and nodded her head. Several others looked sheepishly at Amy, Barb, and Jill, then they looked at each other and said nothing.

"Never mind how this Slippery Rock game sounds," I said. "Let's just see how well we do, and I trust we'll all try to do our best in our next adventure, and what a poetic adventure it is: Slippery Rock tangling with a Golden Tornado. Why, that sounds like a beautiful one-line poem, doesn't it?"

After loading the van for the four o'clock game, we agreed on a code of behavior. All the players promised to refrain from talking to each other, to keep the radio off, and to study, sleep, or enjoy the beauty of Pennsylvania's softly rolling countryside. The players, conscious of their academic pursuits, appreciated the extra time to study, especially in view of approaching tests. Angi offered to sit in her usual place, the bucket seat in the front of the van, and to keep me awake via conversation.

As I began the drive on the country roads leading to Slippery Rock, Angi spoke about a research paper that she was doing for another professor in the English department. She had gathered all her data and was considering casting her paper not in the "standard boring research mold," as she called it, "but into a more creative vessel." Smiling, she said, "Why be an Aristotle if you've got the gift to be a Plato?" She wondered if I knew how her professor, my colleague, would react to her approach.

We drifted out of that topic and landed on a more serious one, one that troubled most of the athletes in the van. Angi spoke slowly as she introduced it: "Sometimes I think—"

"That's good," I interrupted.

"You're not funny, Coach."

"What? Repeat that, please."

"Sometimes I think you're not funny, Coach."

"Okay, you win! Continue." I smiled.

"Sometimes I think that sports in our culture could be compared to those cows that give us the milk that your Henry Aaron—remember him?—once fell in love with."

"Sports and cows?"

"You got it, Coach, and the comparison might seem strange, but it's there, and it's telling," Angi said.

Unable to see an immediate and obvious similarity between the two, I repeated, "Sports and cows: in what sense are they similar?"

"In a certain Angiesque sexist sense," she replied and repeated her reply, obviously delighted by the whistling sounds of the "s."

"Sexist?" I said.

"Yes, sexist."

"I hate to give up so soon, but I don't see what you're driving at."

"I do," she said. "At forty: check your speedometer. Seriously, Coach, you surely must see the similarities between cows and sports."

"Okay, tell me: how exactly does the comparison work? You've got me curious now."

"Yep," Angi said. She tightened her lips, then snapped them, making a popping sound. "I've got you where I want you: confused, puzzled, baffled by three words. Two are all-American words, the other, all-Bombay: sports, cows, sex."

"Mentioning cows and sex," I said, "reminds me of an old doctoral dissertation that someone once wrote that dealt with the history of the dairy industry in the state of Wisconsin from the years 1875 to 1876 or some such narrow time span. The standard joke around our research-conscious graduate school was that the fellow's research was so exhaustive that he must have examined each cow tit by tit."

Angi laughed, then said, "My comparison of sports to cows grows not out of a doctoral dissertation but out of my personal observation of all the emphasis on male sports and the de-emphasis of female sports."

"*De-emphasis* might be the wrong word," I said. "Women's sports, thanks to the hard work of the equity-conscious people in the women's movement—"

"You better say feminist movement, Coach, because the movement has men, too, you know. Men who coach women in college or girls in high school or below are in the movement, whether they like it or not. But go on, you were talking about *de-emphasis.*"

"Yeah, *de-emphasis* is the wrong word because women's sports are being started in many schools in a variety of areas. Witness our brand-new soccer program, for example."

"Yeah, but those that are being started and even those that are already established receive little attention and virtually no resources when compared to what the men get from our male-dominated culture," Angi said.

"But how," I asked, "does your comparison of sports and cows work, and in a sexist context, no less?"

"It works this way," Angi said, tilting her head backward, palming an avalanche of curls, and dumping them on the back of her neck. "People in our culture act as if sports were like cows, with men's sports being white cows and female sports being black cows."

I glanced at Angi and said, "So what?"

"So, you see," she continued, "a lot of people in our male-dominated culture know that white cows give white milk but they act as if black cows gave chocolate milk, presumably an inferior brand of milk, less useful and all."

"Fortunately," I said, "our culture is changing."

"You better believe it," Angi replied. "Opportunities for your daughter should be greater than opportunities were for your wife."

"Indeed, they should be," I said. "I look forward to the day when women's sports occupy a place in our culture that's as precise as pain in our lives, as distinct as the bulge of a late pregnancy, as attention-riveting as rumble strips."

"Love your metaphorical flourish," Angi said. A dash of sarcasm and a smile flavored her words. I smiled and drove on.

When Angi began to read *A Portrait of the Artist as a Young Man*, my thoughts drifted to my role as a women's coach, and I found myself reflecting on the question: Should men coach women in team sports at the college level? If someone asked me this question, how would I reply? My answer would probably tap my experiences as a women's soccer coach and would connect or clash with Angi's feminist thinking. It would probably go something like this: Just as females do not serve as head coaches of male basketball or football teams at the college level, men ought to stay out of coaching women's athletics. (Slightly more than half of the teams we had played against or would play against were coached by men.) I hope that as women's soccer continues to grow, many players, after graduation and further education, will consider coaching the sport. When women's basketball burst on the national scene in the seventies, many men rushed in and claimed the head coaching positions, but now women coaches are beginning to take back those positions. I hope that women will also claim the coaching positions in soccer.

Our trip to Oberlin College had shown me, in a dramatic way, the need for women to coach women. While our players were dressing for the Oberlin game, my son Sam and I were chatting in the parking lot outside the locker room area. Suddenly, two of our players came out. One of them told me, "Coach, I must take her"—pointing to the other player—"to the emergency medical clinic we saw on the way up here. She has a problem that I don't want to explain and that I wish you wouldn't ask about." Needless to say, I did not ask, but I assumed it concerned her menstrual cycle. I had forgotten to check the first-aid kit to make sure it had items that addressed that particular female need; indeed, I had failed to anticipate such a need. A female coach would be more sensitive to such needs and how they might impinge on her players' performance.

Once I had begun a practice by outlining the scheduled drills for the day. Our players, who individually and as a team had a terrific sense of humor, followed my introductory remarks with questions that were prefaced by the rhetoric of parliamentary procedure. "Point of Information," one player said before she asked about the rigorous drills and laps scheduled for that day. "Point of Clarification," another player began her question which footnoted her uneasiness with the day's schedule. When I responded by clarifying and detailing the exercises and all the running that I wanted done on that hot afternoon, a third athlete followed my long response with "Point of Disgust."

Most coaches who work at the college level have usually played the sport that they coach, and that experience is invaluable to a coach. For example, when a female coach assigns certain drills to her players, she is aware of the wisdom of those drills and of the endurance levels of her athletes. That awareness, coming from the perspective of "having been there" as a *female* competitor, is sharper, richer, and more informed than my awareness would be as a male coach. My awareness throughout the season grew through guessing, reading appropriate material, interviewing my wife, recalling past experiences in coaching male football players, and interacting with our players.

Moreover, young athletes—and this I discovered while coaching football, and it certainly applies to women's soccer—often hesitate to confide their problems in college counselors, pastors, parents, or roommates, but they would happily approach their coaches. Fifteen years after graduating from college, most football players may vaguely recall their English professors, history teachers, or psychology instructors, but they will vividly remember their coaches. Players—whether in football or women's basketball, men's baseball or women's soccer—need coaches with whom they feel free to confide their most intimate problems, and a coach of the same sex is likely to invite and stimulate that relationship at a healthy level, a level grounded in trust and sympathetic understanding. A coach must realize that an athlete is not just a person with physical skills but a complex human being.

Still further—and this might be an obvious but important point to note—sports are activities that constantly require touching. I remember one day when a dear friend, Mike Oravitz, and I were sitting behind the visiting team's bench, watching a women's basketball game at Geneva College. Mike and I were horrified to see the visiting male coach constantly holding the women players as he sent them in and took them out of the contest. "He probably does not mean any harm by all this holding and touching of the women players," Mike said, "but I'd never do it if I were a coach. The appearance is so unfortunate, and what fans—or even his own players—infer from a gesture is a lot different than what a coach means or implies by it." From then on, I resolved that if I ever coached a women's athletic team, I would make it a rule never to touch a player for whatever reason, a rule that I followed religiously throughout my tenure as Geneva's women's soccer coach.

Following that rule, however, tortured my natural coaching tendencies. Like other coaches of highly intense team sports, I wanted to maintain literal contact with my athletes by occasionally touching them, by hugging them in victory or putting an arm around their shoulders and consoling them in defeat. These were natural enough tendencies that I had experienced when I coached football. Coaches, moreover, need to be with their players in the locker room before and after a game. The locker room ambience offers a crucial dimension to the total picture of a sports activity, but a male coach has no place in the women's locker room, and of course the reverse is true.

I had no idea if Angi would agree with my argument, and I wasn't about to ask for her response (she was too involved in Joyce's narrative). I suspected she'd label my argument as "unintentionally sexist," and she'd offer one of her own that had women serving as head coaches in men's soccer, baseball, basketball, football, and other sports at the college level.

Women are beginning to assume roles as athletic directors of men's and women's programs at major universities and small liberal arts colleges. I wholeheartedly endorse this trend as one way of making sure that gender equity is realized in given programs. Perhaps such positions of power might lead to women coaching men and the reservations that I have might turn out to be unfounded. If that becomes the case, then I'd have to reassess my position.

"Certainly, women in power," Angi would say, "could help change the color of milk."

•   •   •   •   •

As we neared the town of Wurtemburg, Angi said, "Remember those Oberlin missionaries you once told us about at the end of one of those early practices?"

"Sure do."

"Well, you're chugging along as if you were a relative reluctantly heading to see one of them and happy that you got stuck on a slow boat to China. You can certainly go over forty miles, Coach, can't you?"

"Of course I can, but with all our players in the van, a wife and four kids at home, and all these narrow country roads, I've got to watch my speed."

"Or lack of it," she said.

"When I was single," I said, "I used to drive seventy or even more. After I got married, I continued to do so, and even after little Rita came on the scene, I persisted in driving fast, until one day Rita jolted my attention. She was a little girl then, standing on the front seat of our yellow Opel, resting one hand on my neck, the other on top of the seat. I was driving fast—foolishly fast—on the Kansas prairies, land of her birth. 'Slow down, Daddy,' she said. 'Slow down. The earth looks like it's shivering.' Needless to say, I slowed down and that image comes to mind every time I get the temptation to put pedal to the metal."

"What temptation?" Angi said, and laughed.

"I'll speed up when we get to the interstate up by Portersville," I said.

Whenever we passed a dairy farm, Angi would look at the cows in the field, and I would also. We would frequently snicker and comment on their colors. Angi wondered out loud if any college used a cow for a nickname. "Do you know, Coach?"

"Yes, I do. Williams up in New England uses a nickname with cows in it, but the color of their cows isn't black or white."

"You're serious?"

"Yes, I am."

"What's their color?"

"Purple. Their nickname is the Purple Cows of Williams College."

"Strange," Angi said.

"If you think that's strange," I said, "some colleges even use trees for nicknames."

"Name one."

"The Sycamores of Indiana State."

"How strange."

"There's even a high school in Oklahoma," I said, recalling my years in the land of Woody Guthrie, "that uses the nickname Hens: the Hens of Henryetta High."

"Temple uses Owls," Angi said.

"That's a lot better than Turkeys, though the obligatory alliteration would be there in the Temple Turkeys, wouldn't it?"

"South Carolina uses Gamecocks," Angi said.

"Oregon, Ducks."

"So if there're hens, ducks, gamecocks, and owls, then some schools might well have cows, and your Williams bit is probably for real."

"Oh, it's for real; I'm not kidding about those Purple Cows. There's one nickname that fascinates me but that I suspect no school uses even though it ignites fear and respect in the hearts of people the moment you mention it."

"What's that?"

"Are you ready for this?" I asked, orchestrated a long Paul Harvey–type pause, then said, "It's none other than Cockroaches. If you're a good, solid, punishing team, you should inflict pain on your opposition, and the very word *pain—aches—*is in cockroaches. Now tell me, wouldn't that be a great nickname for a team?"

"I'd hate to see the uniform of the mascot," Angi said.

"Wouldn't it be great if some wealthy donor (a fat feline, as it were) proposed to give a five-million-dollar donation to Geneva for use in their athletic programs provided the college changed its nickname from the Golden Tornadoes to the Fightin' Cockroaches? Do you think the college officials would agree to such a change?" I asked.

"Who knows?" Angi replied. "Colleges do strange things, don't they?"

"They sure do," I said. "Who would've ever thought that a college would name itself after a toothpaste?"

"Or better yet, a lock."

"Or even a rock."

"I can just hear your famous radio announcer saying, 'On to the field go the Cockroaches of Geneva,'"Angi said, laughing.

"Don't laugh," I said. "There's probably a good comic short story in this: A rich trustee gives five million dollars to a college and attaches to it the cockroach name change. Other trustees resist the change but lust for the cash. The athletic department faculty supports the name change; most of the other faculty resist. The president supports it, but her husband resists. The students come in at 80 percent for the change, 12 percent against it, and 8 percent undecided. There's enough tension and potential complication here to make an engaging story line, and the story could have a crisis and a resolution. Don't you think?"

"Speaking of story lines," Angi said, "what're you working on now, Coach?"

"Fiction or creative nonfiction?"

"Creative nonfiction."

"A book that graphs the ways of man—"

"And women—"

"Well, I have too much respect for women, but if you insist—"

"I do, I do," she said.

"But wait till you hear the context before you do, Angi. Whatever, the book graphs the ways of people from the point of view of the animals; it explores the animals' perspectives of us."

The van coasted to a stop at a red light. We made eye contact as she asked, "A serious or comic book?"

"A seriocomic book is probably a good way to describe it," I said.

"Tell me a bit more," she said.

"Well, you know how the various television networks, and PBS especially, have numerous nature programs that delve into the ways of the animal kingdom?" I asked, quickly glancing at the other players in the van.

"Sure do."

"I thought it might be fun to reverse the perspective and have an animal narrate to the animal kingdom the ways of humanity. In other words, how do we appear on animal television? Just what do the animals think of us? How do they portray us?" The van began to move again.

"I see," Angi said.

"A lot of our ways must seem mighty strange, even weird, to the animals. Don't you think?" I asked.

"*Si cogito*, Coach," Angi said, delighting in wedding Spanish and Latin with a Maryland accent. "But give me an example of what you mean."

"Consider this: when we blow our noses, we use a napkin, a tissue, that we often discard. Isn't that right?"

"Right."

"But when we dress up and go to more formal gatherings, the more aristocratic ones in our ranks often use handkerchiefs, and when they blow their noses, they don't discard the handkerchiefs; they neatly fold them and place them in their pockets or purses. They, in effect, save the contents of their noses."

"I suppose that appears to be somewhat strange, if not downright bizarre, to some sensitive animals," she said.

"Imagine what some animals must think of when they see a white handkerchief sticking out of the dark breast pocket of a male suit. Why, they'll probably think, 'There's snot and then there's snot,' kind of like us when we say, 'There's academic excellence and then there's academic excellence.' Snot saved in that pocket square hankie must be award-winning snot."

"From an animal's point of view," she said.

"Right," I responded. "Now, in the book," I added with a soft smile, "animals try to explain to each other our ways and habits. The narrator on animal television explains to the viewers man's nose-blowing, snot-saving phenomenon. The animal television crews, working with some scientists, capture the phenomenon on film. Then the scientists go beyond that: they harness what they label 'the handkerchief humans,' then they tag them and release them to their natural habitats. 'Animal scientists,' the narrator of a TV segment concludes, 'have yet to unlock the mystery of why man saves his snot in this manner. Tagging man, the scientists believe, might increase our understanding of man's behavior.'

"In another TV program, animal scientists corral several humans, male and female, and plant some chimneylike tubes—horns is what we call them—on their nostrils. Then the scientists tag the humans and release them to the wilds of civilization. This procedure is used by the animal scientists in the hope of finding the key to unlock man's snot-saving mystery."

"Inter-r-resting," Angi said, her friendly sarcasm intact.

"And you know what fascinating thing happens after all that, don't you?" I asked.

"What?"

"The activists from the Human Liberation Movement protest, but to no avail. The animal scientists continue their thing."

"Interrrrresting," she said again, this time rolling the "r" on her tongue.

"The way you rolled that 'r' reminds me of a concrete poem that one of my students wrote in Creative Writing. The poem is simply the word *Reproduce* with the 'o' printed not once or twice but nine times."

As we drove on, Angi spoke about several poems she was preparing for publication in Geneva's literary magazine and about a biography of Lawrence Ferlinghetti that she was reading the week of the Slippery Rock game.

When there was a lull in the conversation, I told Angi, "Jock-jock coaches, to use your old label, probably like to talk about their teams or phys. ed. classes on these road trips, but word-jock coaches love to talk about their writings and the academic pursuits of their students." I leaned over and flicked the air-conditioning blower on high. "As long as you're in one of these attentive, long-suffering moods, let me give you another example from that animal-TV book."

"What does this one deal with?"

"Language."

"What?"

"Language."

"Baggage?"

"No, no," I said, raising my voice, "language, the English language."

Angi reached down and readjusted the air conditioner. "Sorry, Coach, I know you just adjusted the blowers on this thing, but they're just too loud now. Anyway, what's this language bit?"

"Consider this: We often say, 'He worked his tail off.' Well, that expression confuses some people at Geneva, and it also confuses almost all the animal linguists in my book," I said.

"Now, wait a minute, Coach. I don't understand. Let's work this out one issue at a time."

"Okay."

"You say it confuses some people at Geneva?"

"That's right."

"And who are these people?"

"They're the folks you see a lot around the mailroom. They lust for their mail with a passion more intense than that of writers, and frankly, I didn't think that was possible. But it is, and they do it."

"Now you've got me curious: To whom are you referring?"

"Foreign students."

"Oh, yes, I agree," she quickly said.

"But there's one important difference between the foreign students' mail and the mail of writers," I said.

"Oh, what's that?"

"Foreign students," I said with a chuckle, "correspond with friends and relatives back home, but a writer—and I certainly speak for myself here—corresponds with himself most of the time. If it weren't for all those writers throughout America corresponding with themselves by enclosing those self-addressed stamped envelopes—the abbreviation is SASE, but I prefer SARL, the more accurate description, which stands for self-addressed rejection letter—then postal rates would be much higher. Writers are to the post office what government is to the wheat or tobacco farmer: a subsidy. You might have never seen what a postal subsidy looks like."

"You're right on that, Coach," she said with a smile.

"Well, you're looking at one; indeed, you're being coached and taught by one," I said.

"Let's get back to that language bit. I want to see how it all fits in your animal-TV book project," she said.

"Yeah, that. In the book, animal linguists hear the expression 'worked his tail off' and they find it strange because they search and search and they fail to locate tails on humans. They speculate on the meaning of the phrase while their scientists continue their indefatigable search for humans with tails, and when they finally find some—in symphonies and proms and weddings—they're thrilled with their discovery. They draw immediate comparisons between people and penguins, and some begin to speculate with certitude on how penguins evolved from man."

"Okay," she said, "I think I'm beginning to see your serio-comic drift."

She pressed me for a few more examples, and I gave her some. We also talked about her work on an upcoming assignment for our creative writing class. Angi and I were the only ones in the van to have a sustained conversation on the road to Slippery Rock.

Once on the Slippery Rock field and moments after concluding our warm-up drills, I overheard Angi tell a teammate who was standing near me as we stared at some sizzling shots at goal being taken by the Slippery Rock players, "I can't believe we put ourselves through this week after week."

Catching the implication of her remark, I asked, "Are you nervous?"

"You bet," she said.

"Look, this is just another game. Just go out there and have fun. You're a good player in your own right," I added as a Slippery Rock player not only hit but drove the ball with her head into the goal's net. "I've seen you handle corner kicks—and with your head—just as well as she did just now. So don't lose your confidence. Go out there and do your best."

Privately I thought: It might be easier to locate a man with three nostrils than for us to beat the women's soccer team that's out there now.

Moments after we broke up our final huddle and our players trotted to their positions on the field, I looked over at the more than twenty Slippery Rock players gathered around their coach, a woman dressed in gym trunks and a green and white Slippery Rock sweatshirt, carrying a clipboard and a whistle. I wondered what their breakup "charge chant" would be, so I listened carefully and even drifted toward their circle. On the count of three, they exhorted, "Go, Rock!"

"Did you hear their charge chant?" I asked Sharon, who remained on the sidelines near me. (She was the writing major who shared my initials and who often called me—as I called her—by those initials.)

"No."

"They said, 'Go, Rock!' An original chant, eh?" I said, pacing the sidelines.

"Oh," she said, unimpressed by the chant. "What do you expect? This is Jock U., remember?"

"It's a versatile chant, too, wouldn't you say?" I asked, clapping my hands and yelling encouraging words at our players on the field.

"A what?" she asked.

"Versatile," I said.

"Versatile?"

"Right. It's the kind of chant that plays well here but would also play well in Florida," I said. The teams started the game by exchanging passes between teammates. "Do you know why I say that?" I asked.

"No," she replied, and yelled encouraging remarks at a teammate who had just made a poor kick.

"Just look at it this way," I said. "When you say, 'Go, Rock!' in Florida, the teens will head to their discos and the senior citizens to their chairs, and they'll rock away. Two birds with one stone—"

"Hey, S.H., that's a cliché," she said triumphantly. "You've caught enough of mine over the years, and I'm happy to nail you for one on the sidelines of the Slippery Rock game."

"Go ahead, nail me for one, and you'd better be ready to go in before long," I said. "I'm going to send you in at fullback; it looks like we're going to be playing a lot of defense today."

Slippery Rock's players took command of the game early. They frequently passed the ball: fast, firm, well-timed passes. When a player received a pass in the clear, she would dribble it until one of our players challenged her, then she'd pass it, flare out, and head downfield. Occasionally, they would loft the ball across the field, stopping it with their heads, chests, or thighs. They impressed me with their quickness in narrowly defined areas and their speed when the ball traveled far away.

At the eleven-minute mark of the first period, a series of passes among three players from Slippery Rock's forward line—passes that had three of their offensive players working against two of our defenders—resulted into a shot at goal. Amy stopped the shot and punted the ball, only to see the three forwards, once again, maneuvering the ball with quick combinations of dribbling and passing, which resulted in a Slippery Rock player taking a hard, low shot at goal. Amy stretched for the shot and blocked it with her right foot. The shooter followed the impressive block by tapping an easy goal past Amy, who was staggering to recover her balance, desperately trying but failing.

Three minutes later, the ball was once again in Amy's area, being kicked around by several Slippery Rock players. Their attack with the ball was physical and occasionally verbal. When I took Angi out for a brief rest in the first half, she told me, "Coach, there's a word in the language that rhymes with 'luck' that some of their players use after a bad kick." They must not be using it often, I told myself, because I'm not seeing many bad kicks out there. Three minutes after scoring their first goal, Slippery Rock registered a second one, thanks to a clean, hard shot by the right wing that soared past the outstretched arms of Amy.

At the thirty-third-minute mark of the first period, the Slippery Rock offense came to life again, and they scored another goal. This time, the left wing was heavily involved in moving the ball, and the score came off a high kick by the left wing to the center of the field. A Slippery Rock player met the ball with her head and drove it into the net past a bewildered Amy.

During those thirty-three minutes, the Rockets looked as if they had played together as a unit for years: they moved the ball downfield, passing it not between two players but among three, in a triangular pattern. The moving triangle—which we had practiced and practiced but failed to execute well because of our mixture of beginners and experienced players—was executed with textbook precision by the Slippery Rock players, all of whom seemed to be well-conditioned, aggressive, confident, and experienced.

After the third goal, Slippery Rock made some substitutions, and the game degenerated into a sluggish, poorly played match of high kicks in the center of the field, inaccurate passes by both teams, and numerous fouls on both squads. Near the end of the first period, with Slippery Rock's defense playing almost at the midfield line, our left wing, Barb, anticipated a pass, received it, and dribbled it toward the Slippery Rock goal. A couple of Slippery Rock players attempted to attack her to steal the ball, but she dribbled around them, set it up to her powerful left leg, and rammed the ball into the net. Her follow-through was so strong, she stumbled and fell to the grass but was pulled up and congratulated by several Golden Tornadoes. The half ended with the score of Slippery Rock, three, Geneva, one.

At halftime, I told our players that they were playing well but that we could be "blown out" if that first unit came back in the second half. I urged our players to play solid and systematic defense. "Be aggressive," I said. "Attack the person with the ball; don't wait for her to come to you."

"Coach, some of those Slippery Rock players are really rough. They use their bodies and legs and lean into you as they dribble the ball in traffic," one player said.

"They're rough, vicious, but if they hurt or hit you inadvertently, they swear and apologize. You've got to like that, at least," another player said.

I continued my rambling halftime speech—at times upbeat, at times realistic, most of the time confidence-building—and when our players took the field at the second half, the first Slippery Rock unit appeared. They drove downfield and took several shots at our goal, all of which were stopped by Amy. One particularly low, fast-moving shot had Amy doing a cheerleader-type leg split; the instep of her right foot stopped the shot, eliciting genuine cheers from the Slippery Rock crowd and bench, including the coach.

Slippery Rock's first unit added two more goals early in the second half, and we managed to add zero goals, even while playing against their second unit. Five to one, I said to myself, is not a bad defeat, given the competition. At least we weren't shut out. For one brief moment after the Wheeling game, I had thought—hoped—that ineptness had left us for good, but we weren't that fortunate. It came back in the Slippery Rock game, much as a smile does to a happy face. I later told myself: Perhaps it wasn't ineptness but stiff competition that had returned. That level of competition was going to remain with us until the final game of the season: the return match with wonderful Wheeling.

After dinner, we rode home. The players sang, teased each other, and appeared jovial. A defeat meant little to them, and that pleased me. I overheard several players comparing Slippery Rock's red-brick, newer-looking campus with Geneva's old stone buildings, historic towers, stained-glass windows, and well-kept lawns. The radio played the latest rock music throughout the trip home, and at one point I asked Angi, who again sat in the bucket seat to my right, to turn it down: "The record seems to be stuck and the disc jockey must have gone to sleep." I said that with a snicker that Angi ignored.

"Listen to this guy," Angi said, laughing. She turned around and shared my comment with the other players. They laughed also. Then she addressed me: "Coach, that's the music; you've got to get with it."

"I am," I said.

"Mercy me," Angi said.

"Next road trip," I said, "we'll have to listen to NPR. That's National Public Radio on the F.M. dial, you know."

"Oh, no," she said.

"Oh, yes. That's high-culture stuff, classical music and all. You'd love it," I said.

"Let me see if I understand you correctly, Coach," Angi said, using a favorite expression of mine. "You mean to say that you want to make these road trips another humanities class?" Angi was referring to Geneva's demanding and excellent twelve-hour core course—required of all students—that traced the history of Western civilization and especially its cultural achievements.

"Why not?" I said, laughing, and then assured Angi, "We'll turn the dial to NPR only if most of the players request it."

"Thank goodness," she said. "Then we're safe, very safe, I'm happy to say, Coach."

"Let me see if *I* understand *you* correctly, Angi: Are you saying that the death of culture at Geneva is alive and well?"

"Yeah," she said, stretching out the word. "But come to think of it, NPR is more likely to play Bob Dylan, Judy Collins, Joan Baez, and Peter, Paul, and Mary than these silly rock stations some of the players like to listen to."

When we were close to Beaver Falls, several players asked me to drop them off at various locations other than the campus. In so doing, I transformed my identity in the minds of the players from a scholar-coach to a driver of a coach in a big city.

"Next stop," one player said, "will be Sammy's Barbershop."

"Get off if you need a haircut," another added.

"Next stop," a player said after we passed the barbershop, "will be the New Brighton YMCA."

"Get off if you need to exercise," another player added.

Once we passed the YMCA, another player shouted, "Next stop will be Athen's Family Restaurant."

"Get off if you're hungry—"

"For great Greek food—"

"And misplaced apostrophes," Angi added. (As we drove past the restaurant, I looked at the lighted blue and white sign, and sure enough, the apostrophe was incorrectly placed.)

Once we passed the restaurant, a player said, "Next stop will be the Carnegie Library."

"Get off if you need an education," came the advice.

When I made a left turn and the players saw a funeral home, one player said, "Next stop will be Campbell's Funeral Home."

And to that another responded, "Get off if you're dead."

"There's no way to top that," I said, laughing. "Next stop will be the dorms." The players began to reach for their soccer bags and books.

At home that evening, I wrote a long entry in the "Soccer Season Diary." What follows is an excerpt from that entry:

Barb scored a goal at Slippery Rock, and she did it in her typical manner. . . . We lost again: five to one. The Rockets were so powerful and impressive. . . . And our Tornadoes were truly golden this day in that they touched down at Slippery Rock, fluffed things a bit, but did little serious damage.

If Geneva's president doesn't wish to speak to our football coach regarding my old idea of having a woman kick an extra point or a field goal in a men's varsity football game, then I'll probably write the Slippery Rock athletic director about the idea. American sports history will be made in such a move, and national television and the print media will cover it. Immense positive publicity will result to the school that does this first. The key word is first.

If Geneva doesn't want to enter the history books in this manner, then maybe Slippery Rock would. I know Slippery Rock has women players—and I base this, in part, on my observation of their corner kicks in practice and during the game—who'll be able to make extra points or field goals; some Rockets might even make good punters.

From our team, Barb, Angi, Amy, and Jill have strong enough legs—and accurate ones, too—to drill field goals or extra points through the football uprights. Oh, I just wish someone in authority here at Geneva decides to give them a chance.

When I first mentioned the idea to several Geneva colleagues, they were enthusiastic about it. "If the kick fails," one faculty member put it, "no one will broadcast it, but if it's good, it's national news, a feature that'll be all over the papers and the other, nonprint media." Several urged me to try the idea on the president (which I had already done in a casual conversation) and others in appropriate positions at Geneva.

I really don't want to approach Gene [Sullivan, the head football coach and the only coach in Geneva's history to take a team to an NAIA national tournament and finish in the Final Four], for I'm another (and an upstart, at that) coach, and I don't want to seem to be meddling in his sport. Maybe a formal memo to the president will do. That'll remind him of the idea and give him time to meditate on it.

Had interesting little dialog with S.H. on the sidelines . . . and with Angi on the way up and back in the van. . . . Players like these—witty and cheerful and intelligent as they are—make coaching the Golden Tornadoes such a joy.

Seldom, however, did I find joy in learning week after week about the character of our opposition. After the Rockets of Slippery Rock came The Big Red of Denison University in Granville, Ohio. The Denison coach called me to confirm the game, and she was also kind enough to mail me—unsolicited material, I might add—a roster and a profile of over twenty players, three of whom were from Sweden. Denison's record impressed me greatly, and the profile of some of the players depressed and intimidated me.

At dinner with one of my favorite Geneva colleagues, a dear friend and a philosopher, I tried to tap his wisdom on how to deal with the awesome might of Denison. Philosophers had earned my respect, for most of the ones I had known had devised a strategy to brave the nonsense of academic life and to do it with a classic simplicity.

Several incidents involving philosophers had compelled me to seek my friend's wisdom. One involved a study in criminology undertaken by a former colleague for his doctorate in sociology. In the study, my colleague had tried to apply highly complicated laws and formulas from physics and mathematics to criminal behavior. The procedure satisfied the sociologists on the Ph.D. committee, but it met a snag in the reaction of the committee's only philosopher, who insisted on knowing how the study was going to help the chief of police.

Another incident occurred at a lecture on ethical relativism held at the University of Wisconsin. After the speaker gave a highly obscure lecture spiked with mathematical formulas supporting the theory of ethical relativism, a philosophy professor seated to my right rose to his feet, pounded his fist in the air, and thundered, "What is the matter with the Ten Commandments?" Then he added softly, "Your lecture today makes them sound like the ten suggestions."

A third incident also happened at a lecture, but this time at Indiana University in Bloomington. The guest lecturer had given an involved treatise elucidating, so he claimed, a difficult aspect of Immanuel Kant's *Critique of Pure Reason*. At the end of the lecture, a philosopher informed the speaker, "You just made a serious error in your interpretation. Could you please tell me on what page that error appears?"

After I had enumerated Denison's strengths to my philosopher-friend, I asked him, "What would you do if you were in my position as the Geneva coach?"

"You're the only coach?" Byron asked.

"Yes."

"That means you're the head coach?"

"Right."

"Well, then," he said, "the answer is easy; it's downright obvious. Take two aspirins and resign, effective immediately, or—"

"You mean there's more?" I asked.

"There's an alternative," he said.

"Which is?"

"Take one aspirin and call the coach requesting a defeat through forfeit," he said, smiling.

To me, resignation seemed unwise, for we still had other games to play, and one of those was against Wheeling Jesuit College. And although Wheeling was improving rapidly, we might be able to beat them again, even at their home field. Forfeiture sounded plausible, though our players would never forgive me for that. Perhaps the wisest thing to do, I told myself, would be to prepare the team for Denison and see what happens.

During the week before the Denison game, the Geneva student newspaper, *The Cabinet,* published an article on the status of the women's soccer team:

Lady Tornadoes Smash and Get Smashed

"Some of the best women soccer players in America will play on the 33rd Street field Friday afternoon at four," according to Dr. Hanna, Geneva's head soccer coach. The players will be representing Denison University of Ohio, a school that features an undefeated team in NCAA division three varsity play. Denison's two losses came at the feet of Division One teams.

"They're loaded with all-American candidates, and they're well-coached and disciplined," Dr. Hanna said, "but we're going to show up for our adventure."

Geneva's soccer team lost to Slippery Rock five to one, but before that they scrambled Wheeling College of West Virginia in the Lady Tornadoes' first victory. The score was Geneva five Wheeling zero. Barb Schwettman led the lady G's with three goals.

"The Wheeling game was particularly rewarding to the team," Dr. Hanna said, "for it was our first victory, and it was attended by a crowd that had more of an emphasis on quality, not quantity. Why the crowd was a gallery of WHO'S WHO of Geneva folks."

At the dinner table on the eve of the Denison game, our family talked about three sports-related topics. I told them about a memo I had written earlier that day, addressed to Geneva's president, suggesting a change in the college's mascot. "The current mascot that has a student wearing that furry whatever-it-is suit," I said, "garners all sorts of ridicule from students, staff, faculty, and visitors."

"Yeah," Sal said. "The mascot's big nose that's supposed to look like a tornado looks like a big nose."

"A caricature of a big nose," my wife added.

"A gigantic symbol or statue for the NRA," Rita said with a smile.

"The what?" Sal said.

"The NRA: the Nose Rubbing Association," Rita told Sal. "Haven't you ever heard of them?" she asked.

"No," Sal said.

"Neither have I," Rita said.

"What did you tell the president?" Sal asked.

"I told the president that he might want to consider assigning a project or running a contest where a group of students would design a Frisbee that had a ribbon or ribbons attached to its center. The trick, of course, would be to design a Frisbee-ribbon that when properly launched would create a tornadolike pattern." I looked up. All seemed to be attending to their food and, I assumed, listening, so I continued, "The Frisbee-ribbon could combine the school's colors. It could be sold at concession booths and thrown into the stands after touchdowns. Cheerleaders could fling it around the gym during basketball time-outs; little kids could play with it behind the soccer bench when the game is in progress."

"Now you're talking," Sam said.

"What was he doing before?" Paul asked his twin.

Sam failed to respond, so I continued, "The ribbon or ribbons could be different colors, and the mascot could be given a positive and pleasant name such as Flying Colors."

"It'll be interesting to see how he responds," my wife said.

"I hope he gets more excited about this idea than he did about that idea of having one of our soccer players kick a field goal or an extra point in the men's football game," I said.

"I do, too," my wife said.

"I still think," I said, in defense of the woman football kicker, "that's a great idea, one that would get us national publicity on all three networks and CNN and throughout the print media— wire services and all. Such publicity would bring attention to our brand-new program in women's soccer and our other well-established sports for women and men at Geneva."

"That it will," Rita said.

"But wait, there's more," I said.

"Oh," Rita said.

"We'll also enter American sports history," I said.

"And that's nothing to sneeze at," my wife said.

"That's right," Rita said. "Kleenex is."

"Seriously," I added, "publicity-starved colleges like ours wait year after year for *U.S. News and World Report*'s annual issue on America's best colleges. Usually, the magazine ends up with a vast array of different—and, in many instances, little-known—schools on their extensive lists. But the editors of that special issue are smart; they also mention the Harvards and Stanfords and Yales and Columbias of this world. Mention of these traditionally outstanding schools give their lists credibility. In any event, many of those publicity-starved schools that make the list end up giving the magazine all sorts of free publicity in their alumni bulletins, their college ads, their admission brochures, and other literature. My point is, we don't have to wait to be listed in *U.S. News*; we can generate our own national publicity with a unique and self-serving publicity stunt, one that'll do wonders for our women's athletic programs in general, and for recruiting women soccer players in particular."

"Now you're sounding not only like the coach," my wife said, "but like the creative writer-coach that you are."

"Sounds to me like a lazy way to recruit players, Dad," Rita said.

"Thanks, honey," I said, smiling, and tapped her hand.

Midway through dinner, the conversation shifted to the forthcoming Denison game. "If we win this game," I said as I sliced my baked potato, "I'll eat—"

"Don't say, 'I'll eat my hat,' Dad," Sal said. "You're supposed to have eaten so many by now for losing all sorts of other bets."

"Okay," I said, "I won't say that, but I *will* say that I'll buy a wig and start parting my hair in a line straight as a hammer's handle."

"I hope you do," Rita said, "because I'm getting pretty darn tired of the way it looks now."

"What does it look like now?" Sal asked.

"A sickle," Rita deadpanned.

"There we go again," Sam said, "making jokes about Dad's hair."

"What hair?" Paul added.

Paul and Sam were born in Virginia. Sal and Rita were born in Lyons, Kansas, one of the docks of America's "amber waves of grain." Addressing Rita, I asked, "Are you suggesting that Wichita State University could use a new mascot, a new Wheat Shocker, as it were?"

"If you want to see it that way," Rita said.

"And what would that mascot be?" Sal asked.

"A man with a bald head," I said. "Or better yet, a platoon of bald men. Why, the 'Bald Is Beautiful' convention could well be a convention of Wichita State Shocker mascots. After all, the part of a bald man does look like a sickle, doesn't it?"

"Whatever," Sal said. "I hope tomorrow's Denison game is a shocker to Denison, of course. But I'm not holding my breath."

As things turned out, the Denison game attracted a large crowd for a Geneva soccer game, women's or men's, and it unfolded a peculiar game plan that shocked many, a game plan that I engineered in my capacity as the unaspirined head coach of the Golden Tornadoes.

Part IV

Denison and Beyond

7

Drano, Geneva, and
the Gipper of Notre Dame

When I taught English and coached football in the mid- and late seventies at Sterling College, a small school on the prairies of central Kansas, a seventy-eight-year-old widow enrolled in my creative writing class. Her reason for taking the class was simple: she wanted to write for her grandchildren all about her exciting journeys to Europe. "Some people," she once told us in class, "capture their memories in slides, snapshots, or even home movies, but I want to do mine in words—in prose."

She had a splendid sense of humor. Her first day in class, for example, she overheard a female student ask another, "Is that unique lady in our class?" The old widow instantly replied, "Girls, girls, I heard that, and I'm so happy you said 'unique' and not 'antique.'"

Her humor often delighted the class. Her enthusiasm about writing was high; her writing talents low, though she refused to recognize that, and I resisted every opportunity to inform her in blunt language. "And you'd better not," the students once told me, "for she might have you in her will."

One day while teaching English and coaching soccer at Geneva, I told my creative writing students all about the widow from Kansas, and I shared with them a typical line that she would use to describe an Italian cathedral: "The cathedral in Rome was so absolutely beautiful and so exceedingly gorgeous that words cannot be used to describe it."

"Now, that's the type of general description," I told the creative writing students at Geneva, "that I hope you'd avoid." Then I added what I frequently told the seventy-eight-year-old Kansan: "It so happens that one of the objects of this course is to use words to describe whatever you're writing about. I really don't want to hear you use this expression: 'Words cannot be used to describe it.'"

On the Thursday after our Slippery Rock defeat, my creative writing students, whose class I had to cancel in order to travel to the ball game, asked me, "Dr. Hanna, what happened to you guys up at Slippery Rock?"

"You better not say 'guys,'" I said.

"All right, what happened to your girls on—"

"And I don't like 'girls' either," I said.

"Well, you use it every time you refer to them as 'the girls of autumn,' don't you?" a male student asked.

"Yes, I do, and I regret that," I said. "But I use that in order to draw the parallel with *The Boys of Summer,* that famous baseball book."

"Well, what should we use then?" the student asked.

"A headline writer at the *Cabinet,*" I said, referring to the campus newspaper, "wants me to use *ladies,* of all words, because, as she once reasoned to me, *women* has the word *men* in it and *females* has *males* in it, but *ladies* has neither."

"Oh, but it has *lad* in it," Angi said. "That's a dumb idea, Coach."

"You're right," I said. "So let's stay with *athletes* or *players,* okay?"

"Come on, Dr. Hanna, please tell us in detail what happened, blow by blow, kick by kick," another student added.

"Well, let me put it this way," I said. "We lost five to one, and we put on a bad show; I'll confess it was really bad, especially when Slippery Rock's first unit was in."

"How bad?" a student asked.

"Yeah, just how bad?" another added.

"Pretty bad, if you'll allow me to use those words together," I said, pacing the room in front of the blackboard.

"Be more specific, Dr. Hanna," a woman said.

"It's hard," I said, looking up at the ceiling and then back at the students, "to be specific about how bad we were."

"I guess we were so bad," Angi said, splicing her comment with a pause and a smile, "that words cannot be used to describe it."

All the students laughed, and so did I. Then I told them, "Come out and see us tomorrow. We play The Big Red of Denison; that, believe it or not, is their creative and highly original nickname. How many of you are planning to be there?" Several students raised their hands. "We need more support than this," I said.

"You need more support in a lot of areas, Coach," a football player said, and added, "I saw your first game against Houghton."

"Did we lose that?" another student asked the football player.

"Sure did," the player replied.

"By what score?" came a question.

"Four field goals to zero," the football player responded.

"So the team hasn't really improved if the difference in the scoring is still four," another student added.

"But it has," I said. "The first game we lost by four field goals in football language; that makes twelve goals in soccer."

"There's a difference," a fellow said.

"I'd say," a woman agreed.

"It's like human years and dog years," Angi said.

"Whatever that is," a student replied.

"Okay," I said, "let's forget about our soccer fortunes—"

"Try misfortunes," Angi said.

"Okay, misfortunes," I said, "and let's get back to creative writing."

"Before we do, Dr. Hanna," a student said, "let me tell you that my roommate is writing an article for tomorrow's *Cabinet*—"

"You mean *Liquor Cabinet*," Angi interjected, "our underground paper with school spirit."

"And that article," the interrupted student continued, "should bring out a good crowd, especially after they read all that All-American stuff you said about Denison in the paper."

"Before we start class, Dr. Hanna," another student said, "aren't you going to make a comment on Jack's haircut?"

The haircut, apparently, had been a topic of conversation among the students before I arrived. Jack was a particularly good-natured young man who participated vigorously in class discussions and whose hair had once reached to his shoulders. He had gone to a barbershop in nearby Pittsburgh and had his hair cut in a crew cut (what we used to call it in the fifties) that needed Wildroot hair tonic to prop it up. When Bob Haldeman, President Nixon's chief of staff, featured such a haircut in the early seventies, his friends and later the national media that covered Haldeman's involvement in the Watergate crisis called it a "brush."

The students felt that Jack's new "flat top" or "spiked hairdo," as some called it, was "cute," "different," "ugly," "in style," "attractive," "super ugly," "a mistake," "horrible looking," "artistic." I said, "I agree with all those comments," and then in due time I invoked the head of Bob Haldeman.

"Well, come to think of it, it does look like a brush of sorts," one student said.

"What a haircut like that does," I added, speaking slowly, my right index finger and thumb cupping my chin, "is it controls Jack's vocabulary." After a long pause, I added, "Not only that, but if you think about it, it really controls his use of clichés."

"Oh," one student said.

"How so?" another asked.

"Use of clichés?" someone asked.

"That's right," I said.

The students seemed puzzled. "Explain, please," Angi told me.

I did. "Consider this," I said, and looked at the eleven students in the small seminar room on the third floor of Geneva's Old Main. "If you get Jack really upset at something, he won't be able to say, 'That makes me so mad it makes my hair stand,' because it's already standing."

"But, Coach, you can't say that either, can you?" Angi asked.

"Yes, I can," I said, stroking my pate with the palm of my left hand. "What I usually say is, 'That makes me so mad it makes my hair stand—on the sides.'"

Bantering with students, teaching classes of fifteen or eleven or eight, calling students by their first names, inviting them to the house for tea or dinner, reading their columns in the newspapers even though they weren't graduate students in journalism, watching them play organized sports even though a pro career was as available to them as a genuine cure for baldness— all these and other factors often reminded me of the contrast between the small liberal arts colleges where I had taught and coached as a gypsy scholar and the large state universities where I had studied for both my undergraduate and graduate degrees.

Denison, though a university by name, was only twice the size of Geneva. It featured a team loaded with talent and a tough schedule. We were on that schedule. I never did like the concept of "guilt by association," but if being on the Denison schedule associated us with their class and the class of the teams they had already beaten, then maybe the concept did have some redeeming dimensions.

If nothing else, I told myself as I left the creative writing class with the Denison game much on my mind, posterity will see us as being guilty of toughness by association, if not participation.

But participate we must.

Practice sessions leading up to the Denison game—and, indeed, for all the games in the latter part of the season—seemed enjoyable and frustrating. The beginners, who made up more than half the team, exhibited increased skill and confidence with each passing day. They seemed to enjoy working on the fundamentals of dribbling and passing the ball, and the enjoyment came partly from seeing progress in the development of their newly acquired skills. Frustration often set in during those drills when the experienced players intercepted the beginners' passes or derailed their dribbles or stole the ball from them.

Enjoyment for the experienced players came from playing the sport regularly. Frustration, on the other hand, resulted from the team's inability—given the vastly uneven talent—to work on sophisticated plays, to establish a certain flow to the offense, and, no doubt, to fully accept the ways of a quirky coach. In my own mind, I sometimes compared our soccer team to two tennis players, one highly talented, the other a beginner, yet both expected to play doubles against an experienced and skilled pair.

On the morning before the Friday afternoon game with Denison, I lounged in my office, rocking on the swivel chair, feet on the corner of the desk, clipboard in lap. I bit a long yellow pencil, giving my mouth fangs, and took stock of the team, noting the five healthy players (the sixth was injured) who were experienced and the remaining nine who were beginners with different levels of potential and athletic abilities. Using both groups, I tried hard to work out a strategy for the Denison game that all the players might see as shrewd and sensible. Occasionally, I would take the pencil away from my teeth and bounce it on the clipboard ever so gently. I would write, then reflect, talk to myself, hum, look at the photograph of James Joyce (he was of no help) that hangs near my desk, and perform the routine all over again.

Thursday afternoon at practice, I shared the strategy with the team. "There's no way," I told the players at the beginning of practice, "that we're going to beat Denison—absolutely none. This is an unimpeachable fact. Given this fact, what do we do?" This was a rhetorical question that I did not expect them to answer. None did. Most seemed uneasy with my brutally frank assessment.

Clutching the clipboard, I looked at the position changes that I had made earlier in the day, then looked up at the players. "We're going to practice today," I said, "in entirely new positions. The two wings—that's Angi and Barb—will have to play fullback along with the regular fullbacks. The regular halfbacks will play in their positions, and the rest of you will play between the halfbacks and the fullbacks. We will have no forwards. None whatsoever. In other words, the minute the game starts, all of you should immediately rush back and play defense. Do you have any questions up to this point?" I asked.

"So we'll never be in a position to score?" Jill, the captain, asked, and looked at the other players, who seemed just as bewildered by the strategy.

"That's right—unless a miracle happens and one of you should dribble down unmolested and take a clear shot at goal," I said.

"So we're conceding the game before it starts?" a player asked, surprised and disturbed a bit by the strategy.

"Yes and no. You see, a tie to us is as good as a win," I said. "Remember, this team is undefeated in NCAA Division III play; their two losses were administered by Division I teams. We may be able to tie them, keep the score at zero-zero, if all you experienced players play excellent defense and if our rapidly developing beginners help out with the defense as well. If all of you do as well in the game as you sometimes do in these practices, we'll hold our own. And if we tie them, I guarantee you we'll make the wire services."

Glancing at the players' faces, I sensed that they were uneasy with the strategy. Every coach, they probably reasoned to themselves, goes into a game intending to win. I added, "I know; I know just how strange it sounds for a coach to tell his players, 'Let's go out there and play for a tie,' but that's exactly what I'm telling you. The three writing majors on the team who know me best will probably say that's as quirky sounding as his prose or poems; they don't know anything about my scholarly output that is shackled by facts, figures, and footnotes. Whatever they say, I think this silly-sounding strategy of mine will work. Now, let's see," I said, staring pensively at the clipboard. "What's tomorrow—Friday? Right?"

"That's right, Coach; it's game day," Jill said. "That's the day we're going to put this strategy of yours to work." She smiled, and others joined her in smiling, and so did I. And they were happy, I think, to see me smile.

"Well, there should be a nice little article in tomorrow's paper about the Denison game and about our Wheeling win and the Slippery Rock fiasco. I gave the reporter who came to see me nice quotes, but whether those quotes will get in remains to be seen. Anyway, I've been talking up this game with my colleagues and I intend to continue to talk it up in my classes. With the *Cabinet* article and with all the talking that, I trust, you'll be doing with your friends, we're likely to have a great crowd out there, perhaps the biggest crowd in the history of women's soccer at Geneva."

"And men's, too," several players mumbled.

"Yea!" most of them shouted.

"Okay, before we break up," I said, "there's a word that I'm going to use, and I have been debating in my mind the wisdom in using it, but I think I'm going to introduce it as the cornerstone of our strategy for the Denison game. Now, again, I know this sounds weird, but then, I'm sure many of you will argue that this entire strategy is weird, too. Remember the early part of the season when I told you you'd never hear me give a 'Win One for the Gipper' speech? Well, I've kept my promise, for what you're hearing now is a 'Tie One for the Gipper' speech."

"I still can't believe we're hearing it, Coach," Angi said. "You're serious about all this?"

"Yes, I am," I said. "I really am. And this 'Tie One for the Gipper' idea is not original with me."

"I'd hate to meet its author," Angi said. She smiled and added, "It's too wacky an idea for a woman, so who's he?"

"Ara Parseghian," I said, "an old Notre Dame football coach."

"That figures," Angi said. "A dumb old football jock gets us again."

"You're right about the dumb part," I said, "because his tie embarrassed Notre Dame. Our tie—if we're lucky enough to get it—will embarrass Denison."

"It will?" two players asked doubtfully.

"Yes, it will," I said. I paused, scanned the players' faces, then added a doubt of my own: "Maybe."

"How did that Ara guy embarrass Notre Dame?" Angi asked.

"He did it on a cold November day in East Lansing, Michigan," I began to reminisce. "I saw it all on TV. The year was 1966. Michigan State and Notre Dame were undefeated and hotly in pursuit of the national championship. They played a tough game for fifty-nine minutes, and the score was ten to ten. For the last minute of the game, Notre Dame had the ball, and rather than pass and run and call time-outs and use the sidelines, they ran into the line and, in effect, ran out the clock. Parseghian said afterward that he was content to play for the tie. Rockne's famous speech called on the troops to go out there and 'win one for the Gipper,' but Parseghian somehow convinced the ghost of George Gipp to revise that deathbed wish from 'win one' to 'tie one' and ordered Our Lady's troops to settle for the tie. And if that strategy was good enough for Notre Dame then, it's good enough for us now."

"Case closed, Coach?" Angi asked.

"Pretty much," I said.

"But, Coach," Jill said, "you know what people always say about a tie, don't you?"

"No, I don't," I said.

"They say it's like kissing your sister," Jill said.

"Let's feminize that," Angi told Jill, "and say it's like kissing your brother. Okay?"

"Let's just say it's like kissing a family member, from grandparents all the way down to that useless family poodle," I said to Angi and Jill, "and let's get back to our strategy and the key word that's going to define that strategy and focus our game plan. It's a word that we often associate with Drano."

The players looked at each other; they seemed puzzled by my strategy or humor or lack of both. Even my choice of words and stars baffled them. One player said, "The Gipper and Drano. Is that right, Coach?"

"Yes, Drano," I said.

"Drano is the key word that sums up our game plan?" another player asked.

"No, no," I replied, hugging my clipboard as if it were my daughter's teddy bear, "that's what we associate the key word with."

"What *is* it? What's the word?" Amy snapped at me with her husky voice.

"What do we associate with Drano?" another thought out loud.

"TV commercials," someone said.

"Cleaning," a second added.

"No, no," I replied, then asked, "Are you ready for this?"

"Sure are," several players said at once.

"Okay, the key word is *clog*." I spelled it a couple of times as if I were in the National Spelling Bee.

"Clog?" one player inquired, disbelief written all over her face. "Clog? Clog, Coach?" she repeated.

"Yes, clog," I said. "We've got to clog up the middle of the field and especially the area near our goal. We've got to do it with our bodies and our feet and our legs, and we've got to do it so nothing gets through. A Denison shooter will have to shoot the ball through so many legs that it will be impossible for it to go through the goal without someone stopping it. You know how every fan is a coach," I said, referring to one of the most irritating but instantly recognizable characteristics of the modern sports fan in the United States. "Well, in our situation, that condition holds true, but it also informs and illuminates another condition for us, and that is, every player is a goalie, but, of course, no one except Amy will have hands privileges."

"Boy, this sounds unusual," I heard one player say.

"There are ordinary ways to play this game, and there are *extra*ordinary ways; this definitely is on the *extra* side," Jill added.

"That's a charitable way of putting it," Angi said.

"Any other thoughtful comments?" I asked. No one responded, so I continued. "Of course, I realize that with so many people in the area of the goal, we might get serious penalty shots and lots of dangerous corner kicks that even a head shot could convert into a goal, but those are the chances and dangers that we'll have to take and live with throughout the match, or at least its early parts." I broke up the prepractice strategy pep talk by saying, "Let's have a nice practice today; and tomorrow, let's do all we can to tie one for the Gipper."

It was a light practice, calculated at getting the players adjusted to their new positions and to the strategy of playing defense and more defense. We practiced long kicks and punts that would at least force Denison to start their assault from midfield as often as possible and keep their defense near or back of the midfield stripe. We practiced defending against corner kicks, and Amy practiced a few punts—booming several high ones that reached the midfield stripe—that would have popped a smile on the face of Geneva's head football coach.

At three o'clock on Friday afternoon, problems began, and they came from unexpected places. The men's soccer team had a scheduled practice that conflicted with our scheduled game on "their" field at four. Normally, the men's practice went beyond four, and the players at practice that day wanted to use their field even on the day of our game. Not being a pushy person, I refused to force the issue to a crisis. I explained our problem to the gentle and considerate Denison coach, apologizing for the situation and asking her if she would kindly consider having her team warm up on the periphery of the men's field, being extra careful not to interfere with the men's practice. Then I told our players to go to the lot of the Campbell Memorial Presbyterian Church, located across the street from the field, and warm up there. "Maybe at four," I told our players, "the men's team will get the hint and leave, permitting us to play our scheduled game as scheduled. If they don't, I'll see about doing something else that'll get us on some field to play this game."

"Coach, if I were you," Angi said as the team members gathered around me, "I'd go to the athletic director and *demand* our rights to the field, rights granted to us by the published and widely circulated schedule."

"That's right," Jill added.

"Yeah," several players said at once.

"We'll see," I said, "but for now let's practice at the Presbyterian church lot." Then I turned to Jill and told her, "Please take them there now." She did.

When the officials assigned to the game arrived at about three-thirty, I gave them their checks, explained the situation, and told them, "We hope to get the field at four, as our schedule indicates. If not, we might have to do something drastic in order to get our show on the field." (I started to say "show on the road," but Sharon, the cliché-conscious writing major, was heading toward us; seeing her led me, subconsciously perhaps, to freshen the cliché by rewording it slightly.)

Fortunately, the men's team left exactly at four. Much to our players' displeasure, I thanked the players for leaving the field and abbreviating their practice. "I hope next year," I told them, "our own field will be ready for varsity play. We still need nets for our goals; otherwise, the field and goals are in excellent shape now, thanks to the hard work of our maintenance department."

As it turned out, the timing of the men's practice increased our attendance. I overheard one male player telling another, "I can't believe all the people who come to these games."

"I can't either," came the response.

"Imagine if these girls start winning," the first person said.

"Their crowd will probably go down; most people are probably here because this is still a new thing on campus. Don't you think?" came the reply.

"Maybe, but this is a good, *good* crowd," the first person stated again. "I wish we got half of this number at our games."

Most of the men's team players and managers stayed to watch our game, yelling encouragement and advice to our players, sneering and jeering and offering their jockish critiques of our peculiar alignment. At the twenty-minute mark, the game remained scoreless. "I can't believe this," I overheard a fan say.

"Neither can I," another added.

"We're holding all these All-Americans scoreless!" another exclaimed.

"They're doing a great job," my trainer-wife-nurse, who paced the sidelines, reminded me several times during the first period. "I can't believe Angi and Barb at fullbacks, the wings at fullbacks, but it's working so far."

"We're clogging up the middle with a veritable forest of legs and bodies," I said, somewhat triumphantly.

"You sure are," she replied.

"Look. Look at this," I said as Amy boomed a long, high punt that bounced beyond the midfield stripe into Denison territory. "That's part of our strategy, you know, to make Denison work the ball down from the midfield stripe as often as possible."

When Amy wasn't booting those long punts, our fullbacks and all the other people playing in the fullback zones were doing so, for they had been instructed by me not to pass the ball but to kick it as hard as they could toward—and if possible beyond—the midfield stripe. True to form, our players carried out the orders, and Denison, a hardworking and determined team, continued their assault on us, passing and dribbling, again and again, then shooting at bodies, heads, knees, thighs, legs, feet—all jammed in front of, near, and on the sides of our goal.

I told my wife, who stood next to me on the sidelines, "I wish Amy would take her time before punting that ball; that would give a lot of our players a bit of rest, and it would kill more seconds off that clock. So far, we're still very much in this game."

"That we are," she agreed.

Our children were playing with a soccer ball behind our bench. I called Rita and told her to run behind our goal and tell Amy, "Daddy wants you to take your time in punting that ball."

Occasionally during the first period, the ball crossed the midfield stripe into Denison territory, and some of our beginning players tried to advance it further, only to have it taken away from them with ease. Almost all the action was on our side of the field.

Moments before the first period ended, Denison managed to force a goal between the tight cracks created by all those legs and bodies and heads in motion. Nuts, nuts! I yelled silently. I tightened the grip on my clenched right fist and pounded it into the palm of my left hand, pumping out an "Oh, nuts, that hurts." Then I encouraged the players as I clapped, nervous, insincere, isolated claps that paced my words: "Okay, let's continue to play good defense. You're doing a great job out there."

At halftime, with the score Denison, one, and Geneva, zero, and with a huge crowd—over ninety people, perhaps— witnessing the affair, I asked our players to head to the side of the field near our goal. Denison went to the other end of the field. We met as a team to rest, get refreshed, and explore our second-half strategy. Before I could say a word, and just as my children began to supply our players with water, ice, and oranges, Jill told me, "Coach, we can score against this team. We can get back into this game, but we need to get Barb and Angi on the wings and the rest of us in our usual positions."

"So what you're saying is that you really want to get back to a more conventional game, right?" I asked.

"Right," Jill said. I saw the nodding heads and pleading eyes of our exhausted players, who were sitting on the grass, sipping water and ice.

"Okay, let me think about that for a minute," I said. After a long moment of silence, I asked, "Do Jill's comments represent most of your feelings?"

"Sure do," came a reply.

"Coach, the tie is gone now," one player said.

"And if we're going to play for that 'Tie One for the Gipper' idea of yours," Sharon reasoned, "then we have to go out and earn it; we no longer have the luxury to fight to preserve it."

"That's reasonable enough," I said, "and what can I do but agree with you people?"

"So, what do we do, Coach?" Jill asked.

"Let's start the second period with the same lineup that started the Slippery Rock game." I named that lineup and positions and wished the team the best.

When the halftime period ended, I walked alone with Amy and warned her to expect a lot more shots and to take her time in releasing or punting the ball. "By the way," I asked Amy, "were you shocked when Rita relayed that message to you in the first half?"

"Not so much shocked but surprised," Amy said. "Why didn't you yell it to me, Coach?" she asked.

"Simple. I didn't want the officials or the Denison players or coaches to hear that comment. It's not exactly what you'd call kosher coaching, is it?"

"That's right," she said, and trotted to her position on the field.

Once the second period started and I took my place on the sidelines, my wife came by and I told her what the players had wanted to see done and that I had agreed to it. "Our players think they can score on this Denison team," I said. "There's no way. This is one of the best small-college teams in America. The reason the ball crossed the midfield stripe on occasions in the first half is because most of our strong players were playing defense, but now with our mix of experienced and inexperienced players spread all over the field, I envision us playing a much weaker second half. But I hope—oh, I hope—I'm wrong."

As the second half unfolded, I discovered that, unfortunately, I was right. The quick and skillful Denison team scored two goals early in the period, and then they flashed their depth by scoring two more goals with their substitutes.

The Denison coach was an extremely charitable woman. When I congratulated her on their victory and apologized once again for the conditions of the pregame warm-ups, she responded, "This merely illustrates the kind of sexist battles that we have to fight in women's sports." Then she complimented our team, singling out several players for special words of praise. She was particularly impressed by the agility and strength of Barb, our left-footed, left wing, left fullback. "Hope to see you next year," she said as we parted ways, "and I'm sure you'll continue to improve."

After giving a brief "good effort" talk to the players, I helped my children and wife load up the soccer gear into our van. Angi helped also. "Coach," she said as we held open the bag and the children gathered the balls and dumped them in, "I can't believe you kept your cool in dealing with that men's team. I know you're laid-back and all, but your patience was incredible. All our players absolutely hated your 'kill them with kindness' routine."

"Certainly their stubbornness wasn't easy for me," I said.

"And not for us either," Angi said. "We were furious at you, sending us to warm up in that church lot." After a pause, she added, "But that might be why we did so well in that first period. What a way to get us pumped up for a game!"

"I'll apologize again to the team come Monday," I said. "I really feel bad about what happened. Maybe I should've reminded the men's team to consult the schedule."

"One angry player said as we warmed up, 'That Hanna is an English prof, and I suppose he can write, and he better write a stiff memo to the president explaining all that happened.' And if I were you, Coach," Angi continued, "I'd send a copy of the memo to the two athletic directors around here."

"Oh, what happened is just a sad misunderstanding," I said.

"But it's deeper than that, Coach," Angi said.

"I suppose the behavior of some players suggests an insecurity on their part," I said.

"A colossal insecurity," Angi added.

"I suppose they feel threatened by the birth of yet another women's sport at Geneva," I said. "After all, our program would compete with theirs for money, fields, scholarships, fan attention, and even space in the student newspaper and yearbook."

"That could well be," Angi said, "but I'd still write the president if I were you."

"Better yet," I said, "I'll go in and see him. He's a great supporter of women's athletics, you know, and I'll probably meet with him at length, not to complain but to make as strong a case as possible for scholarships, for locker room facilities, and for hiring a female coach to replace me. I want to exact from the president a strong commitment to the program, and I'm confident we'll get one."

"That'll be fine if you do," Angi said.

"The president is an old Kansas man," I said, "and as you know, our family has roots in Kansas. When I coached football in Kansas, he officiated football games there. We often reminisce about our days in Kansas. I know he's most—and I mean most—supportive of our soccer program. He comes to our games, you know, but he was out of town today; otherwise, he would have been here, I suspect."

"I know he comes to our games," Angi said, "and that's why writing him or seeing him is so crucial." She smiled as she added, "In sports, when you get a sucker, you lick him to the bone. Just ask any sports person who deals with wealthy alumni."

The kids put the last ball, which they had retrieved from the far end of the field, and several shin guards into the bag, Angi tied it, and I carried it to the van. We boarded the van, and I drove Angi to her dorm and then took my family to the home of Ed and Pearl Bowman, a delightful older couple who had befriended us when we were their neighbors and with whom we remained close friends even after we moved away. The Bowmans were athletic fans from the days when their son, Bruce, played quarterback at Beaver Falls High School just before Joe Namath came on the scene, and they followed our soccer program with great interest. "Let's go and eat now," my wife told Ed and Pearl shortly after we barged into their house on College Avenue. "We'll tell you all about the Denison game at the Pasta Mill in New Brighton."

After dinner and on the drive home, and even later that evening while watching a nature program on PBS, I thought about our soccer season: from that first practice in late August to the first home game against Houghton to the first road trip to Oberlin to the Wheeling, Slippery Rock, and Denison games. I also thought about our remaining games and especially the final game at Wheeling Jesuit College in West Virginia.

Throughout the season, all our players had worked hard. They had improved and developed, though some had improved more than others. One beginner who had worked hard at acquiring and cultivating her soccer skills was Wendy Pillsbury, an eighteen-year-old freshman from Scarborough, Maine. Wendy, slightly taller than five feet, with brownish-blond hair that fell to her shoulders, had rich blue eyes that observed and calculated, guiding her concentration and movement. Wendy's athletic stamina, nurtured by her participation in track, was reflected on the soccer field. She was wiry, agile, shifty, and determined. Beyond her athletic skills, Wendy had a first-rate mind. In my

English composition class, she did outstanding work; her papers and examinations had a uniformly excellent quality. I had invited Wendy to consider English as a major, but she had opted for mathematics, and I had every reason to believe that she would perform brilliantly in that discipline.

Wendy learned to play different positions on the soccer field. She excelled at right halfback, a position that had her on some occasions moving forward to back up the offense and on other occasions going back to help with the defense. Her kicks, though not as strong as, say, Amy's, Angi's, or Jill's, were often firmly asserted and well placed. Unlike most beginners—who after making a decent kick would stand in place to enjoy the act a bit—Wendy would make a good pass, move, and be in a position to receive a pass in order to make another good pass. Clearly, such "soccer sense" on her part showed me that she was a gifted beginner who was likely to develop rapidly and blend in nicely with an experienced squad in the years ahead.

During our last game of the season, Wendy's performance pleased me, but mine disappointed her. The Wheeling Cardinals, the new soccer team that we had beaten on our home field, had continued to improve and develop. That much I had gathered from watching their pregame practice. Either these players, I told myself during the warm-up session, have improved tremendously or some failed to make the trip to Beaver Falls a few weeks ago. I learned later that both suppositions were true. Both of them applied to us as well. For the first Wheeling game, Angi, one of our best players, and two beginners had gone to Canada to attend a Shakespeare festival. All three—along with a squad that had improved in a few weeks' time—made the trip to Wheeling.

At four o'clock on a sunny afternoon in autumn, the game began. For most of the first period, both teams played exceedingly fine defense, with few shots at goal. Wheeling would mount a drive, only to see it sputter near our goal area, where our players would start a drive of their own, only to see it falter near Wheeling's goal. Moments before the period ended, Wheeling's right wing penetrated our defense with the ball, cut to her left, sold our goalie on a shot in that direction, then suddenly twisted her body and slammed a low, hard shot in the opposite direction—scoring the first and only goal of the first forty-five-minute period.

At halftime, I told myself before I spoke to the team: You've got to make a "Win One for the Gipper" speech to get these athletes up for the second period. I wondered if it would be wise to tell our players that the Wheeling game was going to be—in all probability—my last game as their coach. I had hinted this much to Angi while we washed and dried dishes following, of all times, our first win over Wheeling. In the end, I decided to leave my future plans out of the halftime speech. And the thought occurred to me that whatever we did at Wheeling was none of George Gipp's business. So I kept him out of the speech, too.

"Okay," I told the players at halftime, "what we've got here is *not* an insurmountable one-to-nothing lead. We can overcome it, and we can indeed take the lead." I encouraged them to continue to play hard. I named all the players by position and offered warm and positive remarks about their play, and since I had integrated the three nonstarters into the first half, I said nice things about them as well. I felt as if I were giving the squad my farewell remarks and doing it not in the traditional setting at a banquet in their honor but on a road trip in Wheeling, West Virginia. They were not sitting on comfortable chairs with several dinner plates in front of them, and I was not standing behind a podium overlooking their blunders and cataloging their positive achievements. Rather, they sat or sprawled on the lush green grass in or near the soccer goal that we had defended during the first half. They listened, sipped water, munched on ice; they were perhaps too exhausted to ask questions.

Barb, who had scored three goals in the Wheeling game at our home field, had seen three players collapse on her every time she touched or went near the ball. That certainly was a very good coaching move on Wheeling's part. It left Angi and another player wide open most of the time, but Angi failed to take charge and score. I glanced at Barb's face and she appeared frustrated and downright angry. "Look," I told the players as I concluded my halftime remarks, "we've got forty-five minutes to go. We'll start the same unit that started the game, and I'll make appropriate substitutions as we go along. With all of you playing hard, we can certainly hold them and score. Don't you think?" I said with a smile.

"Yea!" they shouted in a staggered unison that made our meeting appear as if it were a Baptist gathering in the South or the House of Lords in England.

"Okay, let's go to it," I said as they sprang to their feet and trotted to their positions on the field.

Wendy joined all of our experienced players and several of our beginners and started the second half. Indeed, she had started all the halves throughout the season. Seldom did I send in substitutes for her. She was developing so rapidly, I considered her in the same category as a player with light experience or even in a higher category. After ten minutes had elapsed, Wheeling still held on to a one-to-nothing lead. Angi, playing at right wing, had missed taking what appeared from my vantage point to be a couple of attractive shots at goal. I pulled her out of the game. Moments after I did that, Jill scored from her position as center forward, thanks in part to a beautifully timed pass from Wendy, who was playing at the right halfback spot.

After that goal, I put Angi back in and pulled Wendy out. The goal seemed to give us some confidence and momentum, for most of the action during the next thirty minutes or so remained in Wheeling's side of the field. While this action was going on, Wendy and two beginners stood next to me on the sidelines. The game was tight; it was the last half of the match, the waning minutes of the entire season. Wendy, speaking mostly for herself (though she included the two beginners in her rhetoric if not sentiment), said, "Please, Coach, please, please put us in." At first I said nothing. I took two steps to my right. Wendy followed me and said, "Please, please, Coach, we promise we won't make mistakes. Please." I looked at her and said, "Wendy, you know it's not a matter of making mistakes; it's just that this combination that's in there now is doing a fine job; besides, I'd like to see a couple of the players in there now experience the thrill of being in a close, highly competitive match. You—and by you, I mean all three of you—did a tremendous job in the first half and the early part of this half." I took two steps to my left, and they followed me; two steps to my right, and they followed. Wendy kept pleading their—her—case. I refused to risk a change. One third of me said: Be fair to all the players; give all of them a respectable amount of playing time. Another third of me said: These players on the sidelines are clearly better than three other players on the field now, and in order to win this game, it might be wise to follow Wendy's uncommon pleading and make the change. The final third of me said, "If it ain't broke, fix it" is a questionable philosophy in life, mechanical objects, and coaching. Or is it? Wendy's persistent pleading bewildered me. What—oh, what—should I do? I asked myself as the game progressed.

With less than two minutes remaining in the game and with Wendy still hoping to get in, Angi dribbled the ball, dodged a tired body here and an exhausted body there (eighty-eight minutes of soccer had sapped the energies of both teams), then she dribbled in traffic, penetrated past two defenders and coasted a soft, low shot that kissed the net. The Wheeling goalie had come out of the goal and tried to scoop the ball as Angi was trying to clear herself past the defenders. Angi's quickness made all the difference that day.

Following our celebration, the last minute and a half needed to be played. I looked at Wendy and the other two players, Sheryl and Andrea, and sent them into the game. Time ran out with the ball near the center of the field and the final score Geneva, two, Wheeling, one.

Our players mingled with the Wheeling players and the fans. I thanked the parents of several of our players who had come to see us play on the road, and I also thanked the Wheeling coaching staff for a splendid match and for their warm hospitality.

As I drove the van in search of a restaurant in Wheeling, West Virginia, Wendy's pleading reverberated in my mind, leading my thoughts to land on all sorts of topics. I thought of those basketball minute men, the players who usually get in for the last minute of a game if the game is out of reach, that is, impossible to win or lose in the last minute or so. I thought of how my friends, colleagues, kids, and I would sit in the bleachers, occasionally glance at the minute men, and poke fun at their sitting and leaning techniques. We would often lampoon them by saying, "Now left, now right, now toilet position." Wendy's pleading focused in my mind those players' plight, leading me to realize how cruel and crass it was for us to make light of their situation.

Wendy's pleading also led me to realize how urgently the players wanted to participate in a game, especially a close, competitive, meaningful game, and not a meaningless blowout. Participating in a close game, I thought, offered the athletes a certain high, a spectacular feeling, a climax to all the hard work of practice. In so doing, participation might well be seen as a passion, a yearning, a lust, a surge, a drive—a drive that on game day at least could be compared to the sex drive.

As I continued steering the van in search of a restaurant, my old buddy Dick Klugh drifted into my mind. I remembered Dick's son, Curtis, who used to play Little League baseball near the Dragon House of the West Mayfield Borough in Beaver Falls. During his first year, Curtis did an outstanding job in hitting and playing second base; in his second year, however, Curtis was shifted to right field by a new coach. Curtis did an excellent job in playing right field, but Dick desperately wanted his son to move to the Little League's prestigious haven: the infield. To Dick (more than to Curtis) right field seemed to be a stigma, even though I often reminded him that Henry Aaron, Darrell Strawberry, Babe Ruth, and Ted Williams all played right field. "But *not* in Little League," Dick would fire back and burst into anger-laced laughter. (One of my sons, a good friend of Curtis's, practiced his leaning techniques on the bench and seldom started a ball game, and when he did, he played right field.) Curtis was an exceptional hitter, and the coach played him regularly because he needed his "strong bat in there," as he would often tell Dick. Aware of his son's strong bat, Dick would plead and plead (and with good humor, to be sure) his son's case with the coach, much as Wendy pleaded her case with me.

While driving Wheeling's crowded streets, I also thought about the football players I had coached in Kansas and all those football players that I had seen at other small colleges, and I remembered that a vast majority of our players had never participated in a close game in college. Many of those players were recruited to play, only to end up standing around, waiting their turn that they knew might never come. Many small liberal arts colleges that are in pursuit of students constantly use their athletic programs to recruit athletes as students, and I thought about how easy it was for small colleges to recruit those high school stars that the major universities had ignored.

My thoughts continued. When the major universities pass up the once mighty high school stars as "too small or slow" to play major college football, basketball, or baseball, a crisis usually develops in the stars' families. Sandy and Terri and Jamie—once the big stars at the local high school program—are suddenly nobodies in the eyes of their friends and neighbors because of the disinterest of recruiters from the major universities.

Just as suddenly, things change when the small-college coach confidently claims, "Jamie could not only play for us, but we'd be happy to give him an athletic scholarship or some form of aid." (The NAIA and the NCAA Division III are the two major associations that govern small-college sports in the United States. The NAIA member colleges do offer athletic scholarships, and the NCAA schools do not grant athletic scholarships as such, but certain schools often create package deals that can land a targeted student-athlete at a given college.) The high school campus heroes that the large universities had trimmed to size by ignoring them become, once again, heroes in the eyes of their neighbors, friends, and parents. When Myrtle talks to Gloria across the backyard fence about her son or daughter, she can honestly claim, "Sandy was recruited by Saint Mary's of the Plains in Dodge City, Kansas." To be sure, Saint Mary's is no Notre Dame, but Sandy will get to play college football or softball just the same. Similarly, Ginger could tell Harriet, "Terri has a basketball scholarship from Houghton College. That's a small college in upstate New York, you know." She would never mention that Houghton's biggest star might be tall enough to play forward in Japan, where the folks—like haiku—are brief.

As my thoughts landed on Japan and Japanese athletes, the image of a sumo wrestler hit me, alerting me to see how a sumo wrestler's belly in the context of his body resembles the rising sun and the earth. Is there a haiku in that? Is the sumo wrestler the mascot of the land of the rising sun? Or is he an ambassador for Weight Watchers International? The creative-writing-teacher side of me thought as the soccer-team-coaching side of me continued to drive the van loaded with happy, hungry, exhausted, chatty players, made chattier by their splendid performance in the soccer match.

Small athletes, I told myself, will play at small colleges, but even there, many end up sitting on the basketball bench or standing on the football sidelines with little participation, save during practice. Not only does this lack of participation characterize the men's programs at most large universities and small colleges, but it also appears to be penetrating the women's programs at both levels. If that's the case, that's sad, very sad indeed. If I should not come back to coach next year, I wondered, would my successor harbor the same "participation-adventure" philosophy that I had tried to cultivate, or would she (or he) be the "win-at-all-costs" type of coach?

Are women's sports (which were once coached mostly by women and governed by a healthy participation philosophy under the direction of the now defunct Association for Intercollegiate Athletics for Women) being hijacked by television contracts and the male-dominated NCAA? As women's sports continue to become more popular and lucrative and as males continue to enter the women's coaching ranks, will the Partial Participation Rip-off Model (with all its attendant pursuits and macho metaphors such as "a gun for an arm," "floor general," "mauled down the enemy," "killer instinct," "put them away early") begin to dominate women's sports? If so, is that a healthy thing? Do teams have to see each other as enemies who must do battle? Are there other models? Is the Full Participation Relay Model, with its maximum-participation principle, really workable? Can the word *play*, with all its attendant pursuits and metaphors, be brought back into sports, and can women's sports contribute to its reappearance? Can one really preach and teach competition without positing winning as the goal? Did Wheeling, in losing to us by a score of two to one, feel as much a winner as we did, given that theirs was also a first-year program and their athletes played an impressive and challenging match?

Just as I drove the van into the parking lot of a Burger King, I thought: When the Geneva College yearbook, the *Genevan*, records our season for posterity, it will record three in the win column and six in the defeat. By conventional analysis, this represents a losing season. But were we losers? Each of our players would have to answer that for herself. I suspected their evaluations of their development in the sport and their assessments of the program's failures and achievements might differ, and differ vastly.

Our players entered the Burger King feeling special and happy. They smiled even as they stood in a long line to order their food. I felt proud of their achievements on the soccer field in Wheeling. I had sensed that pride during the ride from the field to the restaurant, but I had also sensed something leavening that pride, transforming it into pomposity. At the restaurant, I strutted to the front of the line, pointed to the women behind me, and told the waitress, "All these people are with me. Please add their orders together, and I'll take care of the bill."

Angi and Amy were the last ones in line. After they ordered their food, the waitress began to add the bill. "But wait a minute, please," I told the waitress. "I need to place my order."

"At this Burger King, sir," she said, "all bus drivers eat free."

Angi and Amy laughed and laughed. The baffled waitress looked at them and asked, "What's the matter?"

I said nothing, but Amy slapped me on the shoulder and told the waitress in her Texas drawl, "This happy dude is our head coach. We're a soccer team from Geneva."

"You mean you're from Europe?" the waitress said.

"No, no," I said. "That's the Geneva of cuckoo clock fame; we're from Geneva College in Beaver Falls, Pennsylvania."

Beyond Winning

"And he's Dr. S. S. Hanna," Amy spoke slowly, rhythmically pacing her pronunciation of my name. She paused, then added, "He's our skipper, our head soccer coach, and an English professor."

"And bus driver, too," Angi added, laughing.

"Sorry, sir," the waitress told me. "Please forgive me, sir."

Her sir-sir redundancy reminded me of a true southerner or a service academy cadet and led me to say, "No need to be sorry."

"But I *am* sorry, sir," the waitress said, and left the cash register momentarily.

"You shook up that waitress, Coach," Amy said, "and since your meal is free, get me a chocolate milk shake, please."

"And I'll take a large fry on your order, too, Mr. Bus Driver," Angi said, stretching and accentuating her pronunciation of my new status just as the waitress returned to the cash register. Angi, Amy, and I smiled, and that seemed to relax the waitress. I added the two requested items to my order and paid the bill for the entire team.

"Look at it this way," Angi said, as the three of us carried our food and headed to a booth, "your new downward status, Coach, got us a large fry and a shake for free."

We laughed and then relived the high, the low, and the tense moments of the game during dinner. Amy and Angi noted the performance of Sara Smith, a five-foot, six-inch, 130-pound promising beginner who had developed as the season progressed.

Near the end of the season, Sara, one of our regular fullbacks, had expressed interest in becoming the team's backup goalie. I asked her to stay after practice for a few sessions, and I worked with her on her movement, posture, and concentration. From different places on the field, I kicked numerous balls at the goal, and Sara defended it. We worked on the fundamentals of positioning herself in the goal, catching the ball, diving after balls, jumping and punching balls away, narrowing the shooting angle, throwing or rolling a ball to a teammate, and punting and more punting. Sara, an intelligent and hardworking athlete, seemed to enjoy the tense, grueling, courage-quickening tasks of the goalie.

She played goalie in practice for a few sessions, and after that, she felt she was ready to start a varsity game.

Amy, our regular goalie, Jill, our team captain, Angi, our "beatnik-player-without-portfolio," as my wife affectionately dubbed her, and I met and discussed Sara's progress. We agreed that she was ready to assume the role of goalie, and she received the assignment for the final game of the season. Throughout that game, Amy had played just ahead of Sara at middle full-back. She constantly talked to Sara, encouraging her— especially after Wheeling Jesuit took a one-to-zero lead in the first period—and coaching her as the need arose. Sara respond-ed to the game's challenge and made the crucial saves that ulti-mately led to our victory. Sara and Amy illustrated the concept of teamwork that day.

"You're praising Sara now," I told Amy and Angi as we con-tinued to eat, "and what a far cry that is from the day my wife taped ankles in our living room on College Hill. You tore after our beginners then. It's so nice to see Sara do such a good job this afternoon."

"Sure is," Amy said. "The minute the game ended, I went and hugged her."

"I did, too," Angi said, "and she was beaming from ear to ear."

I looked at Sara, sitting with several happy players in a booth near a window, and said, "She still is."

"You are too, Coach," Angi observed.

"And Wendy did a good job today," Amy said.

"They'd both be good players on next year's team," Angi said. "Players do improve, I guess."

"They do," I said, "and if they work at it in the spring and summer months, both should continue to develop. Sports are like writing: you learn the craft and get better at it by doing. You've got to do, do, do."

"It should be a fun ride home, Coach," Amy said. "Expect a lot of singing and joke telling and ripping at teachers and all."

Sure enough, moments after we left Burger King and I drove the van out of the Wheeling city limits, the singing began. And as on previous trips, the singing would either harmonize with or drown popular songs recorded on tapes that Angi would pop into the van's tape deck. When the players would tire of the tapes, they would ask Angi to turn on the radio, and she would.

Throughout the trip home, the players teased each other and, as Amy had predicted, "ripped at"—not viciously but in good fun—several of their male professors, criticizing their teaching styles (one fellow received the award for "excellence in incompetence") or their manner of dress (another was singled out for coming to class "dressed to live"). When I asked what they meant by that expression, a player replied, "It's Goodwill-type clothes, Coach. It's a takeoff on 'dressed to kill.'" The award that caused an explosion of laughter in the van was the "uncoveted IC award."

"You know what that is, Coach?" Angi asked.

"Nope."

"It's an in joke that kids in my dorm use."

"Does it stand for Iron City beer?" I asked.

"Yes and no," she said. "In mixed company, it's the Iron City beer award, given to that rare professor so intoxicated by learning that he sounds mixed up or incoherent."

"I suppose," I said somewhat defensively, "Iron City could also stand for tough and demanding professors." I offered that comment knowing full well that Geneva had a lot of those professors: tough, smart, demanding, and exemplary.

"You may suppose that, Coach," Angi said, "but with Lori, Amy, me, and other women, the IC stands for something else: something less fluid than beer, if you will." A long pause followed her remarks. I expected Angi to unfurl that "something else," and she did it in her own Angiesque manner when she said: "It stands for intellectually unable to go to the bathroom." She smiled, and then slowly and clearly enunciated: "The defined 'c' word rhymes with *emancipated*."

"Oh," I said, laughing. I shook my head and thought: Students can be clever and wickedly funny. Then I told Angi, "These award-happy players must be getting even for low grades or heavy assignments or—"

"Or something," Angi said. She looked at me and continued, "When the professor is the bus driver, he becomes rip-proof, you might say." She paused, then added, "At least rip-proof while driving."

"Oh, I don't know about that," I said. "That 'dressed to live' label and certainly that IC award apply to me, but they're being kind in leaving me out. Let's face it: my teaching in the minds of many students probably makes a great case for home schooling at the college level."

"Listen to this," Angi said, as a couple of players gave an administrator the "tall, dark, and handsome" award.

"Not only is that guy good looking," Angi said, "but he's also a nice guy to boot."

"If that guy gets the 'tall, dark, and handsome' award," I told Angi, "I wonder who'd get the 'short, fat, and fair' one?"

"I've got a few candidates—"

"Leave them to yourself, Angi; that's just a rhetorical question," I said, fully aware that one of those candidates was sitting to her left.

While the athletes sang and joked, teased each other, and mocked their professors, the following thought stroked my mind: We won our last game, and that was fun. And all season we lost not as many games as we won but *twice* as many. But I daresay we weren't losers, not to my way of thinking, at least.

A week after the last game, I sent all the players a letter, thanking them for their hard work and cooperation throughout the season and informing them that their names would be turned in to the women's athletic director with the recommendation that they be awarded varsity letters for soccer. The other letter—a potentially painful one—that I considered writing needed more thought and consultation.

One evening after dinner, I asked my wife and children if they would like me to continue coaching. All the children wanted me to stay with the program, and they wanted to accompany the team on future road trips—"like Sam did to Oberlin," three of them said at once. My wife and I noted that the time involved in practice, in the home and away games, and in recruiting was far too demanding, given my exceedingly high—but normal for Geneva and similar colleges—class load of fifteen hours a semester, plus committee work, research pursuits, advising, and other related activities. "If the administration would slash your class load in half," she reasoned, and I agreed with her, "then coaching soccer would seem to be attractive." She reminded me that when I had applied for baseball coaching jobs, "You did it with the understanding that it would be half-time baseball coach and the other half English teacher. Now, with your fifteen-hour class load, you're a full-time English teacher and a full-time soccer coach, manager, water boy, van driver, cone carrier, recruiter, and what have you. And then there is—and I think this should be a crucial factor in your decision—that point we talked about a while back, that women's sports teams should be coached by women at the college level. I really agree with and applaud the argument you made after that Oberlin game."

Of course, I respected my wife's sentiment, and even though I enjoyed soccer and had learned a great deal from coaching it, I decided to write a resignation letter to the vice president in charge of athletics, the same person who had sent me my formal appointment letter. Before writing the letter, I visited at length with the vice president and explained to him in detail the factors (too much time and the urgency to have a woman coach for the program) that had led to my decision. I typed the letter and held on to it for seven days before I finally mailed it. The entire letter stated:

> Dear Mr. O'Data:
> This is to confirm our conversation of several days ago regarding my wish to resign from my soccer duties for next year. As I mentioned, the time that coaching requires and my belief that the program will be better served by a woman coach are the main factors in my decision.
> I might add that I had enjoyed the soccer coaching experience, and being an English teacher and a practicing writer, I'm sure it will find a happy place in my prose.

Please feel free to call on me in recruiting for next year's team or in any other way in which I might be of service to Geneva.

Permit me please to note that Ms. Gall, Geneva's Women's Athletic Director, provided me a great deal of help throughout the season. Often I turned to her for help and guidance, and she always responded in a cheerful and professional way.

Thank you, again, for asking me to coach, and please be assured that I remain fully supportive of your work and the program.

Cordially,
S. S. Hanna

When I had accepted the head coaching job in soccer at Geneva, I knew little about coaching the sport, though I was able to play the game in an acceptable manner that I knew would elicit the respect of my players, especially when I was demonstrating various techniques and tricks of the game. Given the character of our team, I was both a teacher and a coach. More importantly, perhaps, I was also a "learner." Coaching women's soccer at Geneva taught me all sorts of lessons from all sorts of domains.

Unlike many other colleges, Geneva does not have an all-sports banquet honoring all the college's athletes, females and males. I thought—and I suggested this to the vice president in charge of athletics—that it might be wise to inject each sport's budget with a little extra cash to be used for a postseason banquet. Each sport could have its own banquet at a local restaurant or join with other sports for mini-banquets, or all the sports could join for one colossal banquet to be held at the end of the year in the college's cafeteria.

Occasionally, I sit in my office and imagine myself responding to an invitation from the members of the Downtown Athletic Club of New York, an invitation to be the keynote speaker at the grandest and most prestigious banquet of them all: the Heisman Memorial Trophy Award Dinner. At the dinner, I see myself talking about the lessons I had learned from my experiences as the first scholar-coach of the varsity program in women's soccer at

Geneva. And since it is a football banquet, I see myself quoting and framing the speech on some little-known advice from a well-known football coach: Knute Rockne. "Make your classes," Rockne once told some Notre Dame professors who had complained of apathetic students, "as interesting as football." I have taken Rockne's advice to the classroom and failed at it in the minds of most Geneva students; I'd certainly try to bring it to the Heisman Trophy address and attempt to do a little better.

I even see our athletes sponsoring all sorts of fund-raising projects in order to collect enough money to fly to New York, to be watered and dined (good athletes are teetotalers, you see) at the Heisman the night of the banquet. Of course, I would prefer it if Geneva paid our athletes' way to New York and back, but with our modest faculty salaries and with the fact that we're a women's team and not a male football team, the chances of the college underwriting our expenses, even to such a prestigious event, would be low, very low indeed.

But I could not envision myself going to New York, New York, without our women athletes. After all, whatever I envision myself saying at the Heisman Memorial Trophy Award Dinner will inevitably tap their adventures and mine at Geneva.

8

The Heisman, the Moments, and T. S. Eliot

"And without further ado, it's my pleasure, as president of the Downtown Athletic Club, to present to you our speaker for the evening, the varsity coach of the women's soccer program at Geneva College, Dr. S. S. Hanna."

Good evening, ladies and gentlemen:

Thank you so much for that wonderful introduction. At first I was afraid that I was going to be introduced as that obscure small-college coach who is as unknown as Vanna White is known.

Seriously, it's not often when a small-college coach from a dreary mill town in western Pennsylvania is asked to address this distinguished body that is assembled here tonight to honor the finest college football player in the land. But this is indeed my good fortune this evening, and I do want to thank you for extending to me your thoughtful and courageous invitation.

Western Pennsylvania, as you all know, has produced some of the great football heroes of our country. Broadway Joe Namath is from Beaver Falls, the Chicago Bears' Mike Ditka is from Aliquippa, the incomparable Joe Montana is from Monongahela, the spectacular Tony Dorsett hails from Hopewell, the Dolphins' Dan Marino is from Pittsburgh—these are just a few well-known folks who have come from the western Pennsylvania area where I coach and teach. (In case you're wondering, Howard Cosell, who did not play the game, did not come from the same region.)

231

Yet I'm not standing here before you this evening to speak about the fauna and the flora, the foundry and the philosophy that have produced such great football stars. When your officers first contacted me by letter, wondering whether I would consider giving this keynote address, they wrote the following:

> Frankly, we are looking for ways to bring a breath of fresh air to our Heisman Memorial Trophy Award Dinner, and your name was suggested to us as a possible keynote speaker. You might be asking: How does women's soccer relate to men's football at the college level? Our response is twofold. Kicking is an important dimension of the football game, and we seldom call attention to it. (Most of the past winners of the Heisman have been quarterbacks or running backs. A few who have played these positions and kicked as well have won the prestigious award. Notre Dame's Paul Hornung comes to mind.) By extending our invitation to you, we wish to highlight in a dramatic way the kicking game in college football. We considered inviting a coach of a "special team," but we decided against that. We wanted to tap a candidate whose invitation to speak would shock and startle the national media and the country at large, leading them to take note of new developments at the Heisman. The second part of our response deals with women's sports. Women's soccer, we are told, is the fastest growing sport in America. Colleges throughout the country are playing it. So, we reasoned, why not take our high Heisman visibility and call attention to a real but little known current in contemporary American sport culture?

This was one long paragraph from a lengthy invitation letter I had received. (I suppose it was a lengthy letter because your officers suspected I might refuse the invitation.) They were wrong on that score. Knowing that I was an English professor as well as a soccer coach, and that professors lecture for periods of fifty-five minutes or one hour and twenty minutes (depending on how often a three-credit class meets per week), your officers suspected that I might give a lengthy speech tonight. They were right on that score. Accordingly, they assigned me a thirty-minute time limit.

Aware that you just had a fine meal with alcoholic beverages and aware that snoring silencers, like dog diapers, have yet to be invented, I have agreed to accept the time limit. So if you're wearing a digital watch, don't keep glancing at it, and if you have the older kind, don't glance at it and/or shake it by your ear. You might do all that to your preachers on Sunday morning, but this is Saturday evening at the Heisman.

Before I launch into the speech proper, permit me, please, to mention that I followed the exceedingly generous "P.S." that accompanied the invitation letter and brought along all the members of Geneva's women's soccer team. To give you an idea of how thoughtful and generous the officers of the Downtown Athletic Club were to our team members, let me give you a couple of examples. Not only did they pay for all our players to travel here and to dine with you this evening, but they also covered our hotel expenses, and they put us up not in the Magic Bed Hotel on skid row (although that might have been an interesting adventure for us) but in a magnificent inn near JFK.

In appreciation of all that hospitality, I promised myself to get off my iconoclastic kick and not say a thing tonight about John Heisman's vindictive ways that manifested themselves when his 1916 Georgia Tech football squad beat little Cumberland College of Lebanon, Tennessee, to the tune of 222–0. (In case you're wondering, the halftime score of that game was a mere 126–0.) I also promised myself to quit speaking even before the allotted time is up if this dinner hall begins to appear as if it is being transformed into a studio for a Sominex commercial.

All that, of course, is a fantasy, the way I would probably begin a speech at the Heisman Memorial Trophy Award Dinner, a speech that would likely explore one of several crucial issues in American sports. Given that the Heisman quarters are the last bastion of American "maledom," as it were, I might focus the speech on Title IX and try to assess what that law has meant to college sports. Or I might try to argue for the urgency of having women coach women in team sports at the college level. Or I might try to present a radical approach to reforming college sports that would center on a system of play that requires maximum participation from all the athletes in team sports such as football, basketball, soccer, softball, and baseball. These issues had often occupied my thinking, especially when I coached football, searched for a job to coach baseball, and established and guided the women's soccer team of Geneva College.

The soccer team, however, did not always fill my mind with such weighty issues. It frequently unfolded moments with lighter lessons, several of which I recorded in the "Soccer Season Diary." One such moment came during a close game in West Virginia against the women Cardinals of Wheeling Jesuit. Our right wing, Angi, had considered several shots at goal but failed to take any of them. Her hesitation and failure disturbed me. So at the appropriate moment for sending in substitutes, I told one player standing next to me, "Please go in for Angi at right wing."

When Angi trotted toward the sidelines and ran by me, I clapped my hands—as most coaches tend to do when they're nervous on the sidelines—and I told her, "Good job, Angi."

"If I'm doing such a good job, why did you take me out?" Angi fired back.

"You know the shots that you missed taking," I said. "I don't care if you shoot and miss, but you've got to *take* the shots if they're there. Get a little rest on the bench, and I'll get you back in soon."

"Okay, Coach," she said, as she began to drift toward the bench, "but let's leave the irony to the classroom."

That incident taught me "to mean what I say and say what I mean," especially when dealing with highly intelligent players such as those who joined Geneva's women's soccer team that first year. The "good job" cliché might be an acceptable way to encourage better efforts from Little League baseball players, but it sounds phony if used in a similar context with intelligent college athletes. A woman with integrity and confidence wants to be told the truth: if a certain individual is a petroleum transfer engineer, then he should be called that, but if all the fellow does is pump gas, then obviously the label is phony, equivalent to "Good job" for missed shots.

Soccer also taught me that a coach can acquire wisdom from his players. The season offered several situations that illustrate this. One that comes to mind happened on a Wednesday afternoon in October. That day I thought of dividing the team into two units for a scrimmage. When I had done that in the past, I often asked the players to count off "one-two, one-two," or I divided them by position or other means. That afternoon, I wanted to do things differently. I appointed what I called, in typical professorial language, two ad hoc captains and asked them to rotate their selections of players to form their teams.

"No, Coach," Jill said. "Don't do it this way; it's not a wise move at all."

"Why?" I asked, uneasy that my authority had been questioned.

"It does more harm than good," Jill said. "So please just go ahead and divide us as you always do, but not this way."

"But why?" I persisted, my voice a bit louder than usual.

"Just think about it, Dr. Hanna," Jill said. That was the first time a player had shown disrespect for me by calling me "Dr. Hanna" on the playing field when she should have called me "Coach Hanna."

After hesitating a few seconds, I said, "Okay, I thought about it and I see no objections to it. It's a new and different approach, and it'll tell me what you think of each other."

"But that's the point, Coach," Jill responded. "We don't want each other to know what we think of each other's skills. That's bad for team morale."

"That's right, Coach," Angi said. "Just imagine how you'd feel if you were the last one picked by each so-called 'subtract hoc' capt—"

"Ad hoc," Amy interrupted, igniting laughter among the team members and me, of course.

When the laughter ceased, Lori, an elementary education major, clinched the entire dispute when she said, "Remember, Coach, when you were a little boy on the playgrounds, and the kids picked teams, and how low you felt if you were the last one to be picked?"

"Okay, okay, I'm sorry," I said. "You're right. My idea is a bad one, and I'm sorry for even bringing it up, and thank you for rejecting it so kindly yet so cogently. Count off in twos, please. Barb, you start."

Geneva's women's soccer players were so bright and sensitive, and they taught me such wise lessons that I occasionally found myself admitting my mistakes. The players might have found my admission refreshing for a coach. Similarly, I found it refreshing, though at times annoying, to deal with college athletes who had such a strong interest in academic matters. It was not uncommon for a player to come to me and say, "Coach, I need to miss practice today because I have to study for a test," or "I can't go to the game tomorrow because I have a paper due and some lab reports that I need to get in. I learned that there really is a distinction between scholarships and jockships in college sports. If the author of *A Season on the Brink*, the best-seller on the Hoosiers' Bobby Knight, decides to write a book on the first season of women's soccer at Geneva, there's a good chance that the book might be titled *A Season With Those Who Think*. I suspect that the problems I experienced in this context were similar to those experienced by women's soccer coaches at Denison or Oberlin. I must quickly add, however, that both of these schools were loaded with talent, and their coaches probably seldom experienced the problem that nagged me: complaints from players who were getting *far too much* playing time.

Coaching also taught me to appreciate the unique reasoning people often use in arriving at significant decisions. Angi told me that she planned to forgo playing soccer during her senior year for two reasons. The first reason, predictably enough, was study: soccer took too much time, and she wanted to devote more time to her academic pursuits. The second reason was less predictable, peculiar perhaps, but to her sound and convincing. "Though my experiences were at times frustrating," she told me, "I enjoyed them so very much that I want to protect them. I don't want to risk having them ruined by an injury or a more demanding coach or even a more talented group of players."

"But next year, under a more knowledgeable and aggressive coach—and, if the administration follows my recommendation, under a woman coach—Geneva would probably have a winning season," I said.

"But even a winning season and all the hard work that that might require and the mix of the players, et cetera, might ruin the memory of our first season," she said. "And I really want my soccer experiences to remain just as they're currently crafted. If that sounds strange, that's still me: Angi Moyer, the Golden Tornadoes' first right wing."

Those tiny crowds at our soccer matches were of particular interest to me. The "Soccer Season Diary" is peppered with references to those crowds. Unlike football or basketball games, to which people buy admission tickets, soccer games tend to be free. Most people don't go to soccer matches to cheer and clap, to buy hot dogs, nachos, or beer. Indeed, they don't go to stay for the entire contest; rather, they go to the soccer match as if it were an open house, coming and going—even returning, in some instances—as they please. Some bring newspapers with them that sooner or later they unfurl and read during the game; others might bring dogs, usually on a leash; they bring them not because dogs are intensely interested in soccer matches (they're not) but because soccer matches afford a convenient detour for the dogs during their pooping constitutionals. Dogs in our culture have evolved to such a high state that they seldom venture out and poop on their own. They now require humans to accompany them; not only that, but a certain kind of human—the kind one often sees in New York City, where the pooper-scooper laws are on the books and are enforced, ergo obeyed—the kind willing to salute the dog's pooping performance by first bowing and then scooping the dog's "output." (I hesitate to use that word, for we often speak of a writer's literary output.)

Other fans—and they're few—are the connoisseurs of the game; they'll stay for the entire match, giving it their undivided attention. These fans tend to be as interested in the game as the parents of most of the players are bored by it. Their interest and love of the sport keep them there for the entire game, whereas the players' parents patiently balance their intense boredom with the love of their offspring and remain there for the entire game as well.

While observing our soccer crowds, I occasionally found myself reflecting on certain questions. Why, for example, do parents go to Little League baseball games to watch their sons play? Why do they go to softball games to watch their daughters play? Why do they go to basketball games in high school to watch their kids play? Indeed, why do they go to women's or men's soccer games in college? For the love of their offspring? Surely. But there must be other reasons. For the love of the sport? Maybe. For an interest in the levels of competition? Not exactly. To engage their sophisticated knowledge of the game? Not really.

One balmy autumn day, I watched our team struggle during a home game that had several parents in the crowd. As the game progressed, I thought of writing a short story that explores the reasons why parents go to see their kids play sports. In the story, I expected to bring out the conventional, predictable reasons, but I also hoped to explore the most mysterious reason of them all, one that flew by me, lit up like a lightning bug, and continued its flight. This reason had the parents going to the games in order to participate mystically in the reversal of the aging process. Every kick that their daughters make, every head ball, every pass or shot or punt is watched by the proud parents, who get that strange and pleasant sensation that makes them feel as if they're doing the playing. In the story, the parents watch and silently chant: Oh, to be young again! One part of the story is set in the present; the other part is set in 2043, the year when medical science finally succeeds in making us all into human yo-yos. Parents living in that year and beyond would be able to be young again. One pill taken at sixty-six, the story goes, will reverse the aging process, and people will go down to age six. At six, another pill, and the process will be reversed again as people go up to sixty-six. And again. And again. Up and down. Up and down. As I watched the teams go up and down the field, two possible titles for the story came to mind. One was, "Oh, to Be Young Again!" and the other, "Soccer, Science, and Human Yo-Yos."

Strange thoughts, I learned, go through the mind of a soccer coach who has to watch ninety minutes of soccer, especially when he knows that the match has already been decided in the first ninety *seconds*. But when the coach also dabbles in the writer's craft, the strangeness might be explained, if not excused. To put it differently: our small and special soccer crowds were a source of inspiration for my literary pursuits.

When the yearbook—edited with creativity and insight by Paula Logan, a preministerial student—that covered the first season of varsity soccer at Geneva came out, I was pleased by the account. My colleagues and kids found it slightly amusing. Two pages were given to women's soccer. Indeed, each sport, be it football or women's tennis, received two pages—that's all. "Lady Tornadoes Show Their Skill" serves as the headline for our team's section, and the pages display the official team picture and five photographs of players in action.

Angi, Barb, and Amy—our right wing, our left-footed left wing, and our goalie—are featured in separate action shots. The two other pictures are group action shots taken at practice. In one of those pictures, a beginner is shown kicking the ball that appears in the air, but the kicker's right-footed follow-through appears to be headed to a teammate's butt, much to the amusement of my kids and colleagues. To my wife and me, the picture represents, in a manner of speaking, a poignant metaphor of my coaching throughout the season. The two pages also note the schools that we played and the scores of the games as well as an edited version of the feature article on our goalie that I had written and sent out for newspaper publication.

On the literary front, the manuscript version of *When She Went Men-Bashing* continued to go out and come back like a dedicated parent of six children desperately searching for work in a horribly depressed economy. The manuscript's struggles led me to believe what I had suspected: that first novels are tough to sell, comic first novels are super tough, and comic first novels by unknown writers waiting to be discovered are super-duper tough. The wisdom and humor of a good friend and successful author, Harry Farra, helped me negotiate the despair-mined fields of publishing.

On a more cheerful note, *The Gypsy Scholar: A Writer's Comic Search for a Publisher* came out and the early reviews on it pleased me. *Publishers Weekly* wrote, "Well written, fast paced, funny and enjoyable, it deserves a sizable audience. Hanna paints a humorous picture of educational and social conditions in small colleges, struggles for a livelihood in academia, problems of appealing to jocks and other unwilling students of freshman English. Most delightful of all is his account of attempts to get his manuscript published."

Library Journal called the book "clever," pointed to its "witty prose," noted that it offers "tips the reader won't find in such standard sources as *Writer's Market*," and concluded with the one-word sentence: "Recommended."

The *Chronicle of Higher Education* published a little feature on *The Gypsy Scholar* and quoted from its ironic dimensions. One quote had me recalling the fortunes of two former colleagues who had sent their dissertations to a university press in Texas. The results: "One was accepted and published, and in five years it earned the author $123.29. The other doctoral dissertation was rejected and returned, but it was returned damaged due to a fire at the press. Thanks to an insurance claim, the press enclosed a $300 check with the partly barbecued manuscript."

One of those former colleagues, now a professor at Vanderbilt University, phoned me after he had read the *Chronicle* feature. "I've already told several of my friends and colleagues," he said, a measure of mock pride trembling in his voice, "that my dissertation had been discussed in *The Chronicle of Higher Education*. Marsha," he added, referring to his wife, "even told some of her friends at work." I laughed; he continued. "I haven't figured out how to enter all that on my curriculum vitae yet. Let me know if you get some ideas on that," he kidded.

Angi and Amy traveled all over Europe during the summer months that I spent writing this book. Angi sent me aerogram after aerogram cramming in fine print their adventures in Frank-furt, Paris, Madrid, Amsterdam, and Dublin, among other plac-es. They traveled with backpacks, stayed in hostels, rode trains at times, and hitchhiked at other times. Angi concluded one letter with a quick reference to her and Amy on the road: "hitchhiked to London—made signs FROM TEXAS TO LONDON & stood out by highway. A lot of people laughed, some waved, some pre-tended not to see us." The vigor and details of her letters made it easy for me to see her and Amy all over Europe, the Europe that Angi had come to long for from our study of works by Hemingway, Stein, Joyce, Pound, and Eliot.

When Angi and Amy returned to the United States' Geneva, Angi stayed away from soccer and concentrated on her course work and writing; she also continued to serve as my grading as-sistant in freshman composition. Amy joined Barb, Andrea, Wendy, Jill, Sara, Lori, and Debbie in participating in the soccer program's second year. The college officials went outside the faculty ranks and hired a capable male coach who lived and worked in the Beaver Falls area. I do not know if they seriously considered my recommendation of "doing whatever it takes to attract and hire a qualified female to coach the program."

Geneva's president and the vice president in charge of athlet-ics, both males, strongly supported the women's soccer pro-gram; they made sure that most of the recommendations I had made to improve the program were in place for the second year. Accordingly, locker rooms were added to the field house; porta-ble goals with nets and pipes that could allow one to expand and shorten the field as needed replaced the netless and heavy home-made wooden goals that we had used in practice throughout the first season; scholarships were granted to deserving student-ath-letes; lots of work was done to improve the conditions of the field; an assistant coach–manager was appointed; and gym bags were purchased for the athletes. In its second year, the women's program had acquired all that the men's program had had for years. The women players were happy; the administration was happy; the first-year coach, who was replaced by a coach-and-a-half, was happy; and the compliance with Title IX, in the soccer domain at least, was in place.

That second year, my kids and I would often stroll to the soccer field and watch the team play. Eight of the fifteen team members had played on Geneva's first team, and all of them continued to improve and develop. Watching them was a pleasant and a sad experience for me, a joyful and a painful one. Frequently, I would pace the periphery of the field, watch the game from different angles, look at the grass, and occasionally kick it by way of questioning the wisdom of my decision to leave the head coaching job. When I had paced the sidelines as a coach, I always encouraged our players by shouting, "Good job," "Excellent kick," "Splendid effort"; but walking around the soccer field as an ex-coach, as an interested spectator, as a curious fan, I failed to utter a single word of encouragement. I remained silent and pensive, as if I were alone on a bar stool, brooding and nursing a strong drink that I felt could drown the painful results of a bad decision.

And at times I thought it really was a bad decision. I thought that I should have fought to have my class load lightened and my committee assignments and advising responsibilities changed so that I could continue coaching the soccer players, whom I had come to respect, to enjoy serving, teaching, and coaching. But I also thought that it was a good decision, for the players deserved a more capable coach, a woman who could relate to them better than I could and who could serve as a role model for them and others. My ambivalence led me to tilt to the belief that it was a bad decision, because another male had taken over the program, but then it tilted to the realization that it was a good decision, for the new male coach had stronger soccer coaching experience than I had, albeit in the men's domain.

Whenever I went to see the women play that second year, I never stayed for an entire game, and I seldom asked about the final score of a game. Whenever I saw my former players on campus, I always asked them about their athletic and academic progress, but I never asked them about the scores of games.

Even though our soccer season was played in late summer and early autumn, the opening lines of T. S. Eliot's *The Waste Land* often navigated my mind as I saw my former players perform. I would walk around the field and recite the lines in silence:

April is the cruelest month, breeding
Lilacs out of the dead land, mixing
Memory and desire, stirring
Dull roots with spring rain.

"Mixing memory and desire," I once told my kids as we were leaving a game, "is hard. It really is." They said nothing in response; they might have sensed that I missed, dearly missed, my coaching duties.

Sharon Hasek, the writing major who shared my initials, joined Angi in ending her varsity soccer career after one year. (The other five players from the first-year team had graduated. Suzanne Maslo was the class salutatorian and Sheryl Yost was magna cum laude.) Sharon, unlike Angi, went to most home games, and she and I would occasionally visit while watching our former teammates play. I once told her, "I loved it when I coached, and I'd love to do it now, but I'm now prisoner of a decision that I regret. All I can do now, in Eliot's words, is continue 'mixing memory and desire,' and that's hard and cruel, but it's the order of the day."

Bright and sensitive, Sharon used the time she would have devoted to soccer to help edit another issue of *Chimes*, Geneva's literary magazine, a publication of the Fern Cliffe Literary Society, for which I serve as faculty advisor. Given all the classes she'd taken from me, Sharon had noted how frequently I alluded to Eliot and quoted passages from *The Waste Land* and "The Love Song of J. Alfred Prufrock." Two weeks after graduation, she sent me a piece of needlework on which she had stitched the opening four lines of *The Waste Land*. The words were boxed in an elaborate rectangular needlework design, and the piece was stretched and framed. She included with it a thoughtful letter that offered her appreciation "for all that you had done for me as a teacher and a coach."

If truth be known, I had done nothing that would be considered extraordinary for a teacher or a coach. But then appreciative students—and not wages or teaching loads or research grants or sabbaticals—are part of the rewards of teaching and coaching at small liberal arts colleges like Geneva. Sharon's piece now hangs in my office near a picture of Geneva's first women's soccer team, above a picture of the Sterling College football team that I had helped coach during my years in Kansas.

New women students continue to come to Geneva, and now many of them come not only to get a decent education but to play soccer as well. They come and stay, precisely because soccer involves them in the college's life in a meaningful way, enriching their lives as they discover and develop their physical and social skills. The memory of establishing Geneva's varsity soccer program will linger with me and it will become more pleasant as the years drift by and the women whom I coached graduate and the desire to coach them again fades.

After I wrote the first draft of this book, our daughter Rita started to play on organized sports teams. In time, she played on her high school's basketball, softball, and golf teams and on the Beaver Valley Express softball team. Thanks to the strong coaching of Dick Barns, Chuck Tangora, John McAdoo, Bill Powell, and others, Rita's softball teams won the Pennsylvania State Championship and played in several national tournaments in Indiana, Oklahoma, and Florida.

Our family accompanied Rita to these national tournaments. I was particularly impressed by the exceedingly fine play of many athletes from such states as Georgia, Alabama, Tennessee, Florida, and Arkansas. The southern athletes from the various age groups (fourteen and under, sixteen and under, and eighteen and under) played sound and aggressive ball: hitting with vigor, sliding with gusto, diving for spectacular catches, and throwing with authority and accuracy. As I watched those athletes perform with extraordinary skill, I often wondered if they—and their predominantly male coaches—knew the crucial roles that Nixon's Title IX and equity-conscious women and men of our culture played in providing them with a meaningful alternative to the popular beauty contests of the South, freeing them to play sports, to develop their athletic gifts, to bat, run, and throw their way to college scholarships.

After completing the final draft of this book, I once again experienced the itch to coach men's baseball. Accordingly, I prepared a vita and a cover letter to be mailed to administrators of small colleges. The cover letter stated:

Dear Administrator:

Do you have an inexpensive and de-emphasized varsity baseball program, and would you like to keep it that way? Do you have an overworked athletic director or a head football or basketball coach who *reluctantly* doubles up as a head coach for the baseball program at a time when he should be recruiting for his primary sport?

If you answered "yes" to the above questions, then you might be interested in considering my name for the position of head baseball coach for the next academic year. I'll come with three guarantees: one, your program will remain inexpensive; two, your overworked coaches will be relieved and happy; three—and this is crucial as water—your program will receive national visibility, one that I'm sure will please you.

How would that visibility come about? Easy. I'll write a nonfiction book on the program. It will be a positive book: fun, lighthearted, engaging, very much in keeping with my writing and indeed coaching styles, and—oh, yes—in keeping with the spirit that ought to infuse sports in a liberal arts college.

If wins come along, we'll take them, but we won't lust after them. A central assumption in the book would be that the "rags to riches" story is a cliché, the "riches to rags" decline is too sad a story, but the "rags to rags" shuffle, especially at a strong Phi Beta Kappa–type college, might have an inherent charm about it. In the book, I'll try to tap that charm.

Enclosed is my curriculum vitae. Please note that my first book, *The Gypsy Scholar,* deals with me teaching English, coaching football, and working at the writer's craft. *Beyond Winning,* the second book, deals with women's soccer; it's a salute to the female foot. The third will deal with baseball. If my proposal intrigues you, please consider writing or calling me at your convenience.

Sincerely,
S. S. Hanna

The cover letter and the vita remain poised, ready to sail to all sorts of small-college ports in search of a position to teach English part-time and coach baseball full-time.

"A small college like Geneva can win the small-college World Series," I told my wife as we drank coffee and fought the flies at a local restaurant, "and it'll be lucky if it gets five lines on the wire services to supplement whatever publicity its hometown paper gives it. Most colleges are probably like ours; the local high schools—because they feature the local kids—get far more press than the small college that has many students from a variety of states and few from the local town."

"You're probably right," she said, and assassinated a fly with the yellow legal pad in front of me.

"What I propose to do," I continued, "is write not a few lines on the wire services, not a little article in a local paper, or even a chapter in a book, but an *entire* book on a college's baseball program. With two nonfiction books to my credit, you'd think I'd find a taker now."

"If I were you, I'd first approach those two Phi Beta Kappa colleges in Wisconsin and Indiana and see if their situations had changed. Their administrators, as I recall from their letters, sounded like creative and innovative folks who might see the fun and rewards in your crazy ideas."

"They did sound creative, didn't they?" I said, adding, "You know, the head coaching job in women's softball just opened up right here at Geneva. What do you think? Should I apply for it?"

She looked me straight in the eye, slapped her right palm on the legal pad, and said, "No. Absolutely not." She paused as another fly buzzed us. Then she leaned forward and added a command: "Wait for your pitch."

As I continue to wait, good things continue to happen at Geneva. Our class load has been reduced to twelve hours a semester; a sabbatical system has been installed; and the soccer program is now headed by a woman, a role model for the student-athletes of Geneva College where the motto reads: *Pro Christo et Patria.*